The Emergence of Modern America: 1865–1900

The Structure of American History

Davis R. B. Ross, Alden T. Vaughan, and John B. Duff, Editors

VOLUME I
Colonial America: 1607–1763

VOLUME II
Forging the Nation: 1763–1828

VOLUME III
The Nation in Crisis: 1828–1865

VOLUME IV
The Emergence of Modern America: 1865–1900

VOLUME V
Progress, War, and Reaction: 1900–1933

VOLUME VI
Recent America: 1933 to the Present

The

Emergence of

Modern America:

1865–1900

edited by Davis R. B. Ross
COLUMBIA UNIVERSITY

Alden T. Vaughan
COLUMBIA UNIVERSITY

John B. Duff
SETON HALL UNIVERSITY

THOMAS Y. CROWELL COMPANY

NEW YORK · ESTABLISHED 1834

L. C. Card 78-101951

Series design by Barbara Kohn Isaac

Manufactured in the United States of America

Preface

The Structure of American History is designed to introduce undergraduate students of United States history and interested general readers to the variety and richness of our historical literature. The six volumes in the series offer selections from the writings of major historians whose books have stood the test of time or whose work, though recent, has met with unusual acclaim. Some of the selections deal with political history, some with diplomatic, some with economic, and others with social; all however offer thoughtful and provocative interpretations of the American past.

The volumes, with seven substantial selections in each, cover the following chronological periods:

    I. Colonial America: 1607–1763
   II. Forging the Nation: 1763–1828
  III. The Nation in Crisis: 1828–1865
  IV. The Emergence of Modern America: 1865–1900
   V. Progress, War, and Reaction: 1900–1933
  VI. Recent America: 1933 to the Present

Each volume opens with a general introduction to the period as a whole, in which we have suggested major themes that give coherence to the era and have outlined briefly the direction of past and recent scholarship. An editors' introduction precedes each selection; in these we have not sought to tell the reader what he is about to encounter but rather to identify the selection's author, establish its historical setting, and pro-

vide its historiographical context. Finally, a short bibliographical essay follows each selection, in which the reader is
introduced to a wide range of related literature.

Several criteria guided us in our choice of readings: the distinction of the author, the significance of his interpretation,
the high literary quality of his style. Because we conceived of
the series as a supplement to, rather than a substitute for, the
reading usually assigned in college-level survey courses, we
have tried to avoid material that merely expands in detail the
coverage offered in the traditional textbooks; we have sought,
instead, selections from works that shed new light and raise
new questions, or at the very least provide a kind of reading
experience not customarily encountered in traditional assign-
ments. For, at bottom, *The Structure of American History*
stems from the editors' conviction that the great works of historical writing should not be reserved for the graduate student
or the professional scholar but should be made available to
those readers who can perhaps best benefit from an early
encounter with Francis Parkman, Samuel Eliot Morison, Allan
Nevins, Oscar Handlin, and their peers. We want college students to know from the outset that the stuff of history is
neither the textbook nor the latest article in a scholarly journal. What has often inspired us, as teachers and writers of
history, and what we hope will inspire students and lay readers,
is history written by the great practitioners of the art: men
who have written with vigor and grace the results of their own
meticulous research and meditation.

In order to make our selections as extensive as possible, we
have, with reluctance, omitted all footnotes. We urge readers
to remember that the authority of each historian rests largely
on the documentation he offers in support of his statements,
and that readers who wish to investigate the evidence on which
a historian has based his argument should refer to the original
published version—cited on the first page of each selection.
Readers are also reminded that many of the books recommended in the bibliographical notes appended to each selection are obtainable in paperback editions. We have refrained

from indicating which volumes are currently in paper for the list of paperbacks grows too rapidly. We refer those interested to R. R. Bowker Company, *Paperbound Books in Print,* available at the counter of most bookstores.

D.R.B.R.

A.T.V.

J.B.D.

Contents

Introduction   1

The Black Proletariat in Mississippi   5
    W. E. B. Du Bois

The New York Gold Conspiracy   34
    Henry Adams

Conflict Within the American Labor Movement   72
    John R. Commons and Selig Perlman

Religion in the Immigrant's Life   103
    Oscar Handlin

The Mysteries of the Great Plains   130
    Walter Prescott Webb

The Farmer's Grievances   163
    John D. Hicks

The Triumph of Bryanism   201
    Allan Nevins

Introduction

*H*istorians are fond of identifying dates that mark "turning points," "critical years," or "watersheds" in history. Certain of these dates receive more general assent than others. In European history, 1492, 1789, and 1914 come quickly to mind as the beginnings of new eras. In the history of the American republic, it is almost impossible to avoid 1865. Semester survey courses usually divide at this date, and we tend to compartmentalize our thinking into antebellum and postbellum eras. For textile workers in Massachusetts or farmers in Iowa, life in the 1870's may not have seemed much different from that of twenty years earlier, but change was everywhere around them.

Our mental image of the Gilded Age is one of enormous innovation, bustle, and diversity; of the confusing movements of people into the cities and out into the new West; of belching smokestacks and flamboyant plutocrats. The Civil War had summoned the nation's energies; with its end, the people had turned elsewhere for release. Now that the troubling questions of the nature of the federal Union and the power of the national government had been settled, Americans devoted themselves to pursuits of personal power and wealth. Casting aside the virtues of older America, they now reckoned achievement by the yardstick of material wealth. The small farmer, formerly the exemplar of everything considered worthwhile in the national experience, lost status and respect. Once called by Jefferson "the most precious part of a state," the agriculturist now saw himself become a figure of fun, referred to as a hick or rube or hayseed; he watched helplessly as his children drifted away to the cities. Old cities grew immoderately; new ones, Birmingham and Denver, for example, developed almost overnight. In 1860 one out of every six Americans lived in urban areas; by 1900 more than one in three did. But the cities changed in ways other than size; the vast influx of immigrants after 1890 changed their character as well. The mystifying variety of peoples alarmed many anxious to preserve some sort of Anglo-Saxon homogeneity. Others feared the foreigners' propensity to join labor unions whose demands for a more equitable division of the fruits of economic expansion carried with them a grim intimation of class warfare.

Despite the stubborn resistance of the Indians, the frontier moved steadily westward and disappeared entirely as cow towns dotted the Great Plains, previously believed uninhabitable. Railroads linked all parts of the country, thus providing thousands of new markets for the Eastern and Midwestern industrial complexes and facilitating the fullest exploitation of the country's productivity. The South lagged behind the rest of the nation as that region, devastated by the war, struggled during the Reconstruction period not only to overcome its material disadvantage but to find some solution to the social and moral dilemma created by the presence of four million newly freed black people.

The economic achievements of the age were undeniably immense, producing an almost unimaginable abundance, but as Henry George noted in his wonderfully perceptive study *Poverty and Progress,* it was an abundance in the midst of shocking deprivation. Only a few agreed with him, however, that the cost was fearful. Widespread acceptance of dogmas of Social Darwinism caused most politicians, businessmen, and writers to ignore the glaring inequalities. Darwin's biological concept of survival of the fittest, now applied to the social order, made the millionaire the epitome of the process of natural selection. Criticisms of the system came mainly from embittered workers and angry farmers.

The older histories of the age concentrated on politics and politicians, on business and industrial tycoons, and these topics have not been slighted by the editors. But to deal with them only produces an artificial history and ignores what in the long run is more significant: the story of four million ex-slaves, of the teeming multitude of foreigners in the cities, of the angry and puzzled industrial proletariat, of the dirt farmers of Kansas and the cowhands of Wyoming. Traditional accounts almost invariably treat the immigrant, the worker, and the black man as problems that had to be somehow dealt with rather than as people whose story is worth recording for its own merit. Surely how they lived, worked, and worshipped, what they thought about America, seems more relevant today than much of the standard history of the era.

Accordingly, we have tried to capture some of the complexity and diversity of the times with selections dealing with the Negro in Reconstruction, the emergence of national labor organizations, the process of immigrant acculturation, the civilization of the Wild West, and the grievances of the farmers.

The Black Proletariat
in Mississippi

W. E. B. Du Bois

No era of American history has undergone more reinterpretation in recent years than post Civil War Reconstruction. And no wonder, for the fundamental patterns of race relations in the United States today date from this period. In our age of the Negro revolution, or the Second Reconstruction as it is sometimes called, historians, journalists, politicians, and others have delved into the documentary evidence of the years 1865 to 1877 to find out what happened and what went wrong. This probing has overturned many of the assumptions of the traditional or Dunning school of Reconstruction historiography.

William A. Dunning, a native of New Jersey, attended Dartmouth College, received his doctorate from Columbia University, and spent his entire teaching career (1886–1922) at that institution. Despite his Northern background, he early became convinced of the evil of Radical Reconstruction and devoted his scholarly career

Source: William E. B. Du Bois, *Black Reconstruction in America, 1860–1880* (New York: Harcourt, Brace & Company, Inc., 1935), pp. 431–442, 444–450. Copyright © 1962 by Mrs. Shirley Graham Du Bois. Reprinted by permission of Mrs. Shirley Graham Du Bois. This book has also been published by the World Publishing Company as part of its Meridian Books Series.

to "analysis and extended reflection [on] the struggle through which the Southern whites, subjugated by adversaries of their own race, thwarted the scheme which threatened subjection to another race."

Dunning's own contributions to Reconstruction history were considerable, but even more significant was the work of a number of graduate students attracted to his seminar at Columbia. From this seminar came a series of studies, all thoroughly scholarly, but all of which approached the problem of the restoration of the Union as a particularly Southern dilemma, assumed the innate inferiority of the Negro, and followed a common theme.

The theme became the accepted interpretation of the period for almost half a century and it can be briefly stated: A malevolent Radical Republican leadership in Congress led by Thaddeus Stevens and Charles Sumner destroyed hopes for a happy reconciliation of the sections by preventing Andrew Johnson from implementing President Lincoln's just and generous plan of restoring the South. Instead, the Radicals plunged the South into a nightmare of military satraps and revolution." Governing the South was a weird coalition of ignorant Negroes, rapacious carpetbaggers from the North, and scalawags, despicable Southern whites of the lowest classes who toadied to the new leaders to obtain political prominence and economic advantages. Under direction of Radical Republican leaders in Washington, these governments then entered upon an orgy of misrule, plunder, and corruption without parallel. For ten years a veritable reign of terror engulfed the Southland. At length, conservative, respectable whites, symbolically referred to as redeemers, organized themselves to take back control of their states. The redemption was accomplished earlier in some states than others, but the agony of the South did not completely end until the withdrawal of federal troops following the disputed election of 1876 and the Compromise of 1877. In the works of popular historians the Dunning interpretation grew even more extreme as may be gathered from some of the chapter headings in Claude G. Bowers lurid polemic, *The Tragic Era*: "The Great American Farce," "A Season of Scandal," "Degradation and Depression," "The Falling of Rotten Fruit."

This essentially Southern, anti-Negro interpretation captured academic circles throughout the country with only a few voices raised in dissent. Moreover, the most articulate dissenter, William E. B. Du Bois, was disregarded because he was a Negro militant and a Marxist.

Du Bois (1868–1963)—urbane, cosmopolitan and bitter—did not conform to the turn-of-the-century stereotype of the Negro. A Harvard Ph.D. and one of the founders of the National Association for the Advancement of Colored People, he assailed those of his race like Booker T. Washington who counseled patience and accommodation in dealing with the dominant white society. Du Bois is today regarded as a precursor of the Black Power movement in his advocacy of protest against the white establishment. In addition to politics, Du Bois devoted himself to the study of the sociology and history of the American Negro. *Souls of Black Folk* (1903) is considered a classic, and *Black Reconstruction in America 1860–1880,* although marred by Marxist jargon (the Negroes' departure from the plantations is represented as a general strike; field hands are referred to as the black proletariat), details the role of the blacks in the politics and the economy of the Reconstruction South with such convincing intensity as to demolish the caricature created by the traditional interpretation of the ludicrous, thieving Negro politician.

Most importantly, *Black Reconstruction* forced other historians to reevaluate their own assumptions. Four years after its publication, a Southern historian, Francis B. Simkins, asked his fellow historians to stop describing Reconstruction "as a melodrama involving wild-eyed conspirators whose acts are best described in red flashes upon a canvas." Urging a more critical, creative, and tolerant attitude to such an important period of history, he admitted that historians had not faced up to the main issue, the great American race question. The revisionist argument gained momentum in 1940 when Howard K. Beale called for a rewriting of Reconstruction history without "first assuming, at least subconsciously, that Carpetbaggers and Southern white Republicans were wicked, that Negroes were illiterate incompetents, and that the whole white South owes a debt of gratitude to

the restorers of 'white supremacy'." Thus began an on-
slaught on the Dunning school that has continued un-
abated in a host of books and articles.

The revisionists have directly challenged the traditional interpretation on the severity of Reconstruction,
contending that the South, emerging in defeat from a
bloody Civil War, received a surprisingly lenient settlement. Government by bayonet never really occurred,
military rule ended for the most part by 1870, and even
while in operation appears to have been remarkably
light, just, and efficient. The reputations of the carpetbaggers and the scalawags have undergone rehabilitation.
Many of the former were idealists sincerely interested in
helping the Negro find his place in a world turned upside
down, while the despised scalawag often turns out to be
a prewar Southern Whig of old family and high status,
realistically accepting what the war had wrought. As for
corruption during Reconstruction, it certainly did exist,
but often as not, the conservative white redeemers profited more than their radical opponents. It is well to remember also that corruption was nationwide in America
during the Gilded Age. On the positive side, the revisionists have stressed the accomplishments of Reconstruction in the South, including the establishment or the
revival of free public education, the adoption of more
democratic state constitutions, and the introduction of
the concept of social services for public welfare. The
landed elite controlling Southern politics before the war
opposed public expenditures for such purposes. The new
governments were not afraid to tax to rebuild roads and
bridges and to provide hospitals, asylums, and police and
fire protection.

In the following selection Du Bois presents his case for
the Negro and for the carpetbagger government of Mississippi.

*M*ississippi has been called a peculiarly typical state in
which to study Reconstruction. But this should be modified.
In direct contrast to South Carolina, Mississippi was the place

where first and last Negroes were largely deprived of any opportunity for land ownership. The great black belt plantations on the Mississippi had hardly been disturbed by war. The barons ruling there, who had dictated the policy of the state, were to the last degree reactionary because they entirely misconceived the results of the war. They were determined not to recognize even the abolition of slavery, and as for establishing peasant-proprietors on their land or granting even civil rights, they were adamant. To the proposition of political rights for Negroes, they simply would not listen for a moment.

Mississippi was in all respects a curious state. It was the center of a commercialized cotton kingdom. The graciousness and ease of the plantation system had scarcely taken root there. Mississippi plantations were designed to raise a profitable cotton crop and not to entertain visitors. Here and there the more pretentious slave manor flourished, but, on the whole, the level of the state in civilization and culture was distinctly below that of Virginia and South Carolina, and smacked more of the undisciplined frontier.

In this state there were, in 1860, 353,899 white people and 437,404 Negroes, of whom less than 1,000 were free. The population had only been a few thousand at the beginning of the century and small in 1820. Then from 1840 on, the Cotton Kingdom spread over Mississippi, greatly increasing its population. The result was that after the war, there was in this state a group of planters whose great plantations dominated the rich Black Belt. From Memphis to the Gulf were a succession of counties with 60% or more of black population, while on the poor lands of the northeast and southeast were the poor whites.

The planters had always dominated the state in its political and economic aspects, and it was suddenly required after the war that this state should not only assimilate a voting population of nearly 450,000 former slaves, but also that the mass of poor whites should have a political significance which they had never had before. It was a project at which Mississippi quailed. Sterling Price prayed "to God that my fears for the future of the South may never be realized; but when the right is given to the Negro to bring suit, testify before the courts and vote in elections, you all had better be in Mexico."

Mississippi had a bad financial reputation long before the Civil War; Reconstruction actually improved this. In 1839, less than one-tenth of the money collected from fines and forfeitures by the sheriffs and clerks throughout the state ever reached the treasury. In 1840, the Senate Journal had the names of 26 tax collectors who were defaulters to an average amount of $1,000 each. In 1858, the auditor of the state was a defaulter for $54,000. The endowment of Jefferson College, valued at $248,748, disappeared without record, and the college had to be closed. The money realized from the 16th Section Fund donated to schools by the Congress of the United States was lost or embezzled to the amount of $1,500,000. The Mississippi Union Bank sold bonds to the amount of $5,000,000, and later repudiated the debt.

The effect of war on property in the state was marked. The assessed valuation of Mississippi property in 1860 was over $500,000,000. Subtracting $218,000,000 as the value of the slaves, we have $291,472,912. This was reduced in 1870 to $177,278,890. The whole industrial system was upset, and the cotton crop, which was 1,200,000 bales in 1860, was in 1870 only 565,000 bales.

Naturally, these planter-capitalists proposed to protect themselves from further loss by dominating the labor of their former slaves and getting their work as cheaply as possible, with the least outlay of capital, and selling their crops at prevailing high prices.

William L. Sharkey, former Chief Justice of the State, was appointed Provisional Governor, June 15, 1865, and the state held a constitutional convention the same year, the first to be held in the South under the Johnson plan. The Governor complained that there was "an unprecedented amount of lawlessness in the state." The convention consisted of 100 delegates, most of them representing former Whigs, largely opposed to the secession of 1861. This convention recognized slavery as abolished, but did not wish to assume responsibility "for whatever honor there may be in abolishing it." An ordinance, therefore, was passed declaring that slavery had been abolished by the United States, and that hereafter it should not exist in the state. Further concessions to the Negro were fought. The Negroes of the state met October 7 and protested to Congress, expressing fear lest they be reenslaved. President Johnson wrote to Governor Sharkey suggesting that Negroes of education and property be given the right to vote so as to forestall the Radicals in the North.

Johnson pointed out that such a grant "would completely disarm the adversary," the Radical Republicans in Congress. The suggestion did not "receive any attention whatever" from the convention. "It is highly probable that the unanimous sentiment of the convention was against the idea of political rights for the Negro in any form." But a whole arsenal of reasons against enfranchisement was already prepared. Most of them started from the assumption of a general Negro franchise, and consequent "Negro domination"; the intelligent freedman was considered but "a drop in the bucket."

"It was argued that 'this is a white man's government,' and that in the sight of God and the light of reason a Negro suffrage was impossible."

The real fight in the convention was on the subsidiary question as to whether Negro testimony would be allowed in court, and it was on this question that the campaign for electing a Governor and legislature turned. It was remarkable that throughout the South, far from envisaging Negro suffrage for a moment, the states fought first to see how few civil rights must be granted Negroes; and this gradually boiled down to the momentous question as to whether a Negro could be allowed to testify against a white man in court.

The election took place October 2, 1865, and Humphreys, a general in the Confederate Army, was elected Governor by the party opposed to letting Negroes testify in court, which also secured a majority of the members of the legislature. This defeated Sharkey's candidacy for the United States Senate. Humphreys had received no pardon from the President when elected but received one afterward.

Sharkey notified the President that a Governor and legislature had been elected, but the President made him retain his powers, and warned him that the legislature must accept the Thirteenth Amendment and a code for the protection of Negroes. There was continued friction between the military and civil authorities, and the President allowed the writ of habeas corpus to remain suspended. "Anarchy must in any case be prevented." The presence of Negro troops in the state caused bitter complaint. On January 5, 1886, there were 8,784 Negro troops and 338 Negro officers. The President promised to remove them as soon as possible. Sharkey declared that they encouraged the belief among Negroes that lands were going to be distributed among them. By the 20th of May, 1866, all black troops had been mustered out and removed from Mississippi.

The legislature then proceeded to adopt the celebrated Black Code of 1865, and completed the set of laws by reenacting all the penal and criminal laws applying to slaves, "except so far as the mode and manner and trial of punishment has been ordained by the law." The North was incensed, and the Chicago *Tribune* said that the North would convert Mississippi "into a frog pond before they will allow any such laws to touch one foot of soil in which the bones of our soldiers sleep." Back of this sentiment was the conviction that Mississippi, whose political population for Congressional apportionment was 616,040 in 1860, would now be increased to 900,000, and this new power was going to be arrayed against Northern industry, thrift and power.

The whole reactionary course of Mississippi helped the abolition democracy in the North. General Ord assumed command in Mississippi in March, 1867, and on April 15, he began to register the new electorate, colored and white. Among Ord's appointees was Isaiah T. Montgomery, formerly a slave of Jefferson Davis. He was made a Justice of the Peace and was perhaps the first Negro in the state to hold public office. Ord appointed a number of civil officials, and was compelled practically to nullify the Black Code by military order. The result of the registration showed the white people that contrary to their firm and happy belief, the Negro was not becoming extinct; 46,636 white voters registered, and 60,137 Negroes. This showed the political situation plainly.

In 1867, the cotton crop was almost a total failure on account of weather conditions and other reasons. Ord issued an order requiring investigation of charges against landholders of driving off freedmen in order to prevent paying back wages. There was a great deal of theft of cotton and horses. Later, the abundant crop of 1868 induced Mississippi to begin to believe in free labor.

At Christmas, 1867, there had been widespread rumor of a Negro insurrection due to the idea that land was going to be distributed among them. Humphreys, then Governor, issued a proclamation reciting the apprehensions of combinations or conspiracies formed among the blacks to seize the lands, unless Congress should arrange to plan a distribution by January 1. Ord told General Gillem, commander in the subdistrict of Mississippi, that Congress was not going to seize the lands of planters, but that the Governor had already plenty of land in Mississippi for freedmen and that they could settle on it when they chose to do so.

The election was set for the first Tuesday in November, 1867. Negroes were given representation among the election officials; this brought bitter protest.

"We hoped this shameful humiliation would be spared our people, at least until the freedmen of Mississippi decide whether they will submit to Negro equality at the ballot box or elsewhere. General Ord has heretofore exhibited a wisdom in his administration which has been highly approved by the people, but we doubt not the lovers of peace throughout the country will condemn the order as injudicious, if not insulting, to that race whom God has created superior to the black man, and whom no monarch can make his equal. The general commanding cannot surely have forgotten that the Negro has no political rights conferred on him by the state of Mississippi, although he is given the privilege by a corrupt and fragmentary Congress to cast a ballot in the coming farce dignified by the name of election."

White Mississippi fought Reconstruction tenaciously at every step. The legislature stubbornly refused to adopt the Thirteenth Amendment, declaring that they had already abolished slavery and that they would not consent to the second section, which gave Congress the right to enforce freedom.

"Shall Mississippi ratify the Thirteenth Amendment?" asked the Vicksburg *Herald* on November 9. "We answer, no, ten thousand times, no."

Then came the question as to who might register and who was to decide on the eligibility of a former Confederate. The Commanding General, in accordance with Johnson's instructions, declared that the Board of Registrars had no power; he was overruled by General Grant and by the Act of Congress of July 19.

Immediately, Mississippi tried to bring the matter before the Supreme Court by seeking to enjoin President Johnson from enforcing the Reconstruction Acts. The Supreme Court refused to entertain the case on the ground that it would interfere with a coordinate branch of the government in the performance of its duties. Thereupon, another action was brought by the State of Georgia, which tried to enjoin the Secretary of War, but the court held that it was without jurisdiction. Finally, the celebrated case *Ex parte McCardle* was started on appeal from a military decision at Vicksburg, but Congress forestalled the case by depriving the court of jurisdiction in this particular case and others of similar character.

There had been a plan for the white people to refrain from voting in 1867, a plan widespread through the other Southern states. The idea was that by refraining from taking any part in this convention, the whole thing might go by default and Reconstruction fail. But that seemed to many too much of a risk, and in its place there came a movement on the part of some of the planters to acquiesce in the situation, and to organize and plan the control of the Negro vote. In other words, certain leaders, like the editor of the Jackson *Clarion*, General Alcorn and Judge Campbell, were in favor of recognizing the right of the Negroes to vote in 1868, and said that the policy of the Democrats would drive the Negroes into the Republican Party. Ex-Senator Brown agreed, and many other white leaders. The most advanced Reconstructionist was General Alcorn, who asked if it would not be wise to yield something to black suffrage, and then to control the votes in the interests of such an organization of industry and society as they thought best.

This was no wild scheme. The Negroes were used to subordination to the great planters. If the planters did not form an alliance with the Negroes, the planters would be threatened by the pretensions of the poor whites and possible leadership from Northern white men, ex-soldiers and investors, who were largely represented in the state. It was a matter to consider carefully; in the end Mississippi went further along this line than any other Southern state, and found it easier to do this because of the compulsion and intimidation that could be exercised over the Negro vote on the great plantations of the Black Belt.

The so-called "Black and Tan" convention met at Jackson, January 9, 1868. It was the first political organization in Mississippi with colored representatives. There were in all one hundred delegates, of whom 17 were colored, although 32 counties had Negro majorities. There were 29 native white Republicans, and 20 or more Northern Republicans. This was interesting and characteristic. It showed in the first place that the Negroes were not even trying, much less succeeding, in any effort to use their numerical preponderance in order to put themselves in political power. Under strong economic pressure, the Negro voter designated white men to represent him. The large majority of the members of this convention were elected by black voters.

Seven or eight of the colored delegates were ministers. Four of the Northern Republicans had lived in the South before the war, and two had served in the Confederate Army. It characterizes the times to know that five of the members afterward met violent deaths. Members were paid $10 a day in depreciated scrip worth 65¢–70¢ on a dollar, making their pay about equal to the convention of 1865.

During the organization of the convention, it was moved that the word "colored" be added to the name of each Negro delegate. Thereupon, the Reverend James Lynch, a colored man, afterward Secretary of State, moved to amend it so that the color of each delegate's hair should be added also.

There was here as in South Carolina the same charge against this convention and against succeeding legislatures, that they did not sufficiently represent wealth; they represented poverty; and the majority of the members, white and black, were not taxpayers. They represented labor, and were voting and working as far as they intelligently could to improve their condition and not to increase the profits of the hirers of labor.

In the convention, the colored people clung to the idea that the government intended to divide the land among them. One of the first acts of the convention was to appoint a committee of five to report what legislation was needed to afford relief and protection to the state and its citizens. This committee reported early in February, and found an alarming amount of destitution among the laboring class. They thought that the number of the destitute was at least 30,000, and perhaps was 40,000. There was distress and suffering, which in some cases bordered on actual starvation.

The Commanding General, who was at the time Gillem of Tennessee, sided with the planting interests, refused to cooperate with the convention in this matter, and declared that the demand for labor exceeded the supply. In other words, labor must work for food or starve. It was reported that the Negroes were still expecting the distribution of land. Suspension of taxes imposed upon freedmen prior to January 1, 1868, was demanded, and the repudiation of all debts, contracts and judgments incurred or made prior to April 28, 1865. The Commanding General was requested to issue an order "directing the restoration of property alleged to have been unlawfully taken from colored persons on the grounds that property accumulated by them in a state of slavery belonged to their masters." This the General declined to do.

The Commanding General was again requested, in a report signed by three colored members, to furnish from the public funds means to return slaves sold into Mississippi to their former homes, and Congress was asked to set aside, through the Freedmen's Bureau, one-half of the cotton tax collected in the state. They asked the Governor of the state to let Negroes share in the donations sent him for the relief of the destitute; but the Governor refused, saying that it was a private gift.

After this preliminary discussion, which was afterward criticized as beside the point, when in fact it was the main point, the convention turned toward making a new Constitution, as they had refused to adopt the old. They framed a Constitution under which Mississippi lived for twenty-two years. It did away with property qualifications for office or for suffrage; it forbade slavery; it provided for a mixed public school system; it forbade race distinctions in the possession and inheritance of property; it prohibited the abridgment of civil, rights in travel; and in general, it was a modern instrument based on universal suffrage.

A minority tried to disfranchise the mass of ignorant Negroes, and there was considerable quarreling and some fighting. Universal suffrage was adopted by a large majority, and on account of that, 12 of the white delegates resigned. Other ordinances forbade property qualification for office, or educational qualification for suffrage.

The civil government under Reconstruction increased the powers of the Governor and made a more elaborate governmental organization and function for the state. It provided for a Lieutenant-Governor, a State Superintendent of Education, and numerous other officials. Some of the counties were consolidated to form larger legislative districts. Evidently, the success of the planters in controlling the Negro vote alarmed the carpetbaggers and the poor whites, and they determined to suppress the ringleaders of the rebellion far more drastically than was required by the Reconstruction Acts.

The convention consequently determined to deny the right to vote and hold office to practically all whites who had anything to do with the Rebellion, and thus the proposed Constitution disfranchised perhaps 20,000 or more of the leading white citizens of the state. This has been represented as petty

jealousy and desire for vengeance on the part of the carpetbaggers. It was more than this. It was an attempt to end the
oligarchy of landlords who still advocated slavery and the
rule of wealth.

After sitting 115 days, the Convention adjourned and submitted the Constitution to the people. The proceedings in
this convention had undoubtedly been dominated by the
wishes of the Northern men and the poor whites, with the
support of the Negroes. But instead of cementing the alliance,
the Negroes were ignored, and when preparations were made
for the campaign, were given little recognition. The chief
evidence of this was failure to nominate Negroes for office;
the real policy beneath this was ignoring the plight of Negro
labor, and making the Republican Party chiefly the mouth-
piece of the new Northern capital. The opposition organized
as the Democratic White Men's Party of Mississippi and declared that the Republicans were trying to degrade the Cau-
casian race. The provision for a mixed school system particularly came in for widespread criticism.

Meantime, Humphreys was removed as Governor on account of opposition to the Reconstruction Acts, and General
Adelbert Ames appointed Acting Governor. Humphreys refused to give up, and was removed by the soldiers. But reaction was not beaten. The vote of the Black Belt was cast
largely under the dictation of the landholders and hirers of
black labor. The result of the election was a surprise. Fifty-
six thousand, two hundred and thirty-one votes were cast for
the Constitution, 63,860 were cast against it, and Humphreys
had been reelected Governor.

A committee of five from the Convention announced that
the election had been carried by fraud and intimidation, accompanied by social proscription and threats to discharge
laborers from employment. The Republicans held meetings
in various counties, declaring that the late election had been
the work of terrorism and fraud.

On the other hand, the result of the election was to show
all parties that a more sincere attempt to recognize the Negro
and enable him to vote had to be made. Negroes could not be

ignored. Their right to vote meant something. If they were intimidated and coerced by force and economic means, the planters would soon be back in power. Moreover, even in this election, certain leading Negroes, like John R. Lynch, had deliberately voted with the planters, and an alliance of planters and Negroes was not impossible. It would have been an alliance based partly on labor control and partly on understandings consummated between black labor leaders and white landholders. Working out from the old slavery, it might have gradually negotiated an industrial emancipation for the intelligent blacks, while using the solid black vote to keep white labor and Northern capital subordinate. One group of Negroes recommended, therefore, another constitutional convention. They said they wished to cultivate kindly relations with their white friends, and declared that they would support capable and honorable men, even if they were former Confederates.

The 40th Congress adjourned with the question of Mississippi unsettled. Finally, in April, 1869, a bill was agreed upon which directed that Mississippi was to be admitted when she adopted the Fifteenth Amendment, and that the President was authorized to submit the Constitution as a whole and also the same Constitution with its provisions disfranchising the bulk of Confederates left out. Gillam was removed, and General Ames, who had been acting Civil Governor, was made Provisional Governor of the state. He reported that certain men, backed by public opinion, were committing murders and outrages. Under direction of Congress, Ames removed a large number of officers, and made appointments of state and local officers, including several Negroes. Among other things, he declared freedmen to be competent jurors. He said of his work at this time:

"I found when I was Military Governor of Mississippi, that a black code existed there; that Negroes had no rights, and that they were not permitted to exercise the rights of citizenship. I had given them the protection they were entitled to under the laws, and I believed I could render them great service. I felt that I had a mission to perform in their interest, and I hesitatingly consented to represent them and unite my fortune with theirs."

Ames thus made a counter bid for Negro support, reversing the indifferent stand of the Mississippi Republicans. In July, President Grant issued a proclamation ordering the Constitution to be submitted for ratification November 30. The Radical Republicans held their convention July 2 and attempted a platform of several resolutions. These resolutions declared: "In favor of an impartial and economic administration of the government; the unrestricted right of speech to all men at all times and places; unrestrained freedom of the ballot; a system of free schools; a reform of the 'iniquitous and unequal' system of taxation and assessments which discriminated against labor; declared that all men without regard to race, color or previous condition of servitude were equal before the law; recommended removal of political disabilities as soon as the 'spirit of toleration now dawning upon the state' should be so firmly established as to justify Congress in taking such action; declared in favor of universal amnesty, universal suffrage, and encouragement of immigration."

Ex-Governor Brown and the Conservatives were in favor of ratifying the Constitution without the proscriptive provisions and of accepting the Fifteenth Amendment. They secured Judge Dent, a brother-in-law of Grant, as their candidate, thinking in that way to secure the good will of Grant: But Grant repudiated the party that nominated Dent. The Dent party nominated Thomas Sinclair, a colored man, for Secretary of State. The Republicans nominated General J. L. Alcorn for Governor, and the Reverend James Lynch, a mulatto preacher, for Secretary of State.

The whole election showed the increasing political importance of the Negroes, and this undoubtedly explains the increased activity of the Ku Klux Klan in 1869. There were some riots in three or four counties. The Constitution was ratified almost unanimously, but the proscriptive sections disfranchising members of the Secession Convention and other active Confederates were defeated. The provision forbidding the loan of state funds was ratified.

The first Reconstruction legislature met at Jackson, January 11, 1870. The legislature elected in 1868 had never been convened because of the defeat of the Constitution. Negro membership in the new legislature was larger than in the convention. There were forty colored members, some of whom had been slaves before the war; but among them were some "very intelligent" men. Particularly, there was considerable representation of ministers. In the Senate, there were five colored members.

Many of the wealthiest counties were represented by ex-slaves. Yet as Lynch shows, Negroes never controlled Mississippi. "No colored man in that state ever occupied a judicial position above that of Justice of the Peace, and very few aspired to that position. Of seven state officers, only one, that of Secretary of State, was filled by a colored man, until 1873, when colored men were elected to three of the seven offices, Lieutenant-Governor, Secretary of State, and State Superintendent of Education. Of the two United States Senators, and the seven members of the Lower House of Congress, not more than one colored man occupied a seat in each House at the same time. Of the thirty-five members of the State Senate, and of the one hundred and fifteen members of the House,—which composed the total membership of the State Legislature prior to 1874,—there were never more than about seven colored men in the Senate and forty in the Lower House. Of the ninety-seven members that composed the constitutional convention of 1868, but seventeen were colored men. The composition of the Lower House of the State Legislature that was elected in 1871 was as follows:

"Total membership, one hundred and fifteen; Republicans, sixty-six; Democrats, forty-nine; colored members, thirty-eight; white members, seventy-seven; white majority, thirty-nine.

"Of the sixty-six Republicans, thirty-eight were colored men and twenty-eight, white. There was a slight increase in the colored membership as a result of the election of 1873, but the colored men never at any time had control of the State Government, nor of any branch or department thereof, nor even that of any county or municipality. Out of seventy-two counties in the State at that time, electing on an average twenty-eight officers to a county, it is safe to assert that not over five out of one hundred of such officers were colored men. The State, district, county and municipal governments were not only in control of white men, but white men who were to the manor born, or who were known as old citizens of the state, those who had lived in the state many years before the War of the Rebellion. There was, therefore, never a time when that class of white men, known as Carpetbaggers, had absolute control of state government, or that of any district, county or municipality, or any branch or department thereof. There was never, therefore, any ground for the alleged apprehension of Negro domination as a result of a free, fair, and honest election in any one of the Southern or Reconstructed States."

At the same time, the Negroes were laborers, and if at any time the white and black labor vote united, property and privilege in Mississippi were bound to suffer. And on the other hand, if property controlled black labor, white labor would be as helpless as before the war. These two fears explain Reconstruction in Mississippi.

The legislature ratified the Fourteenth and Fifteenth Amendments and elected three United States Senators, one for the full term, and two for unexpired terms. For the full term, Alcorn was chosen, and for one unexpired term, General Ames; while Hiram R. Revels, a colored minister, was chosen to fill the unexpired term of Jefferson Davis.

Revels came from North Carolina and was educated in Indiana; he was a minister in Baltimore at the opening of the war, and there helped to organize two colored regiments. He came South with the Freedmen's Bureau, and was surprised when selected to represent the state in the Senate. He was a man of intelligence, but the Republican United States debated three days on his credentials. Finally, after one of Sumner's ablest speeches, he was admitted. Even after that, Philadelphia refused the use of her Academy of Music for a meeting at which he was to speak.

Ames now turned over the government to Alcorn and went to the Senate. Alcorn took a firm and advanced stand. In his inaugural speech, he spoke of his attachment tor Mississippi. He declared that it was the duty of the government to protect all its citizens, white and black, before the ballot box, the jury box and public office, and to give industrial opportunity to the honest and competent without discrimination of color. He said:

"In the face of memories that might have separated them from me, as the wronged from the wronger, they offered me their confidence, offered me the guardianship of their new and precious hopes, with a trustfulness whose very mention stirs my nerves with emotion. In response to that touching radiance, the most profound anxiety with which I enter my office as Governor of this state is that of making the colored man the equal before the law of every other man—the equal, not in dead letter, but in living fact." He had a word to say for the poor whites. "Thousands of our worthy white friends have ever remained to a great extent strangers to the helping hand of the state."

Unfortunately, Alcorn instead of staying and finishing this job thus well outlined, had the universal Southern ambition of the day to go to the United States Senate. He was, therefore, in office only a little over a year, when he went to Washington to succeed Revels. The legislature, meantime, went to work to set up the government.

The part which the Negro played in this Reconstruction was as extraordinary as it was unexpected. There were far fewer Negroes of education and ability in Mississippi than in South Carolina or Louisiana. But there were a few, perhaps a bare half-dozen, who gave universal and epoch-making service.

. . . . .

The legislature of 1871 was in session about six months, and passed 325 acts and resolutions. The increase of citizenship, and the revolution through which the state had passed, called without doubt for more laws. The expenses of the legislative department were large and the session long. Yet it can hardly be said, considering the work done and the depreciated value of currency, that it was an extravagant assembly.

The legislature of 1872 had John R. Lynch, a Negro, as Speaker of the House. There were 28 white and 38 colored Republicans and 49 Democrats, and it took a trip of Senator Alcorn from Washington to induce enough white Republicans to support Lynch in order to elect him. At the close of the session, however, Lynch was presented with a gold watch and chain. On motion of a prominent white Democrat, a resolution was adopted thanking him "for his dignity, impartiality and courtesy as a presiding officer." The *Clarion* declared: "His bearing in office had been so proper, and his rulings in such marked contrast to the former conduct of the ignoble whites of his party, who had been aspiring to be leaders of the blacks, that the Conservatives cheerfully joined in the testimonial."

Civil rights measures constituted a considerable part of the legislation between 1868 and 1876. In his inaugural address, Governor Alcorn "asserted positively that so long as he was governor, all citizens, without respect to color or nativity, should be shielded by the law as with a panoply."

In 1870, "all laws relative to free Negroes, slaves and mulattoes, as found in the Code of 1857 and the laws constituting the so-called Black Codes," were declared to be forever repealed. It was declared to be the true intent and meaning of the legislature to remove from the records of the state all laws "which in any manner recognized any natural difference or distinction between citizens and inhabitants of the state."

The legislature elected in 1873 had 37 members of the Senate, of whom nine were colored, and nine white carpetbaggers. In the House over 115 members, of whom 55 were colored and 60 white, including 15 carpetbaggers. This election went further than any toward a fusion of planters and Negroes, and this was only prevented by the rivalry of Alcorn and Ames.

When Alcorn went to the Senate, he was succeeded by a carpetbagger, R. C. Powers. Finally in 1873, Ames, who had been in the United States Senate, was elected Governor over Alcorn, who was again candidate. With Ames, three colored men went to office: A. K. Davis, Lieutenant-Governor; James

Hill, Secretary of State; and T. W. Cardozo, Superintendent of Education. B. K. Bruce had been selected for Lieutenant-Governor, but refused, and afterward went to the Senate.

This greatly disappointed Alcorn, who wished to remain in the Senate, and who, therefore, refused to escort Bruce to take the oath. Bruce had been County Assessor, Parish and Tax Collector in Bolivar County, one of the wealthiest counties in the state.

"Davis, the new Lieutenant-Governor, had made a creditable record as member of the legislature, but he was not a strong man. Hill was young, active and aggressive, and above the average colored man in intelligence. Cardozo was capable but not well-known."

As to the colored men in the Legislature of 1873, Garner says:

"Relative to the course of the colored members in this legislature, a prominent Democrat writes me as follows: 'In my opinion, if they had all been native Southern Negroes, there would have been little cause of complaint. They often wanted to vote with Democrats on non-political questions, but could not resist the party lash. The majority of whites in both parties exhibit the same weakness.' "

The real meaning of this criticism was that the Negroes wanted to cooperate with the planters, but knew that the planters would disfranchise them at the first opportunity, and only welcomed their alliance now for economic reasons. On the other hand, the Republicans were torn with factions, jealousies and suspicions, and the Negroes did not know how far they could be trusted.

With a few exceptions, the colored members took little part in the work of legislation, although some of the principal chairmanships were held by them. There were few educated men among them, and they watched only for efforts to abridge their privileges as voters and citizens. On the other hand, there were no charges of venality or bribery, and their efforts to learn were intense. They were too willing to take advice and follow leadership, once their confidence had been obtained.

The number of prominent planters in Mississippi who entered the Republican Party to lead the Negroes was unusually large as compared with other states.

Ames immediately began a program of retrenchment in expenditures, and recommended many reforms. Taxes had been increased from one mill on the dollar in 1869 to fourteen in 1874. The credit of the state was still impaired. He recommended a cut of 25% in appropriations, and especially curtailing the bill for public printing. "The recommendations," says Garner, "do credit to the Governor who made them. They do not sound like the utterance of a carpetbagger bent on peculation and plunder."

There were the usual charges of extravagance against the Reconstruction government.

"It should, however, be said that if the testimony of Governor Ames may be followed relative to the expenses of the state government during the two years in which he was at its head, his was the most economical administration since 1856, with the exception of two years, 1861 and 1869."

It was charged that the public debt of Mississippi increased from almost nothing to $20,000,000 during the Reconstruction régime, but this was easily disproved by ex-Governor Ames, who had the figures; and the committee of Democratic legislators that sought to impeach him had to acknowledge the truth of what he said.

"Thus it will be seen that the actual indebtedness of the state is but little over a half million dollars, and that during the two years of Governor Ames' administration, the state debt had been reduced from $821,292.82 on January first, 1874, to $520,138.33, on January first, 1876; or a reduction of more than three hundred thousand dollars in two years—upwards of one-third of the state debt wiped out in that time. Not only has the debt been reduced as above, but the rate of taxation for general purposes has been reduced from seven mills in 1873 to four mills in 1875."

"It should also be said by way of explanation, that the work of restoration which the government was obliged to undertake, made increased expenses necessary. During the period of the war, and for several years thereafter, public buildings and state institutions were permitted to fall into decay. The state house and grounds, the executive mansion, the penitentiary, the insane asylum, and the buildings for the blind, deaf and dumb, were in a dilapidated condition, and had to be extended and repaired. A new building for the blind was purchased and fitted up. The Reconstructionists established a public school system and spent money to maintain and support it, perhaps too freely, in view of the impoverishment of the people. When they took hold, warrants were worth but sixty or seventy cents on the dollar, a fact which made the price of building materials used in the work of construction correspondingly higher."

Garner admits there were no great railroad swindles and no charge of excessive debt. The only charge which is perhaps true was that the number of offices and agencies was needlessly increased.

The one center of undoubted graft under Ames was the public printing contracts, which increased from $8,675 a year, 1867–1868, to sums varying from $50,000 to $127,000 in 1870–1875. This seems, however, to have been largely due to one white man and it is not clear whether he was Northern- or Southern-born.

Rhodes declares that few Negroes were competent to perform their duties and that one who was sheriff of DeSoto County for four years could neither read nor write and farmed out his office to a white deputy for a share of the revenue. John R. Lynch proves that this statement is absolutely false. The Reverend J. J. Evans, a colored Baptist minister and a Union soldier, who held that position, gave entire satisfaction; he left office with a spotless record, accounted for every cent of the funds, and he had, as he wrote, a letter from Evans before him, which showed that Evans could read and write.

Mr. Lynch goes on to say that of the seventy-two counties of the state, not more than twelve ever had colored sheriffs, and that he knew ten of these; and that "in point of intelligence, capacity and honesty, the colored sheriffs would have favorably compared with the whites." When one considers that over one-half of the electors had been slaves, now for the first time given a voice in government, Reconstruction in Mississippi certainly seems like a success.

The Negro leaders who came to the front were in most cases admirable and honest men; and only a few were corrupt. The advance of the masses of the people was shown in the increase of marriage licenses. In 1865, licenses were issued to whites, 2,708, and to blacks, 564, while in 1870, 2,204 were issued to whites, and 3,427 to blacks. In those two years, churches built increased from 105 to 283.

A curious feud between the Governor and his colored Lieutenant-Governor began in the summer of 1874, when Governor Ames went North on his vacation. The Lieutenant-Governor discharged certain appointees, and appointed several judges. Governor Ames, upon returning, revoked these appointees. Lieutenant-Governor Davis also issued a large number of pardons to persons in jail.

Singularly enough, while one of the accusations in the attempted impeachment of Ames was his dismissal of Davis' judicial appointees, Davis was also removed from office in 1876. It was alleged that he had accepted a bribe for granting a pardon. On the other hand, the Governor's action in revoking Davis' appointments was called by this legislature of 1876 "willful, corrupt and unlawful."

It was the especial grievance of the whites that officials and voters were not taxpayers, and that a comparatively small number of the colored voters owned real estate. The most that was charged was that the number of offices and agencies with high salaries was needlessly multiplied. The break came, however, between labor and capital inside the Democratic party.

"Of course a stubborn and bitter fight for control of the Democratic organization was now on between the antagonistic and conflicting elements among the whites. It was to be a desperate struggle between former aristocrats, on one side, and what was known as 'poor whites' on the other. While the aristocrats had always been the weaker in point of numbers, they had been the stronger in point of wealth, intelligence, ability, skill and experience. As a result of their wide experience, and able and skillful management, the aristocrats were successful in the preliminary struggles, as illustrated in the persons of Stephens, Gordon, Brown and Hill, of Georgia; Daniels and Lee, of Virginia; Hampton and Butler of South Carolina; Lamar and Walthall of Mississippi, and Garland of Arkansas. But in the course of time and in the natural order of things the poor whites were bound to win. All that was needed was a few years' tutelage, and a few daring and unscrupulous leaders to prey upon their ignorance and magnify their vanity, in order to bring them to a realization of the fact that their former political masters were now completely at their mercy, and subject to their will."

"After the Presidential election of 1872, Southern white men were not only coming into the Republican Party in large numbers, but the liberal and progressive element of the democracy was in the ascendency in that organization. That element, therefore, shaped the policy and declared the principles for which that organization stood. This meant the acceptance by all political parties of what was regarded as the settled policy of the National Government. In proof of this assertion, a quotation from a political editorial which appeared about that time in the Jackson, Mississippi, *Clarion,*—the organ of the Democratic Party,—will not be out of place. In speaking of the colored people and their attitude towards the white, that able and influential paper said:

" 'While they [the colored people] have been naturally tenacious of their newly acquired privileges, their general conduct will bear them witness that they have shown consideration for the feelings of the whites. The race line in politics would not have been drawn if opposition had not been made to their enjoyment of equal privileges in the government, and under the laws after they were emancipated.'

"In other words, the colored people had manifested no disposition to rule or dominate the whites, and the only Color Line which had existed, grew out of the unwise policy which had previously been pursued by the Democratic Party in its efforts to prevent the enjoyment by the newly-emancipated race of the rights and privileges to which they were entitled, under the Constitution and laws of the country. But after the state and congressional elections of 1874, the situation was materially changed. The liberal and conservative element of the democracy was relegated to the rear and the radical element came to the front and assumed charge."

Here is a record which is not bad. There was no violent revolution in Mississippi. There was no attack upon civilization and culture. There was increased expense, partly for legitimate objects, partly, without doubt, by injudicious and careless expenditure; possibly in some cases by corrupt expenditure.

"In the fall of 1875 just at the time when the whole state rang with assertions of Radical misrule, taxation and robbery, the Author traveled through Mississippi, east and west, north and south, traveled quietly and was personally unknown. At every town and village, at every station on the railroads and every rural neighborhood in the country, he heard Governor Ames and the Republican Party denounced for oppressions, robberies and dishonesty as proved by the fearful rate of taxation. He asked what was the per cent of taxes on the dollar, but never got an answer. One citizen replied: 'Our taxes are enormous.' Another said: 'They are ruinous.' Another: 'They amount to confiscation.' Such were the only replies given. Every form of words that could be used to express excessive taxation was employed. 'Awful,' 'Fearful,' 'Intolerable,' 'Monstrous,' 'Unheard of,' 'Incredible,' but no man answered the question. For the true answer would have been: 'The average taxation since Reconstruction has been a little less than nine mills on the dollar, for all purposes. Of this average of less than nine mills on the dollar almost one-fifth was for public schools so that the total annual taxation for all other purposes has been a little over seven mills on the dollar.' This was the true answer, but every White Leaguer knew better than to answer the question, for one of the originators of that order wrote confidentially to an associate that they must appeal to the world 'as a wretched, downtrodden and impoverished people.' "

On the whole, one cannot escape the impression that what the whites in Mississippi feared was that the experiment of Negro suffrage might succeed. At any rate, they began a revolution known as the "Mississippi plan." Here was no labor dictatorship or dream of one. White labor took up arms to subdue black labor and to make it helpless economically and politically through the power of property.

Senator Revels, of Mississippi, said in the 41st Congress:

"Mr. President, I maintain that the past record of my race is a true index of the feelings which today animate them. They bear toward their former masters no revengeful thoughts, no hatred, no animosities. They aim not to elevate themselves by sacrificing one single interest of their white fellow citizens. They ask but the rights which are theirs by God's universal law, and which are the natural outgrowth, the logical sequence of the condition in which the legislative enactments of this nation have placed them. They appeal to you and to me to see that they receive that protection which alone will enable them to pursue their daily avocations with success and enjoy the liberties of citizenship on the same footing with their white neighbors and friends."

John R. Lynch said, when he was counted out of his election:

"You certainly cannot expect them [the Negroes] to resort to mob law and brute force, or to use what may be milder language, inaugurate a revolution. My opinion is that revolution is not the remedy to be applied in such cases. Our system of government is supposed to be one of law and order, resting upon the consent of the governed, as expressed through the peaceful medium of the ballot. In all localities where the local public sentiment is so dishonest, so corrupt, and so demoralized, as to tolerate the commission of election frauds, and shield the perpetrators from justice, such people must be made to understand that there is patriotism enough in this country and sufficient love of justice and fair play in the hearts of the American people to prevent any party from gaining the ascendency in the government that relies upon a fraudulent ballot and a false return as the chief source of its support.

"The impartial historian will record the fact that the colored people of the South have contended for their rights with a bravery and a gallantry that is worthy of the highest commendation. Being, unfortunately, in dependent circumstances with the preponderance of the wealth and intelligence against them in some localities, yet they have bravely refused to surrender their honest convictions, even upon the altar of their personal necessities."

With riot, fraud, boycott and intimidation, Negro rule was overthrown. William L. Hemingway was nominated against Captain George M. Buchanan, an able and well-qualified man. In an honest election, Buchanan would have been given the office, but Hemingway was declared elected. However, he had been in office only a brief time, when the discovery was made that he was a defaulter to the amount of $315,612.19. Thus "Reform" began.

For Further Reading

A good introduction to the traditional interpretation is William A. Dunning, *Reconstruction: Political and Economic 1865–1877* (1907), which may be supplemented with his *Essays on Civil War and Reconstruction* (1897). Both are available in recent paperback editions. Among the large group of state studies from the Dunning school are James W. Garner, *Reconstruction in Mississippi* (1901), Walter L. Fleming, *The Civil War and Reconstruction in Alabama* (1905), J. G. de Roulhae Hamilton, *Reconstruction in North Carolina* (1914), C. M. Thompson, *Reconstruction in Georgia* (1915), and Charles W. Ramsdell, *Reconstruction in Texas* (1910). Fleming's *Documentary History of Reconstruction* (2 vols., 1906–1907) is a most comprehensive collection of source materials.

Any student probing into the revisionist history of Reconstruction might well begin with these articles: Frances B. Simkins, "New Viewpoints of Southern Reconstruction," *Journal of Southern History* (1939), Howard K. Beale, "On Rewriting Reconstruction History," *American Historical Re-*

view (1940), and Bernard A. Weisberger, "The Dark and Bloody Ground of Reconstruction Historiography," *Journal of Southern History* (1959). Full-length reevaluations include Kenneth Stampp, *The Era of Reconstruction* (1965), John Hope Franklin, *Reconstruction after the Civil War* (1961), and Rembert W. Patrick, *The Reconstruction of the Nation* (1966). In addition, there are several excellent monographs on special aspects of the period which should be noted, including W. R. Brock, *An American Crisis: Congress and Reconstruction 1865–1867* (1963), Otis Singletary, *The Negro Militia and Reconstruction* (1957), John H. and La Wanda Cox, *Politics, Principle and Prejudice 1865–1866* (1963), and C. Vann Woodward, *Reunion and Reaction* (1951), a penetrating analysis of the disputed election of 1876 and the Compromise of 1877.

The biographical literature is rich. Milton Lomask, *Andrew Johnson: President on Trial* (1960), and Eric McKitrick, *Andrew Johnson and Reconstruction* (1960), present contrasting interpretations of the seventeenth President. Other valuable biographies include Benjamin D. Thomas and Harold M. Hyman, *Stanton* (1962), Fawn M. Brodie, *Thaddeus Stevens* (1959), and Hans L. Trefousse, *Benjamin Franklin Wade* (1963).

The New York Gold Conspiracy

Henry Adams

For the most part, European historians now reject the term "industrial revolution" because it tends to exaggerate both the rate and extent of industrial changes that occurred in the late eighteenth and early nineteenth centuries. The developments in technology, finance, and organization are seen as part of a continuing, ever widening stream of change beginning in the late medieval period. Similarly in American history, few writers still use the revolutionary frame of reference in referring to the burgeoning economy of the United States in the years after 1865. Most of the elements of change have been traced back to antebellum years, some as far back as 1812 in New England.

Nonetheless, it is indisputable that during these years a rural, agrarian nation transformed itself into an urban industrial one. In the process, the gross national product more than doubled between 1865 and 1890; the amount of capital invested in manufacturing increased from $1 billion to $10 billion and the number of industrial workers increased five times to over five million. With growth came change in organizations, culminating in the estab-

Source: Charles Francis Adams, Jr., and Henry Adams, *Chapters of Erie and Other Essays* (New York: Henry Holt, 1886), pp. 101–136.

lishment of huge combinations or trusts. The term trust
designated a virtual monopoly in the production of a
particular commodity and in most cases came to be
associated in the popular mind with eminently successful
business entrepreneurs—John D. Rockefeller in oil, Andrew Carnegie in steel, Philip Armour in meat-packing.
Their admirers referred to these titans as captains of
industry or prophets of progress; their critics called them
Robber Barons. The latter term appeared perhaps for
the first time in 1869 when E. L. Godkin, editor of the
Nation, described Commodore Vanderbilt as a lineal
descendant of the medieval barons who preyed upon
their neighbors. In the opinion of Godkin, of many of
his contemporaries, and of some later historians, the
epithet perfectly suited the ruthless capitalists who
robbed investors and consumers, corrupted governments,
and fought viciously among themselves. To these charges,
one of those indicted, Andrew Carnegie, retorted that
concentration of power brought great economic advantages to all: "The poor enjoy what the rich could not
before afford." John D. Rockefeller, always believing that
God had intended him to be rich, defended his competitive practices in Darwinian terms: "The growth of a
large business is merely the survival of the fittest. . . .
The American Beauty rose can be produced in the splendor and fragrance which bring cheer to the beholder
only by sacrificing the early buds which grow up around
it." Ida Tarbell, who studied Rockefeller's Standard Oil
Company in a series of muckraking articles published
by *McClure's Magazine* at the turn of the century, con-
ceded his point that "sacrificing the early buds," that is,
eliminating competitors, created certain benefits for the
economy. But she decried the methods used: price cutting
to eliminate the competitor followed by a gouging of the
consumer, industrial espionage, and bribery. In short,
the system resulted in the blunting of a sense of right
and fairness. Although this view has been endorsed by
several modern scholars, another group, known collectively as the entrepreneurial school, while not denying
the existence of sharp and unethical practices, finds the

Robber Baron concept of little utility. Placing the business leaders within the context of their times, they find
many of them to be more constructive than destructive.

Hardly anyone, however, contemporary or afterward,
has found anything constructive about Jay Gould or Jim
Fisk, Jr. By 1868, this duo had established their reputations for lawlessness and chicanery in their ferocious but
successful struggle with Commodore Vanderbilt and
Daniel Drew for the control of the Erie Railroad. Fortunately, for posterity, their operations had been carefully
watched by two descendants of one of the nation's most
favored families, Charles Francis Adams, Jr. (1835–1915),
and Henry Adams (1838–1918) The Adams' attitude
toward business combination was somewhat ambivalent.
They believed much economic good for the country ac-
crued from concentration, but their study of the Erie
"pirates" led them to conclude that the use of corporate
power was almost by equation the use of corruption. In
his essays "A Chapter of Erie" and "An Erie Raid,"
Charles in a superbly ironic style dissected the legal and
moral complexities of the Erie wars, while Henry in his
essay on the gold conspiracy of 1869 tells how the two
notorious corruptionists nearly wrecked the nation's financial system. Gould and Fisk had gained control of the
Erie Railroad chiefly by buying legal immunity from the
Tweed Ring which controlled New York politicos. The
Grant administration provided them with an excellent
opportunity to manipulate government on the national
level. The chance arose not because Grant was dishonest
but because he was obtuse. Of him, Henry Adams remarked, "the progress of evolution from President Washington to President Grant was alone evidence enough to
upset Darwin. An organism as simple as Grant," Adams
went on, "should have been extinct for ages."

With the help of the President's avaricious brother-
in-law and his old crony General Daniel Butterfield,
Gould and Fisk hoped to corner the New York gold
market. Adams' analysis of the scheme is close and penetrating. He is primarily concerned with reporting the
incident to an English audience and the essay is free from
the unsupported, albeit intriguing, generalizations that

characterize some of his later works. His account has stood the test of time and further research has confirmed his investigation in all but a few details. One correction should be noted. At the time he wrote Adams did not know the extent of Gould's profits; he in fact concluded "every person involved in the affair seems to have lost money." This was certainly not true in Jay Gould's case. A recent scholar estimates Gould made $11 million, which he subsequently divided with Fisk.

*T*he civil war in America, with its enormous issues of depreciating currency, and its reckless waste of money and credit by the government, created a speculative mania such as the United States, with all its experience in this respect, had never before known. Not only in Broad Street, the centre of New York speculation, but far and wide throughout the Northern States, almost every man who had money at all employed a part of his capital in the purchase of stocks or of gold, of copper, of petroleum, or of domestic produce, in the hope of a rise in prices, or staked money on the expectation of a fall. To use the jargon of the street, every farmer and every shopkeeper in the country seemed to be engaged in "carrying" some favorite security "on a margin." Whoever could obtain five pounds sent it to a broker with orders to buy fifty pounds' worth of stocks, or whatever amount the broker would consent to purchase. If the stock rose, the speculator prospered; if it fell until the five pounds of deposit or margin were lost, the broker demanded a new deposit, or sold the stock to protect himself. By means of this simple and smooth machinery, which differs in no essential respect from the processes of *roulette* or *rouge-et-noir,* the whole nation flung itself into the Stock Exchange, until the "outsiders," as they were called, in opposition to the regular brokers of Broad Street, represented nothing less than the entire population of the American Republic. Every one speculated, and for a time every one speculated successfully.

The inevitable reaction began when the government, about a year after the close of the war, stopped its issues and ceased borrowing. The greenback currency had for a moment sunk to a value of only 37 cents to the dollar. It is even asserted that on the worst day of all, the 11th of July, 1864, one sale of £20,000 in gold was actually made at 310 which is equivalent to about 33 cents in the dollar. At this point, however, the depreciation stopped; and the paper which had come so near falling into entire discredit steadily rose in value, first to 50 cents, then to 60, to 70, and within the present year to more than 90 cents. So soon as the industrious part of the public felt the touch of this return to solid values, the whole fabric of fictitious wealth began to melt away under their eyes.

Thus it was not long before the so-called "outsiders," the men who speculated on their own account, and could not act in agreement or combination, began to suffer. One by one, or in great masses, they were made the prey of the larger operators; their last margins were consumed, and they dropped down to the solid level of slow, productive industry. Some lost everything; many lost still more than they had, and there are few families of ordinary connection and standing in the United States which cannot tell, if they choose, some dark story of embezzlement, or breach of trust, committed in these days. Some men, who had courage and a sense of honor, found life too heavy for them; others went mad. But the greater part turned in silence to their regular pursuits, and accepted their losses as they could. Almost every rich American could produce from some pigeon-hole a bundle of worthless securities, and could show check-books representing the only remaining trace of margin after margin consumed in vain attempts to satisfy the insatiable broker. A year or two of incessant losses swept the weaker gamblers from the street.

But even those who continued to speculate found it necessary to change their mode of operations. Chance no longer ruled over the Stock Exchange and the gold market. The fate of a battle, the capture of a city, or the murder of a President, had hitherto been the influences which broke

through the plans of the strongest combinations, and put all
speculators, whether great or small, on fairly even ground;
but as the period of sudden and uncontrollable disturbing
elements passed away, the market fell more and more completely into the hands of cliques which found a point of ad-
hesion in some great mass of incorporated capital. Three
distinct railways, with all their enormous resources, became
the property of Cornelius Vanderbilt, who, by means of their
credit and capital, again and again swept millions of dollars
into his pocket by a process curiously similar to gambling
with loaded dice. But Vanderbilt was one of the most respectable of these great operators. The Erie Railway was
controlled by Daniel Drew, and while Vanderbilt at least acted
in the interests of his corporations, Drew cheated equally his
corporation and the public. Between these two men and the
immense incorporated power they swayed, smaller operators,
one after another, were crushed to pieces, until the survivors
learned to seek shelter within some clique sufficiently strong
to afford protection. Speculation in this manner began to
consume itself, and the largest combination of capital was
destined to swallow every weaker combination which ventured to show itself in the market.

Thus, between the inevitable effect of a currency which
steadily shrank the apparent wealth of the country, and the
omnipotence of capital in the stock market, a sounder and
healthier state of society began to make itself felt. Nor could
the unfortunate public, which had been robbed with such
cynical indifference by Drew and Vanderbilt, feel any sincere
regret when they saw these two cormorants reduced to tearing
each other. In the year 1867 Mr. Vanderbilt undertook to
gain possession of the Erie Road, as he had already obtained
possession of the New York Central, the second trunk line
between New York and the West. Mr. Vanderbilt was supposed to own property to the value of some £10,000,000, all
of which might be made directly available for stock operations. He bought the greater part of the Erie stock; Drew
sold him all he could take, and then issued as much more as
was required in order to defeat Vanderbilt's purpose. After a

violent struggle, which overthrew all the guaranties of social order, Drew triumphed, and Mr. Vanderbilt abandoned the contest. The Erie corporation paid him a large sum to reimburse his alleged losses. At the same time it was agreed that Mr. Drew's accounts should be passed, and he obtained a release in full, and retired from the direction. And the Erie Road, almost exhausted by such systematic plundering, was left in the undisturbed, if not peaceful, control of Mr. Jay Gould and Mr. James Fisk, Jr., whose reign began in the month of July, 1868.

Mr. Jay Gould was a partner in the firm of Smith, Gould, & Martin, brokers, in Wall Street. He had been engaged before now in railway enterprises, and his operations had not been of a nature likely to encourage public confidence in his ideas of fiduciary relations. He was a broker, and a broker is almost by nature a gambler, perhaps the very last profession suitable for a railway manager. In character he was strongly marked by his disposition for silent intrigue. He preferred as a rule to operate on his own account, without admitting other persons into his confidence, and he seemed never to be satisfied except when deceiving every one as to his intentions. There was a reminiscence of the spider in his nature. He spun huge webs, in corners and in the dark, which were seldom strong enough to resist a serious strain at the critical moment. His disposition to this subtlety and elaboration of intrigue was irresistible. It is scarcely necessary to say that he had not a conception of a moral principle. In speaking of this class of men it must be fairly assumed at the outset that they do not and cannot understand how there can be a distinction between right and wrong in matters of speculation, so long as the daily settlements are punctually effected. In this respect Mr. Gould was probably as honest as the mass of his fellows, according to the moral standard of the street; but without entering upon technical questions of roguery, it is enough to say that he was an uncommonly fine and unscrupulous intriguer, skilled in all the processes of stock-gambling, and passably indifferent to the praise or censure of society.

James Fisk, Jr., was still more original in character. He

was not yet forty years of age, and had the instincts of fourteen. He came originally from Vermont, probably the most
respectable and correct State in the Union, and his father had
been a pedler who sold goods from town to town in his native
valley of the Connecticut. The son followed his father's calling
with boldness and success. He drove his huge wagon, made
resplendent with paint and varnish, with four or six horses,
through the towns of Vermont and Western Massachusetts;
and when his father remonstrated in alarm at his reckless
management, the young man, with his usual bravado, took
his father into his service at a fixed salary, with the warning
that he was not to put on airs on the strength of his new
dignity. A large Boston firm which had supplied his goods on
credit, attracted by his energy, took him into the house; the
war broke out; his influence drew the firm into some bold
speculations which were successful; in a few years he retired
with some £20,000, which he subsequently lost. He formed
a connection with Daniel Drew in New York, and a new sign,
ominous of future trouble, was raised in Wall Street, bearing
the names of Fisk & Belden, brokers.

Personally Mr. Fisk was coarse, noisy, boastful, ignorant;
the type of a young butcher in appearance and mind. Nothing
could be more striking than the contrast between him and
his future associate Gould. One was small and slight in person, dark, sallow, reticent, and stealthy, with a trace of Jewish
origin. The other was large, florid, gross, talkative, and ob-
streperous. Mr. Fisk's redeeming point was his humor, which
had a strong flavor of American nationality. His mind was
extraordinarily fertile in ideas and expedients, while his conversation was filled with unusual images and strange forms of
speech, which were caught up and made popular by the New
York press. In respect to honesty as between Gould and Fisk,
the latter was, perhaps, if possible, less deserving of trust than
the former. A story not without a keen stroke of satirical
wit is told by him, which illustrates his estimate of abstract
truth. An old woman who had bought of the elder Fisk a
handkerchief which cost ninepence in the New England currency, where six shillings are reckoned to the dollar, com-

plained to Mr. Fisk, Jr., that his father had cheated her. Mr.
Fisk considered the case maturely, and gave a decision based
on *a priori* principles. "No!" said he, "the old man wouldn't
have told a lie for ninepence"; and then, as if this assertion
needed some reasonable qualification, he added, "though he
would have sold eight of them for a dollar!" The distinction
as regards the father may have been just, since the father
seems to have held old-fashioned ideas as to wholesale and
retail trade; but in regard to the son even this relative degree of truth cannot be predicated with any confidence, since,
if the Investigating Committee of Congress and its evidence
are to be believed, Mr. Fisk seldom or never speaks truth at all.

An intrigue equally successful and disreputable brought
these two men into the Erie Board of Directors, whence they
speedily drove their more timid predecessor Drew. In July,
1868, Gould made himself President and Treasurer of the
corporation. Fisk became Comptroller. A young lawyer, named
Lane, became counsel. These three directors made a majority
of the Executive Committee, and were masters of Erie. The
Board of Directors held no meetings. The Executive Committee was never called together, and the three men—Fisk,
Gould, and Lane—became from this time the absolute, irresponsible owners of the Erie Railway, not less than if it had
been their personal property and plaything.

This property was in effect, like all the great railway corporations, an empire within a republic. It consisted of a trunk
line of road 459 miles in length, with branches 314 miles in
extent, or 773 miles of road in all. Its capital stock amounted
to about £7,000,000. Its gross receipts exceeded £3,000,000
per annum. It employed not less than 15,000 men, and supported their families. Over all this wealth and influence,
greater than that directly swayed by any private citizen, greater
than is absolutely and personally controlled by most kings,
and far too great for the public safety either in a democracy
or in any other form of society, the vicissitudes of a troubled
time placed two men in irresponsible authority; and both these
men belonged to a low and degraded moral and social type.
Such an elevation has been rarely seen in modern history.

Even the most dramatic of modern authors, even Balzac himself, who so loved to deal with similar violent alternations
of fortune, or Alexandre Dumas, with all his extravagance
of imagination, never have reached a conception bolder or
more melodramatic than this, nor have they ever ventured
to conceive a plot so enormous, or a catastrophe so original,
as was now to be developed.

One of the earliest acts of the new rulers was precisely such
as Balzac or Dumas might have predicted and delighted in.
They established themselves in a palace. The old offices of
the Erie Railway were in the lower part of the city, among the
wharves and warehouses; a situation, no doubt, convenient
for business, but by no means agreeable as a residence; and
the new proprietors naturally wished to reside on their property. Mr. Fisk and Mr. Gould accordingly bought a huge
building of white marble, not unlike a European palace,
situated about two miles from the business quarter, and con-
taining a large theatre or opera-house. They also purchased
several smaller houses adjoining it. The opera-house cost about
£140,000, and a large part of the building was at once leased,
by the two purchasers, to themselves as the Erie corporation,
to serve as offices. This suite of apartments was then furnished by themselves, as representing the corporation, at an
expense of some £60,000, and in a style which, though called
vulgar, is certainly not more vulgar than that of the President's official residence, and which would be magnificent in
almost any palace in Europe. The adjoining houses were
connected with the main building; and in one of these Mr.
Fisk had his private apartments, with a private passage to his
opera-box. He also assumed direction of the theatre, of which
he became manager-in-chief. To these royal arrangements he
brought tastes which have been commonly charged as the
worst results of royal license. The atmosphere of the Erie
offices was not supposed to be disturbed with moral prejudices;
and as the opera itself supplied Mr. Fisk's mind with amuse-
ment, so the opera *troupe* supplied him with a permanent
harem. Whatever Mr. Fisk did was done on an extraordinary
scale.

These arrangements, however, regarded only the pleasures of the American Aladdin. In the conduct of their interests the new directors showed a capacity for large conceptions, and a vigor in the execution of their schemes, such as alarmed the entire community. At the annual election in 1868, when Gould, Fisk, and Lane, having borrowed or bought proxies for the greater part of the stock, caused themselves to be elected for the ensuing year, the respectable portion of the public throughout the country was astonished and shocked to learn that the new Board of Directors contained two names peculiarly notorious and obnoxious to honest men,—the names of William M. Tweed and Peter B. Sweeney. To English ears these commonplace, not to say vulgar, titles do not seem singularly alarming; but to every honest American they conveyed a peculiar sense of terror and disgust. The State of New York in its politics is much influenced, if not controlled, by the city of New York. The city politics are so entirely in the hands of the Democratic Party as to preclude even the existence of a strong minority. The party organization centres in a political club, held together by its patronage and the money it controls through a system of jobbery unequalled elsewhere in the world. And the Tammany Club, thus swaying the power of a small nation of several million souls, is itself ruled by William M. Tweed and Peter B. Sweeney, absolute masters of this terrible system of theft and fraud, and to American eyes the incarnation of political immorality.

The effect of this alliance was felt in the ensuing winter in the passage of a bill through the State legislature, and its signature by the Governor, abolishing the former system of annual elections of the entire board of Erie directors, and authorizing the board to classify itself in such a manner that only a portion should be changed each year. The principle of the bill was correct. Its practical effect, however, was to enable Gould and Fisk to make themselves directors for five years, in spite of any attempt on the part of the stockholders to remove them. The formality of annual re-election was spared them; and so far as the stockholders were concerned, there was no great injustice in the act. The Erie Road was in the peculiar position of being without an owner. There was no *cestui que trust,* unless the English stockholders could be called such. In America the stock was almost exclusively held for speculation, not for investment; and in the morals of Wall Street speculation means, or had almost come to mean, disregard of intrinsic value. In this case society at large was the injured party, and society knew its risk.

This step, however, was only a beginning. The Tammany ring, as it is called, exercised a power far beyond politics. Under the existing constitution of the State, the judges of the State courts are elected by the people. There are thirty-three such judges in New York, and each of the thirty-three is clothed with equity powers running through the whole State. Of these judges Tammany Hall elected several, and the Erie Railway controlled others in country districts. Each of these judges might forbid proceedings before any and all the other judges, or stay proceedings in suits already commenced. Thus the lives and the property of the public were in the power of the new combination; and two of the city judges, Barnard and Cardozo, had already acquired a peculiarly infamous reputation as so-called "slaves to the ring," which left no question as to the depths to which their prostitution of justice would descend.

The alliance between Tammany and Erie was thus equivalent to investing Mr. Gould and Mr. Fisk with the highest attributes of sovereignty; but in order to avail themselves to the utmost of their judicial powers, they also required the ablest legal assistance. The degradation of the bench had been rapidly followed by the degradation of the bar. Prominent and learned lawyers were already accustomed to avail themselves of social or business relations with judges to forward private purposes. One whose partner might be elevated to the bench was certain to be generally retained in cases brought before this special judge; and litigants were taught by experience that a retainer in such cases was profitably bestowed. Others found a similar advantage resulting from known social relations with the court. The debasement of tone was not confined to the lower ranks of advocates; and it was probably this steady demoralization of the bar which made it possible for the Erie ring to obtain the services of Mr. David Dudley Field as its legal adviser. Mr. Field, a gentleman of European reputation, in regard to which he is understood to be peculiarly solicitous, was an eminent law reformer, author of the New York Code, delegate of the American Social Science Association to the European International Congress, and asserted by his partner, Mr. Shearman, in evidence before a committee of the New York legislature, to be a man of quixotic sense of honor. Mr. Shearman himself, a gentleman of English parentage, had earned public gratitude by arraigning and deploring, with unsurpassed courage and point, the condition of the New York judiciary, in an admirable essay which will be found in the *North American Review* for July, 1867. The value of Mr. Field's services to Messrs. Fisk and Gould was not to be measured even by the enormous fees their generosity paid him. His power over certain judges became so absolute as to impress the popular imagination; and the gossip of Wall Street insists that he has a silken halter round the neck of Judge Barnard, and a hempen one round that of Cardozo. It is certain that he who had a year before threatened Barnard on his own bench with impeachment now appeared in the character of Barnard's master, and issued as a matter of course the edicts of his court.

One other combination was made by the Erie managers to extend their power, and this time it was credit that was threatened. They bought a joint-stock bank in New York City, with a capital of £200,000. The assistance thus gained was purchased at a very moderate price, since it was by no means represented by the capital. The great cliques and so-called "operators" of Wall Street and Broad Street carry on their transactions by a system of credits and clearing-houses with a very limited use of money. The banks certify their checks, and the certified checks settle all balances. Nominally and by law the banks only certify to the extent of *bona fide* deposits, but in reality the custom of disregarding the strict letter of the law is not unknown, and in regard to the bank in question, the Comptroller of the Currency, an officer of

the National Treasury, testifies that on an examination of its
affairs in April, 1869, out of fifteen checks deposited in its
hands as security for certifications made by it, selected at hazard for inquiry, and representing a nominal value of £300,000,
three only were good. The rest represented accommodation
extended to brokers and speculators without security. As an
actual fact it is in evidence that this same bank on Thursday,
September 24, 1869, certified checks to the amount of nearly
£1,500,000 for Mr. Gould alone. What sound security Mr.
Gould deposited against this mass of credit may be left to the
imagination. His operations, however, were not confined to
this bank alone, although this was the only one owned by
the ring.

Thus Mr. Gould and Mr. Fisk created a combination more
powerful than any that has been controlled by mere private
citizens in America or in Europe since society for self-protec-
tion established the supreme authority of the judicial name.
They exercised the legislative and the judicial powers of the
State; they possessed almost unlimited credit, and society was
at their mercy. One authority alone stood above them, beyond their control; and this was the distant but threatening
figure of the National Government.

Nevertheless, powerful as they were, the Erie managers were
seldom in funds. The huge marble palace in which they lived,
the theatre which they supported, the reckless bribery and pro-
fusion of management by which they could alone maintain
their defiance of public opinion, the enormous schemes for
extending their operations into which they rushed with utter
recklessness, all required greater resources than could be furnished even by the wholesale plunder of the Erie Road. They
were obliged from time to time to issue from their castle and
harry the industrious public of their brother freebooters. The
process was different from that known to the dark ages, but
the objects and the results were equally robbery. At one time
Mr. Fisk is said to have ordered heavy speculative sales of stock
in an express company which held a contract with the Erie
Railway. The sales being effected, the contract was declared
annulled. The stock naturally fell, and Mr. Fisk realized the

difference. He then ordered heavy purchases, and having renewed the contract the stock rose again, and Mr. Fisk a second time swept the street. In the summer and autumn of 1869 the two managers issued and sold 235,000 new shares of Erie stock, or nearly as much as its entire capital when they assumed power in July, 1868. With the aid of the money thus obtained, they succeeded in withdrawing about £2,500,000 in currency from circulation at the very moment of the year when currency was most in demand in order to harvest the crops. For weeks the whole nation writhed and quivered under the torture of this modern rack, until the national government itself was obliged to interfere and threaten a sudden opening of the treasury. But whether the Erie speculators operated for a rise or operated for a fall, whether they bought or sold, and whether they were engaged in manipulating stocks, or locking up currency, or cornering gold, they were always a public nuisance and scandal.

In order to explain the operation of a so-called corner in gold to ordinary readers with the least possible use of slang or technical phrases, two preliminary statements are necessary. In the first place it must be understood that the supply of gold immediately available for transfers is limited within distinct bounds in America. New York and the country behind it contain an amount usually estimated at about £4,000,000. The national government commonly holds from £15,000,000 to £20,000,000, which may be thrown bodily on the market if the President orders it. To obtain gold from Europe or other sources requires time.

In the second place, gold in America is a commodity bought and sold like stocks in a special market or gold-room which is situated next the Stock Exchange in Broad Street and is practically a part of it. In gold as in stocks, the transactions are both real and speculative. The real transactions are mostly purchases or loans made by importers who require coin to pay customs on their imports. This legitimate business is supposed to require from £1,000,000 to £1,500,000 per day. The speculative transactions are mere wagers on the rise or fall of price, and neither require any actual transfer of gold, nor even imply its existence, although in times of excitement hundreds of millions nominally are bought, sold, and loaned.

Under the late administration Mr. McCulloch, the Secretary of the Treasury, had thought it his duty at least to guarantee a stable currency, although Congress forbade him to restore the gold standard. During four years gold had fluctuated little, and principally from natural causes, and the danger of attempting to create an artificial scarcity in it had prevented the operators from trying an experiment which would have been sure to irritate the government. The financial policy of the new administration was not so definitely fixed, and the success of a speculation would depend on the action of Mr. Boutwell, the new secretary, whose direction was understood to have begun by a marked censure on the course pursued by his predecessor.

Of all financial operations, cornering gold is the most brilliant and the most dangerous, and possibly the very hazard and splendor of the attempt were the reasons of its fascination to Mr. Jay Gould's fancy. He dwelt upon it for months, and played with it like a pet toy. His fertile mind even went so far as to discover that it would prove a blessing to the community, and on this ingenious theory, half honest and half fraudulent, he stretched the widely extended fabric of the web in which all mankind was to be caught. This theory was in itself partially sound. Starting from the principle that the price of grain in New York is regulated by the price in London and is not affected by currency fluctuations, Mr. Gould argued that if it were possible to raise the premium on gold from thirty to forty cents at harvest-time, the farmers' grain would be worth $1.40 instead of $1.30, and as a consequence the farmer would hasten to send all his crop to New York for export, over the Erie Railway, which was sorely in need of freights. With the assistance of another gentleman, Mr. Gould calculated the exact premium at which the Western farmer would consent to dispose of his grain, and thus distance the three hundred sail which were hastening from the Danube to supply the English market. Gold, which was then heavy at 34, must be raised to 45.

This clever idea, like all the other ideas of these gentlemen of Erie, seems to have had the single fault of requiring that some one, somewhere, should be swindled. The scheme was probably feasible; but sooner or later the reaction from such an artificial stimulant must have come, and whenever it came some one must suffer. Nevertheless, Mr. Gould probably argued that so long as the farmer got his money, the Erie Railway its freights, and he himself his small profits on the gold he bought, it was of little consequence who else might be injured; and, indeed, by the time the reaction came, and gold was ready to fall as he expected, Mr. Gould would probably have been ready to assist the process by speculative sales in order to enable the Western farmer to buy his spring goods cheap as he had sold his autumn crops dear. He himself was equally ready to buy gold cheap and sell it dear on his private account; and as he proposed to bleed New York merchants for the benefit of the Western farmer, so he was willing to bleed Broad Street for his own. The patriotic object was, however, the one which for obvious reasons Mr. Gould preferred to put forward most prominently, and on the strength of which he hoped to rest his ambitious structure of intrigue.

In the operation of raising the price of gold from 133 to 145, there was no great difficulty to men who controlled the resources of the Erie Railway. Credit alone was needed, and of credit Mr. Gould had an unlimited supply. The only serious danger lay in the possible action of the national government, which had not taken the same philanthropic view of the public good as was peculiar to the managers of Erie. Secretary Boutwell, who should have assisted Mr. Gould in "bulling" gold, was gravely suspected of being a bear, and of wishing to depress the premiums to nothing. If he were determined to stand in Mr. Gould's path, it was useless even for the combined forces of Erie and Tammany to jostle against him; and it was therefore essential that Mr. Gould should control the government itself, whether by fair means or foul, by persuasion or by purchase. He undertook the task; and now that his proceedings in both directions have been thoroughly drawn into light, it is well worth while for the public to see how dramatic and how artistically admirable a conspiracy in real life may be,

when slowly elaborated from the subtle mind of a clever intriguer, and carried into execution by a band of unshrinking
scoundrels.

The first requisite for Mr. Gould's purpose was some chan-
nel of direct communication with the President; and here he
was peculiarly favored by chance. Mr. Abel Rathbone Corbin,
formerly lawyer, editor, speculator, lobby-agent, familiar, as he
claims, with everything, had succeeded, during his varied career, in accumulating from one or another of his hazardous
pursuits a comfortable fortune, and he had crowned his success, at the age of sixty-seven or thereabouts, by contracting a
marriage with General Grant's sister, precisely at the moment
when General Grant was on the point of reaching the highest
eminence possible to an American citizen. To say that Mr. Corbin's moral dignity had passed absolutely pure through the
somewhat tainted atmosphere in which his life had been spent,
would be flattering him too highly; but at least he was now no
longer engaged in any active occupation, and he lived quietly
in New York, watching the course of public affairs, and remarkable for an eminent respectability which became the
President's brother-in-law. Mr. Gould enjoyed a slight acquain-
tance with Mr. Corbin, and he proceeded to improve it. He
assumed, and he asserts that he really felt, a respect for Mr.
Corbin's shrewdness and sagacity. It is amusing to observe
that Mr. Corbin claims to have first impressed the famous crop
theory on Mr. Gould's mind; while Mr. Gould testifies that he
himself indoctrinated Mr. Corbin with this idea, which became
a sort of monomania with the President's brother-in-law, who
soon began to preach it to the President himself. On the 15th
of June, 1869, the President came to New York, and was there
the guest of Mr. Corbin, who urged Mr. Gould to call and pay
his respects to the Chief Magistrate. Mr. Gould had probably
aimed at precisely this result. He called; and the President of
the United States not only listened to the president of Erie, but
accepted an invitation to Mr. Fisk's theatre, sat in Mr. Fisk's
private box, and the next evening became the guest of these
two gentlemen on their magnificent Newport steamer, while
Mr. Fisk, arrayed, as the newspapers reported, "in a blue uni-

form, with a broad gilt cap-band, three silver stars on his coat-sleeve, lavender gloves, and a diamond breast-pin as large as a cherry, stood at the gangway, surrounded by his aids, bestarred and bestriped like himself," and welcomed his distinguished friend.

It had been already arranged that the President should on this occasion be sounded in regard to his financial policy; and when the selected guests—among whom were Mr. Gould, Mr. Fisk, and others—sat down at nine o'clock to supper, the conversation was directed to the subject of finance. "Some one," says Mr. Gould, "asked the President what his view was." The "some one" in question was, of course, Mr. Fisk, who alone had the impudence to put such an inquiry. The President bluntly replied, that there was a certain amount of fictitiousness about the prosperity of the country, and that the bubble might as well be tapped in one way as another. The remark was fatal to Mr. Gould's plans, and he felt it, in his own words, as a wet blanket.

Meanwhile the post of assistant-treasurer at New York had become vacant, and it was a matter of interest to Mr. Gould that some person friendly to himself should occupy this position, which, in its relations to the public, is second in importance only to the secretaryship of the treasury itself. Mr. Gould consulted Mr. Corbin, and Mr. Corbin suggested the name of General Butterfield,—a former officer in the volunteer army. The appointment was not a wise one; nor does it appear in evidence by what means Mr. Corbin succeeded in bringing it about. There is a suggestion that he used Mr. A. T. Stewart, the wealthy importer, as his instrument for the purpose; but whatever the influence may have been, Mr. Corbin appears to have set it in action, and General Butterfield entered upon his duties towards the 1st of July.

The elaborate preparations thus made show that some large scheme was never absent from Mr. Gould's mind, although between the months of May and August he made no attempt to act upon the markets. But between the 20th of August and the 1st of September, in company with Messrs. Woodward and

Kimber, two large speculators, he made what is known as a pool, or combination, to raise the premium on gold, and some ten or fifteen millions were bought, but with very little effect on the price. The tendency of the market was downwards, and it was not easily counteracted. Perhaps under ordinary circumstances he might have now abandoned his project; but an incident suddenly occurred which seems to have drawn him headlong into the boldest operations.

Whether the appointment of General Butterfield had any share in strengthening Mr. Gould's faith in Mr. Corbin's secret powers does not appear in evidence, though it may readily be assumed as probable. At all events, an event now took place which would have seemed to authorize an unlimited faith in Mr. Corbin, as well as to justify the implicit belief of an Erie treasurer in the corruptibility of all mankind. The unsuspicious President again passed through New York, and came to breakfast at Mr. Corbin's house on the 2d of September. He saw no one but Mr. Corbin while there, and the same evening at ten o'clock departed for Saratoga. Mr. Gould declares, however, that he was told by Mr. Corbin that the President, in discussing the financial situation, had shown himself a convert to the Erie theory about marketing the crops, and had "stopped in the middle of a conversation in which he had expressed his views, and written a letter" to Secretary Boutwell. This letter is not produced; but Secretary Boutwell testifies as follows in regard to it:—

"I think on the evening of the 4th of September I received a letter from the President dated at New York, as I recollect it; I am not sure where it is dated. I have not seen the letter since the night I received it. I think it is now in my residence in Groton. In that letter he expressed an opinion that it was undesirable to force down the price of gold. He spoke of the importance to the West of being able to move their crops. His idea was that if gold should fall, the West would suffer, and the movement of the crops would be retarded. The impression made on my mind by the letter was that he had rather a strong opinion to that effect. . . . Upon the receipt of the

President's letter on the evening of the 4th of September, I telegraphed to Judge Richardson [Assistant Secretary at Washington] this dispatch: 'Send no order to Butterfield as to sales of gold until you hear from me.' "

Mr. Gould had therefore succeeded in reversing the policy of the national government; but this was not all. He knew what the government would do before any officer of the government knew it. Mr. Gould was at Corbin's house on the 2d of September; and although the evidence of both these gentlemen is very confused on this point, the inference is inevitable that Gould saw Corbin privately, unknown to the President, within an hour or two after this letter to Mr. Boutwell was written, and that it was at this interview, while the President was still in the house, that Mr. Corbin gave him the information about the letter; perhaps showed him the letter itself. Then followed a transaction worthy of the French stage. Mr. Corbin's evidence gives his own account of it:—

"On the 2d of September (referring to memoranda) Mr. Gould offered to let me have some of the gold he then possessed. . . . . He spoke to me as he had repeatedly done before, about taking a certain amount of gold owned by him. I finally told Mr. Gould that for the sake of a lady, my wife, I would accept of $500,000 of gold for her benefit, as I shared his confidence that gold would rise. . . . . He afterwards insisted that I should take a million more, and I did so on the same conditions for my wife. He then sent me this paper."

The paper in question is as follows:—

"Smith, Gould, Martin, & Co., Bankers,
11 Broad Street, New York, September 2, 1869.

"Mr. ——

"*Dear Sir*: we have bought for your account and risk—
500,000, gold, 132, R.
1,000,000, gold, 133⅝, R.
which we will carry on demand with the right to use.
"SMITH, GOULD, MARTIN, & CO."

This memorandum meant that for every rise of one per cent in the price of gold Mr. Corbin was to receive £3,000, and his name nowhere to appear. If the inference is correct that Gould had seen Corbin in the morning and had learned from him what the President had written, it is clear that he must have made his bargain on the spot, and then going directly to the city, he must in one breath have ordered this memorandum to be made out and large quantities of gold to be purchased, before the President had allowed the letter to leave Mr. Corbin's house.

No time was lost. On this same afternoon, Mr. Gould's brokers bought large amounts in gold. One testifies to buying $1,315,000 at 134⅛. On the 3d the premium was forced up to 36; on the 4th, when Mr. Boutwell received his letter, it had risen to 37. Here, however, Mr. Gould seems to have met a check, and he describes his own position in nervous Americanisms as follows:—

> "I did not want to buy so much gold. In the spring I put gold up from 32 to 38 and 40, with only about seven millions. But all these fellows went in and sold short, so that in order to keep it up I had to buy, or else to back down and show the white feather. They would sell it to you all the time. I never intended to buy more than four or five millions of gold, but these fellows kept purchasing it on, and I made up my mind that I would put it up to 40 at one time. . . . . We went into it as a commercial transaction, and did not intend to buy such an amount of gold. I was forced into it by the bears selling out. They were bound to put it down. I got into the contest. All these other fellows deserted me like rats from a ship. Kimber sold out and got short. . . . . He sold out at 37. He got short of it, and went up" (or, in English, he failed).

It was unfortunate that the bears would not consent to lie still and be flayed, but this was unquestionably the fact. They had the great operators for once at a disadvantage, and they were bent on revenge. Mr. Gould's position was very hazardous. When Mr. Kimber sold out at 37, which was probably on the 7th of September, the market broke; and on the 8th the price fell back to 35. Nor was this all. At the same moment, when the "pool" was ended by Mr. Kimber's desertion, Mr. Corbin, with his eminent shrewdness and respectability, told Mr. Gould "that gold had gone up to 37," and that he "should like to have this matter realized," which was equivalent to saying that he wished to be paid something on account. This was on the 6th; and Gould was obliged this same day to bring him a check for £5,000, drawn to the order of Jay Gould, and indorsed in blank by him with a touching regard for Mr. Corbin's modest desire not to have his name appear. There are few financiers in the world who will not agree that this transaction does great credit to Mr. Corbin's sagacity. It indicates at least that he was acquainted with the men he dealt with. Undoubtedly it placed Mr. Gould in a difficult position; but as Mr. Gould already held some fifteen millions of gold and needed Mr. Corbin's support, he preferred to pay £5,000 outright rather than allow Corbin to throw his gold on the market. Yet the fabric of Gould's web had now been so seriously injured that, for a whole week, from the 8th to the 15th of September, he was at a loss what to do, unable to advance and equally unable to retreat without very severe losses. He sat at his desk in the opera-house, silent as usual, and tearing little slips of paper which he threw on the floor in his abstraction, while he revolved new combinations in his mind.

Down to this moment Mr. James Fisk, Jr., has not appeared in the affair. Gould had not taken him into his confidence; and it was not until after the 10th of September that Gould appears to have decided that there was nothing else to be done. Fisk was not a safe ally in so delicate an affair, but apparently there was no choice. Gould approached him; and, as usual, his touch was like magic. Mr. Fisk's evidence begins here, and may be believed when very strongly corroborated:

> "Gold having settled down to 35, and I not having cared to touch it, he was a little sensitive on the subject, feeling as if he would rather take his losses without saying anything about it. . . . . One day he said to me, 'Don't you think gold has got to the bottom?' I replied that I did not see the profit in

buying gold unless you have got into a position where you can command the market. He then said he had bought quite a large amount of gold, and I judged from his conversation that he wanted me to go into the movement and help strengthen the market. Upon that I went into the market and bought. I should say that was about the 15th or 16th of September. I bought at that time about seven or eight millions, I think."

The market responded slowly to these enormous purchases; and on the 16th the clique was still struggling to recover its lost ground.

Meanwhile Mr. Gould had placed another million and a half of gold to the account of General Butterfield, and notified him of the purchase. So Mr. Gould swears in spite of General Butterfield's denial. The date of this purchase is not fixed. Through Mr. Corbin a notice was also sent by Gould about the middle of September to the President's private secretary, General Porter, informing him that half a million was placed to his credit. General Porter instantly wrote to repudiate the purchase, but it does not appear that Butterfield took any notice of Gould's transaction on his account. On the 10th of September the President had again come to New York, where he remained his brother-in-law's guest till the 13th; and during this visit Mr. Gould appears again to have seen him, although Mr. Corbin avers that on this occasion the President intimated his wish to the servant that this should be the last time Mr. Gould obtained admission. "Gould was always trying to get something out of him," he said; and if he had known how much Mr. Gould had succeeded in getting out of him, he would have admired the man's genius, even while shutting the door in his face. On the morning of the 13th the President set out on a journey to the little town of Washington, situated among the mountains of Western Pennsylvania, where he was to remain a few days. Mr. Gould, who now consulted Mr. Corbin regularly every morning and evening, was still extremely nervous in regard to the President's policy; and as the crisis approached, this nervousness led him into the fatal blunder of doing too much. The bribe offered to Porter was a grave mistake, but a greater mistake yet was made by pressing Mr. Corbin's influence too far. He induced Mr. Corbin to write an official article for the New York press on the financial policy of the government, an article afterwards inserted in the New York Times through the kind offices of Mr. James McHenry, and he also persuaded or encouraged Mr. Corbin to write a letter directly to the President himself. This letter, written on the 17th under the influence of Gould's anxiety, was instantly sent away by a special messenger of Fisk's to reach the President before he returned to the capital. The messenger carried also a letter of introduction to General Porter, the private secretary, in order to secure the personal delivery of this important despatch.

We have now come to the week which was to witness the explosion of all this elaborately constructed mine. On Monday, the 20th, gold again rose. Throughout Tuesday and Wednesday Fisk continued to purchase without limit, and forced the price up to 40. At this time Gould's firm of Smith, Gould, & Martin, through which the operation was conducted, had purchased some $50,000,000; and yet the bears went on selling, although they could only continue the contest by borrowing Gould's own gold. Gould, on the other hand, could no longer sell and clear himself, for the very reason that the sale of $50,000,000 would have broken the market to nothing. The struggle had become intense. The whole country was looking on with astonishment at the battle between the bulls and the bears. All business was deranged, and all values unsettled. There were indications of a panic in the stock market; and the bears in their emergency were vehemently pressing the government to intervene. Gould now wrote to Mr. Boutwell a letter so inconceivably impudent that it indicates desperation and entire loss of his ordinary coolness. He began:—

"Sir,—There is a panic in Wall Street, engineered by a bear combination. They have withdrawn currency to such an extent that it is impossible to do ordinary business. The Erie Company requires eight hundred thousand dollars to disburse. . . . . Much of it in Ohio, where an exciting political contest is going on, and where we have about ten thousand employed,

and the trouble is charged on the administration. . . . . Cannot you, consistently, increase your line of currency?"

From a friend such a letter would have been an outrage;
but from a member of the Tammany ring, the principal object of detestation to the government, such a threat or bribe—
whichever it may be called—was incredible. Mr. Gould was, in
fact, at his wits' end. He dreaded a panic, and he felt that it
could no longer be avoided.

The scene now shifts for a moment to the distant town of
Washington, among the hills of Western Pennsylvania. On the
morning of the 19th of September, President Grant and his
private secretary, General Porter, were playing croquet on the
grass, when Fisk's messenger, after twenty-four hours of travel
by rail and carriage, arrived at the house, and sent in to ask
for General Porter. When the President's game was ended,
General Porter came, received his own letter from Corbin, and
called the President, who entered the room and took his
brother-in-law's despatch. He then left the room, and after
some ten or fifteen minutes' absence returned. The messenger,
tired of waiting, then asked, "Is it all right?" "All right," replied the President; and the messenger hastened to the nearest
telegraph station, and sent word to Fisk, "Delivered; all right."

The messenger was, however, altogether mistaken. Not only
was all not right, but all was going hopelessly wrong. The
President, it appears, had at the outset supposed the man to
be an ordinary post-office agent, and the letter an ordinary
letter which had arrived through the post-office. Nor was it
until Porter asked some curious question as to the man, that
the President learned of his having been sent by Corbin merely
to carry this apparently unimportant letter of advice. The
President's suspicions were at once excited; and the same
evening, at his request, Mrs. Grant wrote a hurried note to
Mrs. Corbin, telling her how greatly the President was distressed at the rumor that Mr. Corbin was speculating in Wall
Street, and how much he hoped that Mr. Corbin would "instantly disconnect himself with anything of that sort."

This letter, subsequently destroyed or said to have been

destroyed by Mrs. Corbin, arrived in New York on the morning of Wednesday the 22d, the same day on which Gould and his enemies the bears were making their simultaneous appeals to Secretary Boutwell. Mrs. Corbin was greatly excited and distressed by her sister-in-law's language. She at once carried the letter to her husband, and insisted that he should instantly abandon his interest in the gold speculation. Mr. Corbin, although he considered the scruples of his wife and her family to be highly absurd, assented to her wish; and when Mr. Gould came that evening as usual, with $50,000,000 of gold on his hands, and extreme anxiety on his mind, Corbin read to him two letters: the first, written by Mrs. Grant to Mrs. Corbin; the second, written by Mr. Corbin to President Grant, assuring him that he had not a dollar of interest in gold. The assurance of this second letter was, at any sacrifice, to be made good.

Mr. Corbin proposed that Mr. Gould should give him a check for £20,000, and take his $1,500,000 off his hands. A proposition more calmly impudent than this can scarcely be imagined. Gould had already paid Corbin £5,000, and Corbin asked for £20,000 more, at the very moment when it was clear that the £5,000 he had received had been given him under a misunderstanding of his services. He even had the impudence to represent himself as doing Gould a favor by letting him have a million and a half more gold at the highest market price, at a time when Gould had fifty millions which it was clear he must sell or be ruined. What Gould might, under ordinary circumstances, have replied, may be imagined; but at this moment he could say nothing. Corbin had but to show this note to a single broker in Wall Street, and the whole fabric of Gould's speculation would have fallen to pieces. Gould asked for time and went away. He consulted no one. He gave Fisk no hint of what had happened. The next morning he returned to Corbin, and made him the following offer:—

> " 'Mr. Corbin, I cannot give you anything if you will go out. If you will remain in, and take the chances of the market, I will give you my check [for £20,000].' 'And then,' says Mr. Corbin, 'I did what I think it would have troubled almost

any other business man to consent to do,—refuse one hundred
thousand dollars on a rising market. If I had not been an old
man married to a middle-aged woman, I should have done it
(of course with her consent) just as sure as the offer was made.
I said, 'Mr. Gould, my wife says "No!" Ulysses thinks it wrong,
and that it ought to end.' So I gave it up. . . . . He looked at
me with an air of severe distrust, as if he was afraid of
treachery in the camp. He remarked, 'Mr. Corbin, I am un-
done if that letter gets out.' . . . . He stood there for a little
while looking very thoughtful, exceedingly thoughtful. He
then left and went into Wall Street, ... and my impression
is that he it was, and not the government, that broke that
market.' "

Mr. Corbin was right; throughout all these transactions his
insight into Mr. Gould's character was marvellous.

It was the morning of Thursday, the 3d; Gould and Fisk
went to Broad Street together, but as usual Gould was silent
and secret, while Fisk was noisy and communicative. There
was now a complete separation in their movements. Gould
acted entirely through his own firm of Smith, Gould, & Martin, while Fisk operated principally through his old partner,
Belden. One of Smith's principal brokers testifies:—

" 'Fisk never could do business with Smith, Gould, & Martin
very comfortably. They would not do business for him. It was
a very uncertain thing of course where Fisk might be. He is
an erratic sort of genius. I don't think anybody would want to
follow him very long. I am satisfied that Smith, Gould, &
Martin controlled their own gold, and were ready to do as
they pleased with it without consulting Fisk. I do not think
there was any general agreement. . . . . None of us who knew
him cared to do business with him. I would not have taken
an order from him nor had anything to do with him.' Belden
was considered a very low fellow. 'I never had anything to do
with him or his party,' said one broker employed by Gould.
'They were men I had a perfect detestation of; they were no
company for me. I should not have spoken to them at all
under any ordinary circumstances.' Another says, 'Belden is a
man in whom I never had any confidence in any way. For

months before that, I would not have taken him for a gold transaction.' "

And yet Belden bought millions upon millions of gold. He himself says he had bought twenty millions by this Thursday evening, and this without capital or credit except that of his brokers. Meanwhile Gould, on reaching the city, had at once given secret orders to sell. From the moment he left Corbin, he had but one idea, which was to get rid of his gold as quietly as possible. "I purchased merely enough to make believe I was a bull," says Gould. This double process continued all that afternoon. Fisk's wild purchases carried the price up to 144, and the panic in the street became more and more serious as the bears realized the extremity of their danger. No one can tell how much gold which did not exist they had contracted to deliver or pay the difference in price. One of the clique brokers swears that on this Thursday evening the street had sold the clique one hundred and eighteen millions of gold, and every rise of one per cent on this sum implied a loss of more than £200,000 to the bears. Naturally the terror was extreme, for half Broad Street and thousands of speculators would have been ruined if compelled to settle gold at 150 which they had sold at 140. It need scarcely be said that by this time nothing more was heard in regard to philanthropic theories of benefit to the Western farmer.

Mr. Gould's feelings can easily be imagined. He knew that Fisk's reckless management would bring the government upon his shoulders, and he knew that unless he could sell his gold before the order came from Washington he would be a ruined man. He knew, too, that Fisk's contracts must inevitably be repudiated. This Thursday evening he sat at his desk in the Erie offices at the opera-house, while Fisk and Fisk's brokers chattered about him.

"I was transacting my railway business. I had my own views about the market, and my own fish to fry. I was all alone, so to speak, in what I did, and I did not let any of those people know exactly how I stood. I got no ideas from anything that was said there. I had been selling gold from 35 up all the

time, and I did not know till the next morning that there
would probably come an order about twelve o'clock to sell
gold."

He had not told Fisk a word in regard to Corbin's retreat,
nor his own orders to sell.

When the next day came, Gould and Fisk went together to
Broad Street, and took possession of the private back office
of a principal broker, "without asking the privilege of doing
so," as the broker observes in his evidence. The first news
brought to Gould was a disaster. The government had sent
three men from Washington to examine the bank which
Gould owned, and the bank sent word to Mr. Gould that it
feared to certify for him as usual, and was itself in danger of a
panic, caused by the presence of officers, which created distrust
of the bank. It barely managed to save itself. Gould took the
information silently, and his firm redoubled sales of gold. His
partner, Smith, gave the orders to one broker after another,—
"Sell ten millions!" "The order was given as quick as a flash,
and away he went," says one of these men. "I sold only eight
millions." "Sell, sell, sell! do nothing but sell!—only don't sell
to Fisk's brokers," were the orders which Smith himself ac-
knowledges. In the gold-room Fisk's brokers were shouting
their rising bids, and the packed crowd grew frantic with terror and rage as each successive rise showed their increasing
losses. The wide streets outside were thronged with excited
people; the telegraph offices were overwhelmed with messages
ordering sales or purchases of gold or stocks; and the whole
nation was watching eagerly to see what the result of this convulsion was to be. All trade was stopped, and even the President felt that it was time to raise his hand. No one who has not
seen the New York gold-room can understand the spectacle it
presented; now a perfect pandemonium, now silent as the
grave. Fisk, in his dark back office across the street, with his
coat off, swaggered up and down, "a big cane in his hand," and
called himself the Napoleon of Wall Street. He really believed
that he directed the movement, and while the street outside
imagined that he and Gould were one family, and that his

purchases were made for the clique, Gould was silently flinging away his gold at any price he could get for it.

Whether Fisk really expected to carry out his contract, and force the bears to settle, or not, is doubtful; but the evidence seems to show that he was in earnest, and felt sure of success. His orders were unlimited. "Put it up to 150," was one which he sent to the gold-room. Gold rose to 150. At length the bid was made—"160 for any part of five millions," and no one any longer dared take it. "161 for five millions,"—"162 for five millions." No answer was made, and the offer was repeated,—"162 for any part of five millions." A voice replied, "Sold one million at 62." The bubble suddenly burst, and within fifteen minutes, amid an excitement without parallel even in the wildest excitements of the war, the clique brokers were literally swept away, and left struggling by themselves, bidding still 160 for gold in millions which no one would any longer take their word for; while the premium sank rapidly to 135. A moment later the telegraph brought from Washington the government order to sell, and the result was no longer possible to dispute. Mr. Fisk had gone too far, while Mr. Gould had secretly weakened the ground under his feet.

Gould, however, was saved. His fifty millions were sold; and although no one yet knows what his gains or losses may have been, his firm was now able to meet its contracts and protect its brokers. Fisk was in a very different situation. So soon as it became evident that his brokers would be unable to carry out their contracts, every one who had sold gold to them turned in wrath to Fisk's office. Fortunately for him it was protected by armed men whom he had brought with him from his castle of Erie; but nevertheless the excitement was so great that both Mr. Fisk and Mr. Gould thought it best to retire as rapidly as possible by a back entrance leading into another street, and to seek the protection of the opera-house. There nothing but an army could disturb them; no civil mandate was likely to be served without their permission within these walls, and few men would care to face Fisk's ruffians in order to force an entrance.

The subsequent winding up of this famous conspiracy may be stated in few words. But no account could possibly be complete which failed to reproduce in full the story of Mr. Fisk's last interview with Mr. Corbin, as told by Fisk himself.

"I went down to the neighborhood of Wall Street, Friday morning, and the history of that morning you know. When I got back to our office, you can imagine I was in no enviable state of mind, and the moment I got up street that afternoon I started right round to old Corbin's to rake him out. I went into the room, and sent word that Mr. Fisk wanted to see him in the dining-room. I was too mad to say anything civil, and when he came into the room, said I, 'You damned old scoundrel, do you know what you have done here, you and your people?' He began to wring his hands, and, 'Oh!' he says, 'this is a horrible position. Are you ruined?' I said I didn't know whether I was or not; and I asked him again if he knew what had happened? He had been crying, and said he had just heard; that he had been sure everything was all right; but that something had occurred entirely different from what he had anticipated. Said I, 'That don't amount to anything; we know that gold ought not to be at 31, and that it would not be but for such performances as you have had this last week; you know damned well it would not if you had not failed.' I knew that somebody had run a saw right into us, and said I, 'This whole damned thing has turned out just as I told you it would.' I considered the whole party a pack of cowards, and I expected that when we came to clear our hands they would sock it right into us. I said to him, 'I don't know whether you have lied or not, and I don't know what ought to be done with you.' He was on the other side of the table, weeping and wailing, and I was gnashing my teeth. 'Now,' he says, 'you must quiet yourself.' I told him I didn't want to be quiet. I had no desire to ever be quiet again, and probably never should be quiet again. He says, 'But, my dear sir, you will lose your reason.' Says I, 'Speyers [a broker employed by him that day] has already lost his reason; reason has gone out of everybody but me.' I continued, 'Now what are you going to do? You have got us into this thing, and what are you going to do to get out of it?' He says, 'I don't

> know. I will go and get my wife.' I said, 'Get her down here!'
> The soft talk was all over. He went up stairs and they re-
> turned, tottling into the room, looking older than Stephen
> Hopkins. His wife and he both looked like death. He was
> tottling just like that. [Illustrated by a trembling movement
> of his body.] I have never seen him from that day to this."

This is sworn evidence before a committee of Congress; and
its humor is perhaps the more conspicuous, because there is
every reason to believe that there is not a word of truth in the
story from beginning to end. No such interview ever occurred,
except in the unconfined apartments of Mr. Fisk's imagination. His own previous statements make it certain that he was
not at Corbin's house at all that day, and that Corbin did
come to the Erie offices that evening, and again the next morning. Corbin himself denies the truth of the account without
limitation; and adds, that when he entered the Erie offices the
next morning Fisk was there. "I asked him how Mr. Gould
felt after the great calamity of the day before." He remarked,
"O, he has no courage at all. He has sunk right down. There
is nothing left of him but a heap of clothes and a pair of
eyes." The internal evidence of truth in this anecdote would
support Mr. Corbin against the world.

In regard to Mr. Gould, Fisk's graphic description was probably again inaccurate. Undoubtedly the noise and scandal of
the moment were extremely unpleasant to this silent and im-
penetrable intriguer. The city was in a ferment, and the whole
country pointing at him with wrath. The machinery of the
gold exchange had broken down, and he alone could extricate
the business community from the pressing danger of a general
panic. He had saved himself, it is true; but in a manner which
could not have been to his taste. Yet his course from this point
must have been almost self-evident to his mind, and there is
no reason to suppose that he hesitated.

His own contracts were all fulfilled. Fisk's contracts, all except one, in respect to which the broker was able to compel a
settlement, were repudiated. Gould probably suggested to

Fisk that it was better to let Belden fail, and to settle a hand-some fortune on him, than to sacrifice something more than £1,000,000 in sustaining him. Fisk therefore threw Belden over, and swore that he had acted only under Belden's order; in support of which statement he produced a paper to the following effect:—

> "September 24.
>
> "DEAR SIR,—I hereby authorize you to order the purchase and sale of gold on my account during this day to the extent you may deem advisable, and to report the same to me as early as possible. It is to be understood that the profits of such order are to belong entirely to me, and I will, of course, bear any losses resulting.
>
> "Yours,
> "WILLIAM BELDEN.
>
> "JAMES FISK, JR."

This document was not produced in the original, and certainly never existed. Belden himself could not be induced to acknowledge the order; and no one would have believed him if he had done so. Meanwhile the matter is before the national courts, and Fisk may probably be held to his contracts: but it will be far more difficult to execute judgment upon him, or to discover his assets.

One of the first acts of the Erie gentlemen after the crisis was to summon their lawyers, and set in action their judicial powers. The object was to prevent the panic-stricken brokers from using legal process to force settlements, and so render the entanglement inextricable. Messrs. Field and Shearman came, and instantly prepared a considerable number of injunctions, which were sent to their judges, signed at once, and immediately served. Gould then was able to dictate the terms of settlement; and after a week of complete paralysis, Broad Street began at last to show signs of returning life. As a legal curiosity, one of these documents, issued three months after the crisis, may be reproduced, in order to show the powers wielded by the Erie managers:—

"SUPREME COURT.

H. N. SMITH, JAY GOULD, H. H. MARTIN,
and J. B. BACH, Plaintiffs,
against
JOHN BONNER and ARTHUR L. SEWELL,
Defendants,

Injunction
by order.

"It appearing satisfactorily to me by the complaint duly verified by the plaintiffs that sufficient grounds for an order of injunction exist, I do hereby order and enjoin . . . . That the defendants, John Bonner and Arthur L. Sewell, their agents, attorneys, and servants, refrain from pressing their pretended claims against the plaintiffs, or either of them, before the Arbitration Committee of the New York Stock Exchange, or from taking any proceedings thereon, or in relation thereto, except in this action.

"GEORGE G. BARNARD, J. S. C.

"NEW YORK, December 29, 1869."

Mr. Bonner had practically been robbed with violence by Mr. Gould, and instead of his being able to bring the robber into court as the criminal, the robber brought him into court as criminal, and the judge forbade him to appear in any other character. Of all Mr. Field's distinguished legal reforms and philanthropic projects, this injunction is beyond a doubt the most brilliant and the most successful.

The fate of the conspirators was not severe. Mr. Corbin went to Washington, where he was snubbed by the President, and at once disappeared from public view, only coming to light again before the Congressional Committee. General Butterfield, whose share in the transaction is least understood, was permitted to resign his office without an investigation. Speculation for the next six months was at an end. Every person involved in the affair seemed to have lost money, and dozens of brokers were swept from the street. But Mr. Jay Gould and Mr. James Fisk, Jr., continued to reign over Erie, and no one can say that their power or their credit was sensibly diminished by a shock which for the time prostrated all the interests of the country.

Nevertheless it is safe to predict that sooner or later the
last traces of the disturbing influence of war and paper money
will disappear in America, as they have sooner or later disappeared in every other country which has passed through the
same evils. The result of this convulsion itself has been in the
main good. It indicates the approaching end of a troubled
time. Messrs. Gould and Fisk will at last be obliged to yield
to the force of moral and economical laws. The Erie Railway
will be rescued, and its history will perhaps rival that of the
great speculative manias of the last century. The United States
will restore a sound basis to its currency, and will learn to deal
with the political reforms it requires. Yet though the regular
process of development may be depended upon, in its ordinary
and established course, to purge American society of the worst
agents of an exceptionally corrupt time, there is in the history
of this Erie corporation one matter in regard to which modern
society everywhere is directly interested. For the first time since
the creation of these enormous corporate bodies, one of them
has shown its power for mischief, and has proved itself able
to override and trample on law, custom, decency, and every
restraint known to society, without scruple, and as yet without
check. The belief is common in America that the day is at
hand when corporations far greater than the Erie—swaying
power such as has never in the world's history been trusted in
the hands of mere private citizens, controlled by single men
like Vanderbilt, or by combinations of men like Fisk, Gould,
and Lane, after having created a system of quiet but irresistible
corruption—will ultimately succeed in directing government
itself. Under the American form of society, there is now no
authority capable of effective resistance. The national government, in order to deal with the corporations, must assume
powers refused to it by its fundamental law, and even then
is always exposed to the chance of forming an absolute central
government which sooner or later is likely to fall into the very
hands it is struggling to escape, and thus destroy the limits of
its power only in order to make corruption omnipotent. Nor
is this danger confined to America alone. The corporation is in
its nature a threat against the popular institutions which are

spreading so rapidly over the whole world. Wherever there is a popular and limited government this difficulty will be found in its path, and unless some satisfactory solution of the problem can be reached, popular institutions may yet find their very existence endangered.

For Further Reading

Matthew Josephson's *The Robber Barons* (1934) is the classic portrayal of the businessman as predator. Other works of this genre are Henry Demarest Lloyd, *Lords of Industry* (1910), and Gustavus Myers, *History of the Great American Fortunes* (1910). At the opposite end of the historiographical scale from these critical studies is Stewart Holbrook, *Age of the Moguls* (1953), and Jonathan Hughes, *The Vital Few* (1966). For more balanced general appraisals of the era, see Thomas C. Cochran and William Miller, *The Age of Enterprise* (rev. ed., 1961), and P. W. Hidy and M. W. Hidy, *Pioneering in Big Business 1802–1911* (1955). Also recommended but much shorter is Samuel P. Hays, *The Response to Industrialism 1885–1914* (1957). Three books by Edward C. Kirkland deserve special recommendation. *Men, Cities and Transportation: A Study in New England History, 1820–1900* (1948) is a model regional study; *Industry Comes of Age, Business Labor and Public Policy 1860–1897* (1961) is excellent social history, and *Dream and Thought in the Business Community 1860–1900* (1956) illuminates the views and the bias of businessmen on topics as varied as public schools and universities and their own mansions. Other informative books are Thomas C. Cochran's *Railroad Leaders 1845–1890: The Business Mind in America* (1953), which dissects the attitudes of the leadership of a vital group, and Sigmund Diamond, *The Reputation of the American Businessman* (1955), a study of the changing historical perspective on six leaders. Superior biographies include Allan Nevins, *John D. Rockefeller* (1940); Burton J. Hendrick, *The Life of Andrew Carnegie* (1932); Frederick Lewis Allen, *The*

Great Pierpont Morgan (1949), and William T. Hutchinson, *Cyrus Hale McCormick: Harvest 1856–1884* (1935). Jim Fisk's flamboyant life is described by William A. Swanberg in *Jim Fisk: The Career of an Improbable Rascal* (1960). For Gould, see Julius Grodinsky, *Jay Gould: His Business Career 1867–1892* (1957).

Conflict Within the American Labor Movement

John R. Commons and Selig Perlman

*W*orker organizations existed in the United States before the Declaration of Independence and the earliest successful strike took place no later than 1786 when a group of Philadelphia printers secured a minimum wage of six dollars a week. However, it was not until the unprecedented industrial expansion that began with the Civil War that organized labor came into its own as an economic and political force to be reckoned with. By ending the depression that followed the panic of 1857 and restoring almost full employment, the war strengthened several national trade unions founded during the 1850's, including the typographers (1852), machinists and blacksmiths (1857), and molders (1859). At the same time the failure of wages to keep pace with prices in the decade after 1860, the growth of mechanization that threatened the jobs of skilled craftsmen in certain industries, such as clothing and boots and shoes, and the influx of immigrants willing to accept lower pay and poorer working conditions combined to create a demand for a national coalition of workers. Ob-

Source: John R. Commons and Others, *History of Labour in the United States, 1896–1932* (4 vols.; New York: The Macmillan Company, 1918–1935), II (1921), 396–423. Copyright 1918 by The Macmillan Company and renewed 1946 by John A. Commons. Reprinted by permission.

serving the huge industrial combinations springing up around them, the workers came to an obvious conclusion: they would have to organize to secure their ends. But agreeing on the need for unity and solidarity in the laboring class was one thing, a consensus on the objectives of the labor movement was quite another. Two fundamentally opposite ideologies struggled for dominance. One view was represented by the trade unions, which drew the great bulk of their members from the skilled craftsmen; the other position advocated bringing all workers into one big union.

The trade unions interpreted labor's goals simply and pragmatically: better wages, shorter hours, and improved working conditions. Testifying before a Senate committee in 1883, Adolph Strasser, president of the Cigar Makers Union, then one of the most powerful of the trade unions, declared: "We have no ultimate ends. We are going on from day to day. We are fighting for immediate objects that can be realized in a few years." Samuel Gompers, destined to serve for more than forty years as president of the American Federation of Labor, put it even more succinctly when he expressed the ambitions of labor in the single word, more! Also, the skilled workers in the trade unions, whether mechanics or carpenters or molders, believed that their skills gave them an advantage in negotiating with employers and feared a dilution of this power would result from association with the great mass of unskilled workers.

The advocates of an all-inclusive organization took their inspiration from the labor reform movements of the Jacksonian era. Their philosophy found expression in the National Labor Union founded in 1866 by William Sylvis. The Union preached cooperation between labor and capital; it also interested itself in broad areas of social reform, advocating among other things abolition of slums and rights for Negroes and women. But within a few years the National Labor Union went directly into politics by transforming itself into the National Labor Reform Party, and what little union aspect it had possessed disappeared entirely. But the principle of cooperation soon found new expression in the Noble Order of the Knights of Labor organized in Philadelphia in 1869 by Uriah Stephens. The leaders of the Knights have been accused of Utopianism and failing to come to grips with the realities of the industrial order in America. Certainly they saw the emancipation of labor coming not from higher wages or reduction in hours. From the first they advocated the abolition of the wage system. There was no good reason, argued Terrence V. Powderly, who succeeded Stephens as leader or Master Workman of the Knights, "why labor cannot through cooperation, own and operate mines, factories and railroads." The structure of the Knights corresponded to this ideology. The organization was divided geographically by districts with a General Assembly to coordinate activities. Membership was open to almost anyone who worked, notable exceptions being bankers, lawyers, and liquor dealers. This contrasted with the horizontal organization of the trade unions, whose membership believed it essential that stonecutters in Chicago belong to the same union as stonecutters in Boston in order to insure the best possible conditions for their craft. The Knights and the unions also disagreed on strikes. To the former, strikes betrayed the principle of cooperation, while to the trade unions, although they hoped to achieve their purposes through collective bargaining, strikes and boycotts were viewed as almost the only effective weapons against recalcitrant employers.

Ironically, although the 1884 constitution of the Knights declared "strikes at best afford only temporary relief," a large part of the early success of the Knights derived from its support of the successful Southwest Railroads shopmen's strike of 1885 when, for the first time, a large corporation negotiated an agreement with a national labor organization. The victory brought thousands of workers into the Knights; by 1886 it boasted a membership of over 700,000 in 5500 local assemblies. Decline, however, set in almost as rapidly, partly because 1886 was the year of the Haymarket Riot in Chicago, which enabled conservative newspapers and employers to unfairly identify the Knights of Labor with anarchism, but also because the irreconcilable differences between the

Knights and the trade unions came to a head during the same year, resulting in the formation of craft-oriented American Federation of Labor.

In John R. Commons' *History of Labour in the United States 1896–1932*, the restiveness of the trade unions and their challenge to the Knights is described. Professor Commons (1862–1945), although primarily an economist and for many years chairman of the economics department at the University of Wisconsin, attempted in his many works to broaden the scope of his discipline by employing the methods and techniques of the other social sciences. The titles of some of his major studies, for example, *Social Reform and the Church* (1894) and *Races and Immigrants in America* (1907), are in themselves evidence of these influences as well as indications of an enduring interest in current social questions. Commons' multi-volume history of American labor is a cooperative series, and Professor Selig Perlman is the associate author of the chapter from which the following selection is taken.

$\mathcal{D}$uring 1886 the combined membership of labour organisations was exceptionally strong and for the first time came near the million mark. The Knights of Labor had a membership of 700,000 and the trade unions at least 250,000, the former composed largely of the unskilled and the latter of the skilled. Still, the leaders of the Knights realised that mere numbers were not sufficient to defeat the employers and that control over the skilled, and consequently the more strategic occupations, was required before the unskilled and semi-skilled could expect to march to victory. Hence, parallel to the tremendous growth of the Knights in 1886, there was a constantly growing effort to absorb the existing trade unions for the purpose of making them subservient to the interests of the less skilled elements. It was mainly this that produced the bitter conflict between the Knights and the trade unions during 1886 and 1887. Neither the jealousy aroused by the success of the unions nor the opposite aims of labour solidarity and

trade separatism gives an adequate explanation of this conflict. The one, of course, aggravated the situation by introduc-
ing a feeling of personal bitterness, and the other furnished
an appealing argument to each side. But the struggle was one
between groups within the working class, in which the small
but more skilled group fought for independence of the larger
but weaker group of the unskilled and semi-skilled. The skilled
men stood for the right to use their advantage of skill and
efficient organisation in order to wrest the maximum amount
of concessions for themselves. The Knights of Labor endeavoured to annex the skilled men in order that the advantage
from their exceptional fighting strength might lift up the
unskilled and semi-skilled. From the viewpoint of a struggle
between principles, this was indeed a clash between the principle of solidarity of labour and that of trade separatism, but,
in reality, each of the principles reflected only the special interest of a certain portion of the working class. Just as the
trade unions, when they fought for trade autonomy, really
refused to consider the unskilled men, so the Knights of Labor
were insensible to the fact that their scheme would retard the
progress of the skilled trades.

The conflict was held in abeyance during the early eighties.
The trade unions were by far the strongest organisations in
the field and scented no particular danger when here or there
the Knights formed an assembly either contiguous to the
sphere of a trade union (such as organising the machine moulders whom the union ignored) or even encroaching upon it
(such as the organisation of an assembly of iron workers at
Braddock, which included unskilled as well as some tonnage
men). The Federation of Organised Trades and Labor Unions
and the Knights of Labor mutually endeavoured to remain on
as friendly terms as possible. We have had occasion to note
that the Federation in 1880 extended to district assemblies of
the Knights an invitation to affiliate, and again, as we saw in
1884, it invited the Order to co-operate in the eight-hour
movement. This friendly feeling was largely reciprocated by
the Knights of Labor. The General Assembly in 1882 ordered
a communication to be sent to the Amalgamated Association

of Iron and Steel Workers with the assurance that the Order would not admit a seceding faction from that union. The next General Assembly voted against recognising a printers' trade district and rejected the proposal of District Assembly 64 (practically composed only of printers) that all printers should be required to join it. The assembly also authorised the appointment of a committee to draw up a platform for an alliance of the various labour unions of the country, having power to confer with the representatives of existing unions.

Even with the expansion of the Order, beginning in 1884, when the local assemblies grew aggressive towards trade unions, the General Assembly for a long time maintained this friendly attitude. In 1884 a resolution was passed, as follows: "No local Assembly of the Order, or any of its members, shall antagonise any trade and labor organisation, or any of its members if known to be faithful workers in the cause of labor, by refusing to work with those holding membership cards in any factory and non-co-operative industry under the control of the Knights of Labor." In 1885 the General Executive Board ruled that District Assembly 41, Baltimore, could not force one of its locals to refrain from sending delegates to the convention of the Federation of Organised Trades and Labor Unions. The General Assembly of 1885 decided that Local Assembly 3834 under District Assembly 1, formerly a local union affiliated with the granite cutters' national union, should return to that organisation provided this could be done without a fine or humiliating conditions, and that the label of the Knights of Labor should never be placed upon goods manufactured at less than union prices.

However, complaints made by trade unions became numerous after 1884. The *Furniture Workers' Journal* accused the furniture workers' assembly at Grand Rapids of trying to win over the members of the union in that place, on the plea that its dues were lower than those of the union. The *Journal* claimed that the same situation existed in several other localities. *John Swinton's Paper* reported early in 1885 from Philadelphia that "the open unions are quietly fighting the Knights of Labor, who in return break up organised unions by taking out a few men and organising an Assembly." The greatness of the drawing power of the Order is illustrated by the fact that during 1885–1886 several local unions in such a highly skilled trade as that of custom tailors went over bodily to the Knights. This had almost ruined the national union.

The Knights were in nearly every case the aggressors; only such a powerful trade union as the Brotherhood of Locomotive Engineers could afford to issue the aggressive order of Grand Chief Engineer Arthur, during the Wabash strike in 1885, that all members withdraw from the Knights of Labor. He soon thereafter declared that the brotherhood was not a labour organisation.

It is significant that among the local organisations inimical to trade unions, District Assembly 49, of New York, should prove the most relentless. This assembly in 1887 during the longshoremen's and coal-miners' strike did not hesitate to tie up the industries of the entire city for the sake of securing the demands of several hundred unskilled working men. The action of the assembly furnishes another proof that the conflict between the Knights and the trade unions was really one between the classes of the unskilled and the skilled.

Though District Assembly 49, New York, came into conflict with not a few of the trade unions in that city, its battle royal was fought with the cigar makers' unions. There were at this time two rival national unions in the cigar making trade, the International and the Progressive, and the aggressive interference by the Knights of Labor created a series of situations of such complexity that at times they almost resembled some of the most involved problems with which modern European diplomacy has been obliged to deal. The split in the cigar makers' union, dating from 1881, occurred in No. 144, New York, turning on the policy of the international officers, which was to support candidates of the existing parties who pledged themselves to the prohibition of tenement-house work. The socialist element in the union at first tried to block this policy, but carried the fight over into the next election of officers where it won by electing a socialist as president of No. 144. He was, however, immediately suspended by Strasser, the inter-

national president, on the ground that he was a manufacturer
and consequently ineligible. But the socialists refused to submit either to the suspension of this chosen officer or to the
order issued by the international executive board to turn over
the funds to the union pending a new election. They formally
seceded by assuming the name, Progressive Union No. 1. The
Progressive Union grew very rapidly because it took in the
tenement-house workers and adopted lower dues than those
of the International Union. It soon spread outside of New
York and thus became in fact, as well as in name, a rival
national union to the older organisation. Naturally its membership was recruited from among the socialists and the recent
immigrants, who also were largely tenement-house workers.
Efforts at reconciliation were repeatedly made, and in December, 1885, a small part of the Progressives united with the
International. Strasser stated in January, 1886, that the trade
union element had come back to the fold "under the resolutions of the Rochester Conference and the restrictions adopted
at the last Convention," but that the "anarchists" and the
"tenement-house scum" still continued to form a union of
their own. However, the "anarchists" and the "tenement-house
scum" constituted nearly the entire membership of the Progressive Union.

As early as 1883, District Assembly 49 took a hand in the
struggle to support the Progressive Union. But the most active
aggression came with the beginning of 1886, when District
Assembly 49, its membership multiplying by leaps and bounds,
gained great confidence in its own prowess. On January 2,
1886, the manufacturers' association, embracing fourteen firms,
declared a reduction in wages. Both the International and the
Progressive unions refused to submit, and, in consequence, the
association started a lockout which threw out of work about
10,000 employees. However, the intense rivalry between the
unions made durable co-operation impossible, and ten weeks
later the Progressive Union, with the aid of the Central Labor
Union, entered into an agreement with the employers. The
other union continued the strike. Thereupon the manufacturers applied to District Assembly 49 for settlement and for

the label of the Knights of Labor. District Assembly 49 readily met the proposal, gave them the white label, and besides allowed the use of the newly introduced bunching machine in exchange for a promise to abolish tenement-house work. Neither the International nor the Progressive cigar makers desired to accept the machine. But the Progressive Union could ill afford to go against its powerful ally, District Assembly 49. On the contrary it felt so hard-pressed by its rival that on March 14, 1886, it decided to join District Assembly 49 as a body and become Local Assembly 2814 with 7,000 members.

The events in New York at once let loose the dogs of war. Already in 1885 the International Union and the Order had come into conflict over the label. In February, 1886, the International Union instituted a general boycott on all cigars which did not bear the label of that union, including those which bore the Knights of Labor label. Similar struggles developed in a large number of cities, notably in Milwaukee and Syracuse. There is ample proof that each side "scabbed" on the other.

The conflict between the Knights of Labor and the cigar makers' union brought to a climax the sporadic struggle that had been going on between the Order and the trade unions. The trade unions finally awakened to a sense of the danger from the rapidly growing Order. The common danger created unity of feeling, and the indifference previously felt for federated action now gave way to a desire for closer union.

Another highly important effect of this conflict was the ascendency in the trade union movement of Samuel Gompers as the foremost leader. Gompers had first achieved prominence in 1881 at the time of the organisation of the Federation of Organised Trades and Labor Unions. But not until the situation created by the conflict with the Knights of Labor did he get his first real opportunity, both to demonstrate his inborn capacity for leadership, and to train and develop that capacity by overcoming what was perhaps the most serious problem that ever confronted American organised labour.

Gompers was the leading emissary sent out early in 1886 by the cigar makers' union to agitate in favour of a closer federation with other unions. The appeal found a ready response. McGuire, of the carpenters' brotherhood, stated before the special meeting of the General Assembly in May, 1886, that from 150 to 160 unions had grievances against the Knights of Labor, and these included iron moulders, brick makers, bakers, miners, printers, carpenters, and granite cutters. In granite cutting the national union engaged in a controversy over a boycott with District Assembly 99 of Providence. On the other hand, the Seamen's Benevolent Union of the Great Lakes, being hard pressed by the employers, voluntarily joined the Order in the expectation that this might gain for it recognition from the vessel owners. The glass industry was practically under the control of the Knights of Labor. In addition to the window-glass blowers' organisation, Local Assembly 300, both the Druggist Ware Glass Blowers' League of America and the Western Green Bottle Blowers' League became district assemblies in 1886. The Flint Glass Workers' Union, on the other hand, came into violent conflict with the Order when the latter admitted a seceding faction from that union.

From the standpoint of the trade unions fighting for preservation, the voluntary assimilation of the weaker unions spelled no less danger than the attempted forcible assimilation of the cigar makers' and the granite cutters' unions. Already the convention of the Federation of Organised Trades and Labor Unions in 1885, at a secret session, had instructed the secretary to raise the question with Powderly. Powderly replied in a friendly and reassuring tone, but, as the report of the legislative committee at the convention of 1886 put it: "Mr. Powderly's power for good was sadly overestimated by the delegates to the last session of the Federation."

The agitation carried on by the emissaries of the cigar makers' union bore fruit and in the spring of 1886, P. J. McGuire, of the carpenters, A. Strasser, of the cigar makers, P. J. Fitzpatrick, of the iron moulders, Jonah Dyer, of the granite cutters, and W. H. Foster, secretary of the Federation of Organised Trades and Labor Unions, issued a call for a general trade union conference in Philadelphia on May 17. Besides the above named unions, it was attended by the officers of the Amalgamated Association of Iron and Steel Workers, the typographical union, the National Federation of Coal Miners and Labourers, the Amalgamated Association of Coal Miners and Labourers, Boiler Makers' International Union, Lasters' Protective Union of New England, German-American Typographia, Tailors' National Union, Nailers' National Union, Bricklayers' and Masons' International Union, Stereotypers' Association and McKay Shoe Stitchers' Union of New England. For the first time in the eighties, did the combined trade union movement of the entire country come together for common action. What the drawing power of the legislative programme put forth by the Federation of Organised Trades and Labor Unions fell short of accomplishing, the common menace from the Knights was sufficiently strong to realise.

William H. Weihe, of the iron and steel workers, was made chairman and William H. Foster and P. J. McGuire, secretaries of the conference. A proposed treaty of peace with the Knights of Labor was then drawn up and McGuire, Weihe, Strasser, Fitzpatrick, Chris Evans (of the miners), and Daniel P. Boyer (of the printers) were selected as a committee to conduct negotiations with the Order. It was also voted that the conference of the executive officers of the national trade unions should meet annually thereafter.

The conference stated "the conviction of the chief officers of the National and International Unions here assembled that, inasmuch as trades unions have a historical basis, and in view of the success that has attended their efforts in the past, we hold that they should strictly preserve their distinct and individual autonomy, and that we do not deem it advisable for any trade union to be controlled by or to join the Knights of Labor in a body, believing that trades unions are best qualified to regulate their own internal trade affairs. Nevertheless, we recognise the solidarity of all labor interests." That the trade union conception of the "solidarity of all labor interests," however, meant no promise of active support to the unskilled class can plainly be seen from the address to the trade unions issued later, which described their task as follows: "Through the development of industry and the aggregation of capital, the tendency is to monopolise the business of the country. Hence the various trades have been affected by the introduction of machinery, the sub-division of labor, the use of women's and children's labor and the lack of an apprentice system, so that the skilled trades were rapidly sinking to the level of pauper labor. To protect the skilled labor of America from being reduced to beggary, and to sustain the standard of American workmanship and skill, the trades unions of America have been established." The address goes on to say that "When they [the trade unions] are founded on such grounds, there need be no fears of their destruction, nor need there be any antagonism between them and the Knights of Labor." The last conclusion, though it may have been entirely legitimate and in strict conformity with abstract logic and justice, went, nevertheless, contrary to the concrete logic of the situation. The trade unions could hardly expect that the Knights of Labor at a critical period such as this, when the fate of their movement was hanging in the balance, could allow the skilled men to remain within the narrow circle of their special trade interests. It was, therefore, a matter of natural sequence that, using the words of the resolution passed by the conference, it became "the avowed purpose of a certain element of the Knights of Labor to destroy the trades unions."

But though the trade unions seem to have failed to grasp the nature of the class struggle conducted by the Knights of Labor, and, therefore, viewed the latter merely as an encroaching organisation, no one can deny that they were acting within their right when they strenuously opposed the policy of forcible assimilation applied by the Knights of Labor. The proposed treaty of peace drawn up by the conference as the basis for future negotiations read as follows:

First, That in any branch of labor having a national or international organisation, the Knights of Labor shall not initiate any person or form any assembly of persons following said organised craft or calling without the consent of the nearest national or international union affected.

Second, That no person shall be admitted to the Knights of Labor who works for less than the regular scale of wages fixed by the union of his craft, and none shall be admitted to membership in the Knights of Labor who have ever been convicted of 'scabbing,' 'ratting,' embezzlement or any other offence against the union of his trade or calling until exonerated by the same.

Third, That the charter of any Knight of Labor Assembly of any trade having a national or international union shall be revoked and the members of the same be requested to join a mixed assembly or form a local union under the jurisdiction of their respective national or international trades unions.

Fourth, That any organizer of the Knights of Labor who endeavours to induce trades unions to disband, or tampers with their growth or privileges, shall have his commission forthwith revoked.

Fifth, That whenever a strike or lockout of any trade unionist is in progress no assembly or district assembly of the Knights of Labor shall interfere until the difficulty is settled to the satisfaction of the trades unions affected.

Sixth, That the Knights of Labor shall not establish nor issue any trade mark or label in competition with any trade mark or label now issued or that may hereafter be issued by any national or international trades union.

The General Assembly met in special session, May 25, 1886, at Cleveland. The prime object of this session was to settle the question of the relation to the trade unions. Powderly remained neutral. Nearly one-third of the delegates were trade unionists. Nevertheless the delegates from District Assembly 49 laboured so diligently that it required four days to secure the passage of an address to "Brothers in the Cause of Labor." The executive board laid the proposed treaty before the convention and the trade union's special committee was given a hearing before the committee on the state of the Order. The treaty was rejected, but a conciliatory address, largely the work of George E. McNeill and Frank K. Foster, with approval by Powderly, was issued "To the Officers and Members of all National and

International Trades' Unions of the United States and Canada," as follows:

> We recognise the service rendered to humanity and the cause of labor by trades-union organisations, but believe that the time has come, or is fast approaching, when all who earn their bread *by the sweat of their brow* shall be enrolled under one general head, as we are controlled by one common law—the law of our necessities; and we will gladly welcome to our ranks or to protection under our banner any organisation requesting admission. And to such organisations as believe that their craftsmen are better protected under their present form of government, we pledge ourselves, as members of the great army of labor, to co-operate with them in every honourable effort to achieve the success which we are unitedly organised to obtain; and to this end we have appointed a Special Committee to confer with a like committee of any National or International Trades Union which shall desire to confer with us on the settlement of any difficulties that may occur between the members of the several organisations.

The practical aspects of the co-operation were to be, according to the address, the interchange of working cards, "the adoption of some plan by which all labour organisations could be protected from unfair men, men expelled, suspended, under fine, or guilty of taking places of union men or Knights of Labor while on strike or while locked out from work," the adoption of a uniform standard of hours and wages throughout each trade whether controlled by a trade union or by the Knights of Labor, and finally, a system of joint conferences and of common action against employers, provided that "in the settlement of any difficulties between employers and employees, the organisations represented in the establishment shall be parties to the terms of settlement."

Obviously, the majority of the Knights of Labor preferred that the trade unions should affiliate with them. It cannot be said, however, that this preference sprang from the mere desire for expansion common to all organisations. The address that the convention ordered to be sent to the president of the Amalgamated Association of Iron and Steel Workers shows that the expansionist policy of the Knights was dictated by its solicitude for the interests of unskilled labour. It said in part: "In the use of the wonderful inventions . . . your organisation plays a most important part. Naturally it embraces within its ranks a very large proportion of laborers of a high grade of skill and intelligence. With this skill of hand, guided by intelligent thought, comes the right to demand that excess of compensation paid to skilled above the unskilled labor. But the unskilled labor must receive attention, or in the hour of difficulty the employer will not hesitate to use it to depress the compensation you now receive. That skilled or unskilled labor may no longer be found unorganised, we ask of you to annex your grand and powerful corps to the main army that we may fight the battle under one flag."

But apparently the skilled iron workers evinced no desire to be pressed into the service of lifting up the unskilled, for when a special committee of the Knights of Labor submitted the proposal to the convention of the amalgamated association, it was voted down practically unanimously. It met with like treatment at the national conventions of the typographical union, the plumbers, steam and gas fitters, the flint glass workers, the coal miners, the stationary engineers, and at the hands of the New York telegraphers, German confectioners, and the jewelers.

During the summer months of 1886 the conflict between the trade unions and the Order was held in abeyance pending negotiations. The committee appointed at the Philadelphia trade union conference convened again at Philadelphia on September 29 and held a joint meeting with Powderly and the executive board of the Knights of Labor regarding the appointment by the latter of a special negotiating committee. Powderly's position was unsatisfactory. Nevertheless, the trade union leaders decided to postpone action until after the meeting of the General Assembly at Richmond, Virginia, in October, 1886, and to meet again at Columbus, in December.

The Richmond General Assembly, which met October 9, presented a unique spectacle. It was thoroughly typical of the great labour upheaval at its highest point. The number of the delegates had more than quadrupled since the session in May, 658 delegates representing a constituency of over 700,000. The overwhelming majority were attending a convention for the first time. They possessed no parliamentary experience and totally lacked cohesiveness. Consequently, District Assembly 49, New York, the leader of the "union haters" with its 61 delegates bound by the unit rule, found it a comparatively easy matter to dictate the proceedings of the assembly, particularly since it secured the co-operation of Charles H. Litchman, the most influential leader in District Assembly 30, Massachusetts, with 75 votes. Powderly, who had been at all previous sessions independent of any combination and thoroughly out of sympathy with the Napoleonic tendencies of District Assembly 49, was now lined up with the latter.

Here is how Joseph R. Buchanan, of Denver, the leader of the minority faction which favoured amicable relations with the trade unions, describes the Richmond session:

It was at Richmond that the seal of approval was placed upon the acts of those members who had been bending every energy since the Cleveland special session to bring an open warfare between the order and the trades-unions. The contest between the exclusivists and the bi-organisation representatives was fierce, and it never waned for one moment during the two weeks of the session. The bitterness of feeling engendered by the strife between these two elements entered into every matter of any consequence which came before the body.... While the question at issue was the Knights against the whole trades-union movement, the discussions covering every possible phase of the subject, one trade only was named in the action taken by the General Assembly—the cigar makers. A resolution was adopted ordering all members of the order who were also members of the Cigar Makers' International Union to withdraw from the latter organisation; failure to comply with said order meaning forfeiture of membership in the Order of the Knights of Labor. The majority by which the resolution was adopted was not, comparatively, large, but it was enough; and the greatest labor organisation up to that time known in this country received its mortal wound at Richmond ... Powderly ... was unequivocally with the anti-unionists. This was Mr. Powderly's first serious mistake as General Master Workman, though he had been criticised because of his course in the Southwestern strike and during the eight-hour movement of May 1, 1886. ... The General Master Workman desired harmony in the order, and he permitted himself to be deceived into the belief that harmony could be secured by killing the influence of the trades-unionists who were Knights.

The open declaration of war by the Knights furnished the last impetus necessary for the complete unification of the trade unions already begun at the Philadelphia conference. The conference of the trade union officials scheduled for Columbus, Ohio, in December, 1886, came together on the eighth of the month. The legislative committee of the Federation of Organ-ised Trades and Labor Unions changed the place of meeting of the annual convention from St. Louis to Columbus, where it met on the seventh. The report of the legislative committee, of which Samuel Gompers was chairman, reviewed with satis-faction the part the organisation had played in the eight-hour strikes. The movement had greatly stimulated the growth of trade unions, which had doubled their membership during the year. It would have been more successful but for the fickle attitude of the "leading members of the Knights of Labor." Among the legislative achievements of the year were the estab-lishment of bureaus of labour statistics in several States, child labour laws, etc. An important place was occupied by the new Federal law for the incorporation of trade unions. The report saw in it a recognition of the "principle of the lawful character of Trades Unions, a principle we have been contending for years," though "the law is not what was desired, covering only those organizations which have, or may remove their headquarters to the District of Columbia, or any of the Ter-ritories of the United States."

The delegates to the convention of the Federation attended in a body the conference of the trade union officials, the latter representing 25 organisations claiming to represent "316,469 members in good standing."

On the second day, having effected a permanent organisation, the conference declared itself as the first annual convention of the American Federation of Labor and devoted the three remaining days of the session to the constitution and to the relations with the Knights of Labor.

A committee was appointed to meet with a similar committee chosen by the convention of the Federation of Organised Trades and Labor Unions and the latter consented to merge itself with the American Federation of Labor.

The new federation was not to be, like its predecessor, a mere association for legislation, but was entrusted with important economic functions. The national or international trade union was made the sole basic unit, and local unions remained entitled to independent representation only in trades where no national union existed. The place of the former legislative committee was taken by a president, two vice-presidents, a secretary, and a treasurer, together forming an executive council, with the following duties: first, to watch legislation; second, to organise new local and national trade unions; third, while recognising "the right of each trade to manage its own affairs," to secure the unification of all labour organisations; fourth, to pass upon boycotts instituted by the affiliated organisations; and fifth, in cases of strikes and lockouts, to issue after an investigation, general appeals for voluntary financial contributions in aid of the organisation involved. The revenue of the Federation was to be derived from charter fees and from a per capita tax of one-half cent per month for each member in good standing. The president's salary was fixed at $1,000 per annum.

Bitter feeling towards the Knights of Labor at once manifested itself, when the delegate from the window-glass workers' association was refused a seat on the ground that "said organisation is affiliated with the Knights of Labor, and is not a Trade Union within the meaning of the call for the Convention." Another attempt was made to negotiate with the Order, and a special committee of the convention met December 11 with a committee of the Knights of Labor. The meeting led to no results, since the trade unions would be satisfied with nothing less than the acceptance of the treaty, and the

Knights of Labor took the attitude that they not only did not have the right to consider it again after it had been rejected by the General Assembly, but that they would refuse to make a definite promise that organisers should not interfere in strikes ordered by trade unions or should not try to organise assemblies from among the members of trade unions. Thereupon the Federation in its turn unanimously declared war upon the Knights and announced the decision to carry hostilities into the enemy's territory: "We condemn the acts [of the Knights] above recited, and call upon all workingmen to join the Unions of their respective trades, and urge the formation of National and International Unions and the centralisation of all under one head, the American Federation of Labor." Along with this went a resolution, likewise unanimously adopted, refusing to patronise the label of the Knights of Labor. After electing Samuel Gompers as president, P. F. Fitzpatrick, of the iron moulders, first vice-president, J. W. Smith, of the journeymen tailors, second vice-president, P. J. McGuire, of the carpenters, secretary, and Gabriel Edmonston, also of the carpenters, treasurer, the convention adjourned to meet the following year at Baltimore.

Although the negotiations between the Knights and the trade unions were rendered fruitless by the arrogance of the trade unions on the one side, and by the apparent indifference of the Order on the other, the fact that out of the conflict had arisen a closely knitted trade union federation practically guaranteed that in the future a bridle would be put upon the aggressiveness of the organisers of the Knights. Of course, District Assembly 49 made the fullest use of the victory at Richmond, and pushed its anti-trade union policy to extremes. It even ordered the members of the Progressive Cigar Makers' Union, its faithful ally against the International Cigar Makers' Union, which had become affiliated as Local Assembly 2814, in March, 1886, either to leave the Order or to give up their union. This arbitrary action was too much even for the Progressives, and, rather than submit, they reunited with the International Union, their bitter enemy of the past six years.

However, the Order as a whole, by the time of the next session of the General Assembly at Minneapolis in October, 1887, clearly saw its mistake, and Powderly handed down a belated decision declaring unconstitutional the action taken at Richmond which expelled all members of the International Cigar Makers' Union. The decision was upheld by the General Assembly. Besides the growing strength of the Federation, this change of policy must have contributed also to the decreasing membership of the Order, which had fallen off one-third in one year. But the Order's conciliatory attitude met with but little response. The trade unions, now feeling their advantage, were not prone to accept the outstretched hand. The Amalgamated Association of Iron and Steel Workers had ordered that none of its members should belong to the Knights of Labor after April 1, 1888. At the convention of the American Federation of Labor in December, 1887, a report was adopted which said: "The attitude of the Knights of Labor towards many of the trades unions connected with the American Federation of Labor has been anything but friendly. . . . While we agree that a conflict is not desirable on our part, we also believe that the party or power which seeks to exterminate the trades unions of the country should be met with unrelenting opposition, whether that power consists of millionaire employers or men who title themselves Knights of Labor." Gompers, in the presidential report, recalled that the Knights of Labor had been present at the Pittsburgh convention in 1881, where the Federation of Organised Trades and Labor Unions had been established, and added: "Let us hope that the near future will bring them back to the fold, so that all having the grand purposes in view, as understood and advocated by the American Federation of Labor, may work for their realisation."

The Subsidence of the Knights

As a basis for this hope Gompers said: "It is noticeable that a great reaction and a steady disintegration is going on in most all organisations of labor which are not formed upon the basis that the experience of past failures teaches, namely, the benevolent as well as the protective features in the unions."

He was not in the least exaggerating. At the end of 1887 the disintegration in the Knights of Labor had reached an advanced stage. The tide of the uprising, which in half a year had carried the Order from 150,000 to over 700,000 members, began to ebb before the beginning of 1887 and the membership had diminished to 510,351 by July 1. While a share of this retrogression may have been due to the natural reaction of large masses of people who had been suddenly set in motion without experience, a more immediate cause came from the employers. Profiting by the lessons of May, they organised strong associations and began a policy of discriminations and lockouts, directed mainly against the Knights. "Since May last," said John Swinton in September, "many corporations and Employers' Associations have been resorting to all sorts of unusual expedients to break up the labor organisations whose strength has become so great within the past two or three years. Sometimes they attack them in the front, but more often on the flanks or in the rear. Sometimes they make an assault in force, and sometimes lay siege to the works; but more often they seek to carry their point by petty subterfuges that can be carried on for a long time without arousing resistance."

The form of organisation of these employers' associations clearly indicated that their main object was the defeat of the Knights. They were organised sectionally and nationally, but the opposing force, the district assembly, operated over only a limited area. In small localities, where the power of the Knights was especially great, all employers regardless of industry joined in one association. But in large manufacturing centres, where the rich corporation prevailed, they included the employers of only one industry as, for instance, the association of shoe manufacturers of Worcester County, Massachusetts, or the Manufacturing Knit Goods Association of New York State. An exception to this rule was the state employers' association in Rhode Island, which was a general association.

The common object of these associations was to eradicate whatever form of organisation existed among the wage-earners.

For instance, the association of shirt manufacturers of James-
burg, New Jersey, locked out 2,000 employes when it was discovered that they had joined the Knights. Likewise the manufacturers of silver goods of New York, Brooklyn, and Providence formed an association and locked out 1,200 men for
joining the Knights. It is therefore not surprising that the
association generally refused to negotiate with the Order and
to arbitrate disputes. In an appeal for aid issued by the
Knights of Labor in 1886, instances where employers refused
to negotiate were cited in Georgia, Massachusetts, Delaware,
Montana, Pennsylvania, Maryland, New Jersey, and Mississippi. Out of 76 attempts at arbitration investigated by the
Illinois Bureau of Labor, 38 offers were rejected—6 by labour
and 32 by capital. The New York commissioner of labour
affirmed that the irreconcilable attitude of the employers was
"the first obstacle in the way of successful introduction of
arbitration." Trade agreements, where they were entered into,
were held no more sacred by the employers than by the rank
and file of the Knights. For instance, the association of leather
manufacturers of Newark, New Jersey, which had entered into
a trade agreement with the leather workers' council of the
Knights, selected one of its members to violate it, assisted
him in the hire of strike-breakers, turned over to him a large
portion of the work of the other members, and forthwith
ordered a systematic discharge of the organised men.

Other important elements in this policy of repression were
the blacklist, the "iron-clad," and the use of Pinkerton detectives. The following is a typical case. The Champion
Reaper Company of Springfield, Ohio, locked out its 1,200
employes upon discovering that they were members of the
Knights, and, with the exception of a small number who were
blacklisted, the remainder were permitted to return to work
upon signing an "iron-clad" oath never to belong to a labour
organisation. The common use of the blacklist is confirmed by
the bureaus of labour of Ohio, Connecticut, Pennsylvania,
and New Jersey.

The Pinkerton detectives, who had first begun to specialise
in labour disputes during the seventies, now became an almost

indispensable factor. A confidential circular sent around by
the Pinkerton agency to employers announced that "corporations or individuals desirous of ascertaining the feeling of their
employees, and whether they are likely to engage in strikes or
are joining any secret labor organisations with a view of com-
pelling terms from corporations or employers, can obtain, on
application to the superintendent of either of the offices, a
detective suitable to associate with their employees and obtain
this information."

Notwithstanding the wide-spread and bitter hostility between the employers and the Knights, the movement resulted
in a considerable number of trade agreements with employers'
associations and with individual employers. The national
officers of the Order strongly urged the idea of conciliation
and trade agreements. In 1885 they induced the General Assembly to declare in favour of compulsory arbitration. Ralph
Beaumont, chief lobbyist for the Order before Congress, explained the long-continued and steady demand for the incorporation of trade unions on the ground that it would give the
Order a legal right to speak for its members in the proceedings
of compulsory arbitration. It is true that, when, following the
Southwest and eight-hour strikes, the leaders realised that
public opinion had turned against the Knights, the demand
for compulsory arbitration was rescinded. Still there can be
no better proof of the strong partiality of the leaders in the
Order for trade agreements.

Trade agreements multiplied, especially beginning with
1887. They generally provided for the recognition of the Order
and of the authority of its chosen committees, prohibited
discrimination against Knights, and obligated the employer to
submit to arbitration in the case of disagreement with his
employees. They included no closed-shop provision, and the
employer retained the right to discharge Knights for any good
cause, except incompetence, in which case he had to arbitrate.
Other agreements also included specific provisions for wages
and hours.

However, the trade agreement was the exception; the rule
was the strike and the lockout.

The control over strikes was an important question for the organisation. As in previous years, contributions to the "defence" fund were compulsory, and each district assembly administered the fund separately. Each one, however, was liable to an assessment by the General Executive Board for the relief of any district assembly whose funds had been exhausted by reason of lockouts or strikes. But this provision was in no case carried out, for each district assembly had its fund constantly depleted by its own strikes. The complete control of strikes by district assemblies was at once a source of strength and of weakness for the Order; of strength, because the local freedom to strike aided the extension of the organisation; of weakness, because it prevented concentrated efforts by the Order as a whole. But prior to the great mass movement of 1886, the dark side of local strike autonomy was not yet obvious. The Order was more careful in the matter of the boycott. Absolute local autonomy in boycotting stood more open to abuse than it did in striking, since the boycott had a tendency to spread beyond local limits and was inexpensive to its originators. So in 1885, the General Executive Board was given jurisdiction over all boycotts that were not strictly local. The General Assembly adopted a rule providing that as long as a boycott affected no one outside of the territory of a local, district, or state assembly, these respective units should retain "the privilege to institute a boycott." In all other cases the approval of the general executive board was made imperative.

The disputes during the second half of 1886 ended, for the most part, disastrously to labour. The number of men involved in 7 months, as estimated by *Bradstreet's*, was 97,300. Of these, about 75,300 were in 9 great lockouts, of whom 54,000 suffered defeat at the hands of associated employers. The most important lockouts were against 15,000 laundry workers at Troy, New York, in June, 20,000 Chicago packing-house workers, and 20,000 knitters at Cohoes and Amsterdam, New York, both in October.

The Troy lockout grew out of a strike on May 15, 1886, for higher wages by 180 women. These women had been organised shortly before as the "Joan of Arc" assembly of the Knights of Labor. Immediately the employers, who sensed in this demand the beginning of a general movement, united in a manufacturers' association and, on May 18, declared a general lockout against the members of the Knights of Labor. Although only one-sixth of those employed in the industry were Knights, the others left work. After five weeks, General Secretary Hayes accepted the price list presented by the manufacturers' association and the lockout and strike were called off.

The lockout in the knit goods industry at Amsterdam and Cohoes, New York, arose on the ground that an apprentice had been promoted to take charge of a new machine. There existed a contract previously entered into by Barry, of the executive board of the Knights of Labor, and the trade manufacturers' association of fifty-eight leading firms, which provided for the open shop and gave to the employer the unlimited right of discharging and promoting men. However, the district master workman of District Assembly 104 declared that his assembly had not been a party to the agreement, and, notwithstanding Powderly's injunction, declared a strike against the mill. This immediately led to a general lockout of the Knights, October 16. Barry and T. B. McGuire, the latter of District Assembly 49, took charge of the dispute and succeeded for over five months in preventing a large portion of the locked-out from going back to work on the conditions prescribed by the employers. Early in May, 1887, the strike was declared off.

More widespread attention than either the Troy or Cohoes lockout was attracted by the lockout of 20,000 Chicago butcher workmen. These men had obtained the eight-hour day without a strike during May. A short time thereafter, upon the initiative of Armour & Company, the employers formed a packers' association and, in the beginning of October, notified the men of a return to the ten-hour day on October 11. They justified this action on the ground that they could not compete with Cincinnati and Kansas City, which operated on the ten-hour system. On October 8, the men, who were organised in District Assemblies 27 and 54, suspended work, and the memorable lockout began. The negotiations were conducted by T. P. Barry, who had been especially commissioned by the General

Assembly then in session in Richmond, and M. J. Butler, the master workman of District Assembly 54. The packers' association, however, rejected all offers of compromise and, October 18, Barry ordered the men to work on the ten-hour basis. But the dispute in October, which was marked by a complete lack of ill feeling on the part of the men and was one of the most peaceable labour disputes of the year, was in reality a mere prelude to a second disturbance which broke out in the plant of Swift & Company, on November 2, and became general throughout the stock yards on November 6. The men demanded a return to the eight-hour day, but the packers' association, which was not joined by Swift & Company, who formerly had kept aloof, not only refused to give up the ten-hour day, but declared that they would employ no Knights of Labor in the future. The Knights retaliated by declaring a boycott on the meat of Armour & Company. The behaviour of the men was now no longer peaceable, as before, and the employers took extra precautions by prevailing upon the governor to send two regiments of militia in addition to the several hundred Pinkerton detectives employed by the association. To all appearances, the men were slowly gaining over the employers, for, on November 10, the packers' association rescinded its decision not to employ Knights, when suddenly on November 15, like a thunderbolt out of a clear sky, a telegram arrived from Powderly ordering the men back to work. Powderly had refused to consider the reports from Barry and Carlton, the members of the General Executive Board who were on the ground, but, as was charged by Barry, was guided instead by the advice of a priest who had appealed to him to call off the strike and thus put an end to the suffering of the men and their families.

The outcome of the Chicago packing-house lockout not only aided materially in reducing the organisation in Chicago, but it had a demoralising effect elsewhere. It taught the lesson that the centralised form of government in the Order, which meant practically a one-man government, was bound up with the greatest danger. Powderly did not possess the aggressive qualifications required for a successful leader in strikes. His eight-hour circular, his telegram in the Chicago lockout, and his later refusal to allow the Order to plead for mercy for the condemned Chicago anarchists, show that, in his reverence for public opinion and especially the opinion of the general press, he had come to overlook the sentiments of the masses whom he led. At a time when his organisation was coming to the front as the fighting organisation of a new class, he endeavoured to play the diplomatist rather than the fighting general.

The Chicago packers' lockout showed in an unfavourable light the centralised form of government. It remained for the great New York strike in January, 1887, to reveal the drawbacks and inefficiency of the mixed district assembly.

The strike began as two separate strikes, one by coal handlers at the Jersey ports supplying New York with coal, and the other by longshoremen on the New York water front, both starting on January 1, 1887. Eighty-five coal handlers employed by the Philadelphia & Reading Railroad Company, members of the Knights of Labor, struck against a reduction of 2½ cents an hour in the wages of the "top-men," and were joined by the trimmers with grievances of their own. Soon the strike spread to the other roads, and the number of striking coal handlers reached 3,000. The longshoremen's strike was begun by 200 men, employed by the Old Dominion Steamship Company, against a reduction in wages and the hiring of cheap men by the week. The strikers were not organised, but the Ocean Association, Knights of Labor, took up their case and was assisted by the longshoremen's union. Both strikes soon widened out through a series of sympathetic strikes of related trades and finally became united into one. The Ocean Association, Knights of Labor, declared a boycott on the freight of the Old Dominion Company, and this was strictly obeyed by all of the longshoremen's unions. The International Boatmen's Union refused to allow their boats to be used for "scab coal" or to permit their members to steer the companies' boats. The longshoremen joined the boatmen in refusing to handle coal, and the shovellers followed. Then the grain handlers on both floating and stationary elevators refused to load ships with grain on which there was scab coal, and the bag-sewers stood with them. The longshoremen now resolved to go out and refused to work on ships which received scab coal, and finally they decided to stop work altogether on all kinds of craft in the harbour until the trouble should be settled. The strike spirit spread to a large number of freight handlers working for railroads along the river front, so that in the last week of January the number of strikers in New York, Brooklyn, and New Jersey reached approximately 28,000: 13,000 longshore-men, 1,000 boatmen, 6,000 grain handlers, 7,500 coal handlers, and 400 bag-sewers. Master Workman Quinn, with his *aides de camp* in District Assembly 49, was in complete control of the strike from the beginning and had the active sympathy of the Central Labor Union and the trade unions.

On February 11, August Corbin, president and receiver of the Philadelphia & Reading Railroad Company, fearing a strike by the miners working in the coal mines operated by that road, settled with District Assembly 49 and restored to the eighty-five coal handlers, the original strikers, their former rate of wages. District Assembly 49 felt impelled to accept such a trivial settlement for two reasons. The coal strike, which drove up the price of coal to the consumer, was very unpopular, and the strike itself had begun to weaken when the brewers and stationary engineers had refused to come out on the de-mand of the assembly. The situation was thus unchanged, as far as the coal handlers employed by the other companies, the long-shoremen, and the many thousands of men who went out on sympathetic strike were concerned. The men began to return to work by the thousands and the entire strike collapsed. Swin-ton attributed the failure to the grave blundering of the com-mittee leaders in District Assembly 49, who, instead of calling out the railroad men and thus stopping all traffic at once, or-dered out the engineers and brewers, who could help but little and stood to sacrifice their agreements with their employers. Although Swinton ordinarily refrained from taking sides in the internal fights of the labour movement, he summarised the out-come of this strike as follows: "We do most sincerely regret the unfortunate collapse of the great strikes alongshore. . . . We are not surprised to hear of the deep and wide dissatisfaction with those braggarts and bunglers who so often forced themselves to the front as 'strike managers' for District Assembly 49, and whose final subterfuges were the laughing stock of the satanic press; but it is to be regretted that the powerful District must be made to suffer through such obtrusive incompetency as we have seen. We trust that the organised labor of New York will never again be damaged as it has been by such displays. Tens of thousands of poor men made sacrifices during the strike, without either whining or boasting."

The determined attack and stubborn resistance of the employers' associations after the strikes of May, 1886, coupled with the incompetence displayed by the leaders, caused the turn of the tide in the labour movement in the first half of 1887. This, however, manifested itself during 1887 exclusively in the large cities, where the movement had borne in the purest form the character of an uprising of the class of the unskilled and where the hardest battles were fought with the employers. District Assembly 49, New York, fell from its membership of 60,809, in June, 1886, to 32,826 in July, 1887. During the same interval, District Assembly 1, Philadelphia, decreased from 51,557 to 11,294 and District Assembly 30, Boston, from 81,197 to 31,644. In Chicago there were about 40,000 Knights immediately before the packers' strike in October, 1886, and only about 17,000 on July 1, 1887. The falling off of the largest district assemblies in 10 large cities practically equalled the total loss of the Order, which amounted approximately to 191,000, of whom not more than 20,000 can be accounted for as having withdrawn to trade assemblies, national or district. At the same time the membership of the smallest district assemblies, which were for the most part located in small cities, remained stationary and, outside of the national and district trade assemblies which were formed by separation from mixed district assemblies, thirty-seven new district assemblies were formed, also mostly in small localities. In addition, state assemblies were added in Alabama, Florida, Georgia, Indiana, Kansas, Mississippi, Nebraska, North Carolina, Ohio, West Virginia, and Wisconsin, with an average membership of about 2,000 each. Balancing these new extensions, however, was a decrease from 122,027 to 61,936 in the total membership of the local assemblies directly affiliated with the General Assembly.

It thus becomes clear that, by the middle of 1887, the Great Upheaval of the unskilled and semi-skilled portions of the working class had already subsided beneath the strength of the combined employers and the centralisation and unwieldiness of their own organisation. After 1887 the Knights of Labor lost their hold upon the large cities with their wage-conscious and largely foreign population, and became an organisation predominantly of country people, of mechanics, small merchants, and farmers, an element more or less purely American and decidedly middle-class in its philosophy. This change serves, more than anything else, to account for the subsequent close affiliation between the Order and the "Farmers' Alliance," as well as for the whole-hearted support which it gave to the People's party.

For Further Reading

Although Commons' history remains the most detailed and comprehensive study of American labor, the following one-volume works are also excellent. Joseph G. Rayback's *A History of American Labor* (1939) is carefully done; Thomas R. Brooks' *Toil and Trouble: A History of American Labor* (1964) is original and penetrating, and Foster Rhea Dulles' *Labor in America* (1960) is an excellent summary in a felicitous style, while Henry Pelling in *American Labor* (1960) is able as an Englishman to identify what is distinctly American in our labor history.

The student wishing to study the subject in depth might take a chronological approach beginning with Richard B. Morris, *Government and Labor in Early America* (1946) and continuing through Walter Hugins, *Jacksonian Democracy and the Working Class* (1960); Lloyd Ulman, *The Rise of the National Trade Union* (1955), and Norman Ware's two volumes, *The Industrial Worker 1840–1860* (1924) and *The Labor Movement in the U.S. 1860–1890* (1929). The modern story is then told by Philip Taft in *The A. F. of L. in the Time of Gompers* (1957) and *The A. F. of L. from the Death of Gompers to the Merger* (1959), which may be supplemented with Irving Bernstein, *The Lean Years: A History of the Worker 1920–1933*, and Harry Miller and Emily C. Brown, *From the Wagner Act to Taft-Hartley* (1950). Two recent books have offered new interpretations of controversial topics: Wayne J. Broehl, *The Molly Maguires* (1964), and Gerald N. Grob, *Workers and Utopia: A Study of the Ideological Conflict in the American Labor Movement, 1865–1900* (1960).

An alternative, highly fruitful method of studying labor history is through autobiography. Recommended are Terence V. Powderley, *The Path I Trod* (1940), Samuel Gompers, *Seventy Years of Life and Labor* (one volume edition 1957), and William D. Haywood, *Bill Haywood's Book* (1929).

Studies of the more important unions include Sam Romer, *The International Brotherhood of Teamsters* (1962); Louis Levine, *The Women's Garment Workers* (1924); Paul F. Brissenden, *The I.W.W.: A Study in American Syndicalism* (1920), Patrick Renshaw, *The Wobblies* (1967), and David Brody, *Steelworkers in America: The Non-Union Era* (1960).

Religion
in the Immigrant's Life

Oscar Handlin

The nineteenth century witnessed the most dramatic population shift in the whole course of civilization. Between 1820 and 1930 more than sixty million people left ancestral homes in Europe and Asia. A few, like the German Forty-Eighters, fled political proscription; others, the Jews of Czarist Russia for example, were driven away by religious pogroms, but for most economic necessity propelled them outward in search of a better life. And for the majority of these the United States offered the best opportunities. Almost thirty-eight million reached the republic before this great *Völkerwanderung* ended. Although the newcomers came in large numbers throughout the century, there were two peak periods: one in the decade and a half before the Civil War following famine in Ireland and peasant dislocation in Germany, and the other in the generation between 1890 and the outbreak of World War I.

The two huge inpourings differed in origin. Those who came before 1860 were natives of northern and western Europe: Irish, Germans, English, Scots, and Scandina-

Source: Oscar Handlin, *The Uprooted: The Epic Story of the Great Migrations That Made the American People* (New York: Little, Brown and Company, 1951), pp. 117–143. Copyright 1951 by Oscar Handlin. Reprinted by permission of Little, Brown and Company.

vians. The latecomers emigrated from Russia, Poland, Austria, Hungary, Italy, Greece, and other southern and eastern European countries. Numerically, many more people came in the second wave; after 1900 the average reached the amazing total of a million and a half a year. But if we consider the proportion of foreign-born to the total population, the rate of difference between 1860 and 1910 is not great. The thirteen million immigrants living in the United States in 1910 represented 14.5 per cent of the population; fifty years earlier, the four million foreign-born composed 13.2 per cent of all Americans.

But the newer immigrants were undeniably more visible. The incredible variety of peoples, bringing with them strange languages and cultures, transformed American cities. Jacob Riis, himself a Danish immigrant, imagined that the map of New York resembled nothing so much as a colorful mosaic with large patches of green for the Irish, and blue for the German, trying to hold their sections against the pushing red of the Italians, the yellow of the Chinese, and the somber gray of the Jews. Riis, understandably, loved the vitality of this polyglot civilization. But others were outraged. Henry Adams, out for a Sunday stroll on the Boston Common, complained about the people he encountered: "The types and faces bore them out; the people before me were gross aliens to a man, and they were in serene and triumphal procession." And while Emma Lazarus had the Statue of Liberty implore "Give me your tired, your poor, your huddled masses yearning to breathe free," Thomas Bailey Aldrich asked, "O Liberty, White Goddess, is it well to leave the gates unguarded?" These contrasting sentiments symbolized antagonistic positions in what developed into a fierce debate over the limits of immigration.

Those favoring exclusion declared the foreign-born to be the cause of the worst aspects of American politics— the corrupt city machines and a growing radicalism. They raised the bugaboo of the foreigner taking jobs from the native worker and charged that unscrupulous employers had dredged labor from the slums of Europe to beat down American wages. Ironically, this argument won the support of Samuel Gompers, president of the American

Federation of Labor and himself an immigrant. The
A.F. of L. regularly came out against unlimited immigration. The immigrant also found himself charged by the
restrictionists with responsibility for most of the social
ills besetting the country—alcoholism, crime, poverty, dis-
ease. Above all, organizations such as the Immigration
Restriction League contended that the newcomers under-
mined the traditional social order and diluted the national character. In an age when the Teutonic or
Anglo-Saxon theory of history (the idea that the success
of Great Britain, Imperial Germany, and the United
States could best be explained by their common Anglo-
Saxon heritage) had become an article of faith, nativists
asked: Should America commit race suicide through free
admission of inferior peoples from southern and eastern
Europe?

The Dillingham Commission created by Congress in
1907 aided the restriction movement by positing fundamental differences between the old and new immigrants,
producing statistics purporting to show the latter to be
more illiterate and transient and less skilled and assim-
ilable than the older peoples. The restrictionists received
further support from a spate of pseudoscientific books on
the particular excellence of the Nordic race, and Congress, in the xenophobic and anti-foreign atmosphere
following World War I and the Red Scare, enacted a
series of savagely discriminatory laws. Often collectively
referred to as the National Origins Acts, these laws remained the basis of the nation's immigration policy until
1965. Their final repeal came about in large part through
the work of historians and social scientists who step by
step demolished the restrictionist case.

No single historian contributed more to the new interpretation of immigration than Oscar Handlin (b. 1915),
Charles Warren professor of American history at Harvard
University. Handlin convincingly demonstrated how the
Dillingham Commission had lied with statistics. He
established also the essential political conservatism of
the immigrants, and while not excusing the corruption
of the machines, emphasized their social utility in an age
absent of welfare programs or unemployment insurance.

We now know that when the newcomer took a native's
job, it usually meant the latter advanced up the occu-
pational ladder; and, of course, it would be difficult to
find today an anthropologist or biologist who believes
that there are superior or inferior races.

In *The Uprooted,* his most imaginative, seminal, and
controversial work, Handlin departs from the usual re-
flections on how the immigrants altered America to consider how America altered the immigrant—history "seen
from the perspective of the individual received rather
than of the receiving society." He has been criticized for
generalizing too broadly about the immigrant experience, especially for regarding the enormous diversity of
peoples as a collective entity, and of not appreciating
the distinctiveness of each ethnic group. In a sense, this
criticism is valid, but it does not really detract from the
value of the work as a study from within. Handlin cele-
brates the distinctiveness of the immigrant experience.
In the early decades of this century, concurrent with the
restrictionist drive, a tremendous effort was made to
Americanize the foreign-born already in the country.
The program aimed to blend all peoples into a homoge-
neous whole. In the end, Americanization failed of its
purpose. Handlin and most students of the nation's ethnic groups are glad that it did. The preservation of cultural identities is no longer deplored, and they are now
recognized for their contributions to the richness of
American life.

The following selection deals with one of the areas
of our society that has most strongly felt the immigrant
impress, religion. Handlin shows how the needs of the
immigrant shaped the character of American religion,
particularly Roman Catholicism and Judaism, rather than
the other way around, as has sometimes been imagined.

A man holds dear what little is left. When much is lost,
there is no risking the remainder.

As his stable place in a whole universe slipped away from
under him, the peasant come to America grasped convulsively

at the familiar supports, pulled along with him the traditional bulwarks of his security. He did not learn until later that, wrenched out of context, these would no longer bear the weight of his needs.

Even in the Old World, these men's thoughts had led ineluctably to God. In the New, they were as certain to do so. The very process of adjusting immigrant ideas to the conditions of the United States made religion paramount as a way of life. When the natural world, the former context of the peasant ideas, faded behind the transatlantic horizon, the newcomers found themselves stripped to those religious institutions they could bring along with them. Well, the trolls and fairies will stay behind, but church and priest at very least will come.

The more thorough the separation from the other aspects of the old life, the greater was the hold of the religion that alone survived the transfer. Struggling against heavy odds to save something of the old ways, the immigrants directed into their faith the whole weight of their longing to be connected with the past.

As peasants at home, awed by the hazardous nature of the universe and by their own helplessness, these people had fled to religion as a refuge from the anguish of the world. Their view of their own lives had generated a body of conceptions and of practices that intimately expressed their inmost emotions. It was not only that they held certain theological doctrines; but their beliefs were most closely enwrapped in the day-to-day events of their existence. The specific acts of being religious were the regular incidents of the village year. Their coming needed no forethought, indeed no consciousness. Their regularity was an aspect of the total order of the village. That was a feature of their attractiveness.

The peasants found also attractive the outward aspects of their religious institutions. The very formality of structure and organization had a meaning of consequence to them. They were all communicants of established churches, whether Roman Catholic, Lutheran, Anglican, or Orthodox. In some lands, where the monarch professed the same faith, to be "established" meant that the Church and State were closely united. That was true in Italy, Germany, Scandinavia, England, and Russia. But that link was not the essential element in establishment which also existed in countries such as Poland and Ireland, where Catholic peasants lived under non-Catholic rulers.

Recognition by the government and special treatment in law were only the surface indications of a deeper significance. To the peasants, establishment meant that their religion held a fixed, well-defined place in their society, that it was identified with the village, that it took in all those who belonged, all those who were not outcasts. Establishment in that sense gave these people a reassuring conviction that they belonged, were parts of a whole, insiders not outsiders.

The other attributes of establishment were appropriate also. About these churches was no confusing cloud of uncertainty. Their claim to men's allegiance rested on a solid basis of authority. It was not an individual choice that was involved in the process of belonging, but conformity. So, everyone else did. So it had been done year before year, generation before generation, as far back as the peasant could reckon . . . ever. The very rights and privileges of the Church, its lands and possessions, were evidence of its legitimacy and longevity. It was unthinkable not to be a member; it demanded a considerable feat of the imagination to conceive of what it would mean to be excluded, to draw down the censure of the entire community, to be barred from every social occasion.

There was no need to argue about these matters, to weigh alternatives, to consider. The Church gave no reasons for being; it was. Its communicants were within it not because they had rationally accepted its doctrines; they had faith because they were in it. Explanation in terms of reasonable propositions was superfluous; the Church was accepted as a mystery, which called for no explanation. These peasants felt the attractiveness of the demand on their faith as of the demand on their obedience to authority. Such, their own ideas had led them to believe, were the sources of certainty.

Village religion was, as a matter of course, conservative.

Peasants and priests alike resisted change. They valued in the Church its placid conviction of eternal and universal sameness, of continuity through the ages, of catholicity through Christendom. The very practices that stirred them now reached back to the earliest times. Here and in precisely this manner, generations of untold ancestors had worshiped. Dimly over the gap of years, fathers and sons engaged in a common communion, assured by the permanence of forms.

The peasants were certain of the fixity of their church in space as well as in time. This priest who ministered to them in this parish was not an isolated individual but one who had an established place in a great hierarchical structure that extended through society. Above the priest was a sequence of other dignitaries rising to loftier and loftier eminence to the one supereminent above all, pope or patriarch, king or emperor. When the retinue of the bishop pranced through the village, when that personage himself appeared attired in all the magnificence of his vestiture, when his distant countenance framed in the miter of his majesty looked down on the assembled community, then the people humbly in his presence were elevated through the dignity of his own imposing power. He had ordained the priest, stood guarantor of the efficacy of the parish rites, brought the village into communion with the whole world of true believers, made the peasant certain there was order in the Church and security of place for each soul within it.

Yet the grandeur of religion did not leave it aloof from its communicants. Splendid though it was in appearance, extensive and powerful in its compass, it was still close to the life of each man. The hierarchy that reached up to the most exalted also reached down to the most humble.

The Church was familiar to the peasants' day-to-day existence. Its outward forms and ceremonies were established in the round of the year. By long usage, each festival had a seasonal connotation through which, in the same celebration, were commingled the meanings of the distant Christian event and of the proximate changes in the immediate world of nature. All the acts of worship were embedded in a setting of which the landscape, the weather, and the sight of the heavens all were aspects. Each holiday thus had substance and individuality, a whole and entire character of its own. Its coming filled the whole place and the whole day, spread out from the church through the road where the procession passed to the blessed field around, extended on from the early service at the altar to the feast and the accompanying jubilation. Each occasion was thus local to the particular village, the possession of each participant, a part of his way of life. This the peasants had in mind when they hoped, most eagerly, to re-establish their religion in the New World.

It was not only the attractiveness of such elements of form that moved the immigrants to reconstruct their churches in America; it was also the substance embraced in those forms. These people were anxious that religion do and mean in the United States all that it had back there before the Atlantic crossing.

At home, worship had brought to the worshiper a pleasure that was aesthetic in nature. If in the new land he had the occasion, which he had rarely had in the old, to talk about the quality of that satisfaction, the peasant put the words of his description around specific impressions of the service—the stately manners, the inspiring liturgy, the magnificent furnishing. But such descriptions he knew were inadequate; for beyond the beauty that adhered to these things in their own right was a beauty of essence that grew out of their relationship to his own experience as a human being. Lacking the habit of introspection, the peasant could not set words to that satisfaction. He could only feel the lack of it.

How comforting were the ceremonial movements of the priest and how stirring his sermon—not at all a bickering argument but a be-gestured incantation! Here was not so much an effort to persuade man to be good as a reminder that he was bad, in effect magically to cleanse him. Indeed, magical qualities inhered in all the acts of worship. Touching on sin and the remission of sin, on evil and the warding-off of evil, these practices made sense in terms of peasant ideas.

In the rite before his eyes, the man could see that the

world in which he lived was not whole, did not of itself
justify itself. No. This was merely a dreary vestibule through
which the Christian entered the life eternal that lay beyond
the door of death. Long and narrow was the passage and
bitter dark. With utmost striving was the crossing made, and
little joy was in it. But there was a goal, and there would be
an arrival. The bells that tolled at the culmination of each
service would toll also at each soul's release, when the hard
journey, over, would lead to its own compensation for the
troubles of the way.

The promise of life to come, and the meaning of the life
of the present, was consolation. At that expected future,
retribution, rewarded good and punished evil, would make
whole the order of mundane things, explain the lapses of
justice, the incongruity of achievements, the neglect of merit
in the existence of the peasant. To the congregation, devoutly
silent under the plaster images, the monotonous chant affirmed over and over that the perspective of eternity would
correct all the disturbing distortions in the perspective of
today.

Faith brought the affirmation that man, though the crea-
ture of change that appearance made him to be, was also
actor in the great drama that had begun with the miracle of
creation and would end in the miracle of redemption. For
him, God had come to earth, had suffered, and had sacrificed
Himself to save all humanity. That sacrifice, repeated at every
mass, was the visible assurance of meaning in the universe.

The same sacrifice transfigured the communicants who
shared the mystery. Wafers and wine, blood and flesh, united
them in the togetherness of their common experience. Not
only they within the village, but through the village to the
uncounted numbers elsewhere, to their own ancestors in
the churchyard who had also once shared, still shared. In the
salving rite of Communion, there mingled with the satisfaction of the act itself the sentiments of village loyalty, the
emotions of family love, and the awareness of fulfillment of
the ideal of solidarity.

If the peasants made a way of life of the establishment of

their religion, so those who were not peasants made a way of life of their dissent.

The dissenting churches made no claims to universality, could imbue their members with no general sense of belonging, indeed left them with the consciousness of being outsiders. But, as outsiders, the Jews or Quakers or Baptists had to cherish the differences which were the marks of their election. Such sects could not take their membership for granted; they had to stress a continuing process of conversion and dedication, whether that be intellectually or emotionally arrived at. Out of the desire to protect their distinctive differences from obliteration in societies so much oriented around the peasant and out of the need to lend dignity to the process of conversion, these groups had also achieved an order of holidays, a formality of services, and a rigid mode of observances that, together, constituted a way of life.

Religion for these people was not as much tied to a locality as for the peasants. The appearance of things played not so prominent a role in the dissenting as in the established churches. Chapel and synagogue by their nature were not so likely to make a visual appeal, and rite was not so conspicuous in their practices. The congregations were more likely to be attached to the evidences of their own participation in worship as individuals—how they sang this psalm or offered up this prayer. For these evidences reminded them of their own consciousness of community as a group; and though they were a community of noncommunicant outsiders, still that consciousness was precious to them, worthy of preservation wherever they were.

Become immigrants and arrived in America, peasants and dissenters therefore alike struggled to reconstruct their churches. In the manner of doing, there were differences among the various groups. But the problem of all was the same: how to transplant a way of religious life to a new environment.

The immigrants began with the determination that their emigration would not destroy the ties that bound them to

the church. For years they kept alive a connection with the
Old Country parish. Letters from the other side brought news
of the place and the people; letters from this side brought
gifts to embellish the building, and sometimes, requests for
counsel from the priest.

But the immigrants thought it more important still to
bring their churches to the United States, to reconstitute in
their new homes the old forms of worship. At heavy cost and
despite imposing obstacles, they endeavored to do so. Often
when a phase of the struggle was over—say, a new edifice
dedicated—they would look back with relief and surprise at
the height of the difficulties surmounted.

The conditions of emigration and the hardships of the
crossing were immediate sources of confusion. On the way,
in the ships, the terrible disorder made troublesome any ritual
observance. The prolonged lapse of unsettled time obscured
the calendar; on the move, no day was individual from any
other. Without the ministrations of a priest, without the sus-
tenance of a whole community, the worshiper was limited to
his own humble resources of prayer. It would take an effort
to regain the richness of experience he had once enjoyed.

The end of the journey was the start of new tribulations.
In the United States the immigrants encountered a most dis-
couraging situation. All the conditions of religious life in
America were different from those in the Old World. As the
newcomers struggled to adjust themselves, they discovered a
maze of barriers that separated them from the desired objective, transplantation of the old churches.

It was difficult, for instance, to understand the diversity
of religious affiliations. In Europe the established church was
universal; only a few outsiders dissented. Here a vast variety
of sects divided the population, and did so according to no
meaningful pattern of social, economic, or sectional status.
In outward aspect, in occupations, in respectability, one could
not distinguish the members of one denomination from another. All these people furthermore associated with each other
on terms of complete equality. There seemed no reason there-

fore why a man should not change his church as freely as his hat. Indeed, to the immigrants it seemed the Americans were perilously near to doing so all the time.

Every religion therefore was in open competition for adherents with every other. There was no establishment in the United States; no church was connected with the State or favored by the laws. What was more, no sect had so secure or commanding a position in any other way that it could compel members to come to it or penalize those who did not. In all the great cities, throughout the West, and in many parts of the South, the churches were almost all equally new and stood on approximately the same footing. Even rural New England, where the Congregationalists had at first held an exceptional position, after 1850 approached the general condition.

The absence of an authoritative national, or even a regional or local, church was unfamiliar and disturbing. The privacy of beliefs, the freedom to enter what denomination he wished —or none at all—placed before the immigrant the necessity of giving answers to questions that had never been asked of him before. Without the aid of priests, for it was in the nature of the movement that laymen came in advance of the clergy, these humble people had to make the most difficult of decisions. That they insisted on re-creating the old churches testifies to the strength of the old ties.

Such decisions involved not principles alone, but all sorts of concrete, practical considerations. With the most devout will in the world, a churh would not appear unless there were funds for an edifice and a staff for its service.

The problem of finances was sufficiently oppressive. At home the peasants had never to consider the means of paying the expenses. The Church supported itself by grants either from the State or from the income of its own lands; the communicants contributed only the fees for particular services and these were fixed by the force of age-old custom. All such revenues disappeared with immigration. New ones to replace them were the minimal cost of reconstituting the churches in America.

Then the immigrants discovered that costs could not be minimal in the New World which compelled them to take on many additional charges not known in the Old. Here the pious had to create afresh, and at once, what in Europe had always been at hand, the product of centuries of growth. Everywhere the newcomers went they purchased buildings or, where they were able, erected new ones. They accumulated all the furnishings and the appurtenances necessary for the service and for all that raised what funds their own efforts brought them.

They could count on little help. The Roman Catholics occasionally benefited from the assistance of philanthropic monarchs like King Ludwig of Bavaria, or from the donations of missionary organizations, the Austrian Leopoldine Verein and the French Society for the Propagation of the Faith, or most of all, from the services of the international orders. But such aid, valuable as it was, was trifling against the enormity of the need. By and large, the money that built the churches and other religious institutions was assembled from the earnings of humble laborers who painfully accumulated what they scarcely could spare and devotedly gave what they could.

The magnitude of the task was multiplied by the circumstance that it was executed without the support of the kind of authority that had familiarly operated on the peasants at home. There was, to begin with at least, only a skeletal hierarchy and no corps of clerics to supply leadership. Under the American voluntary system, the churches had no sanctions. They counted for support on the good will and loyalty of their communicants. A bishop could not simply command and expect to be obeyed; his orders evoked a response only to the degree that he catered to the wishes of his flock. Law in the United States increased the uncertainty by defining the congregation as the church incorporate, and naming the laymen rather than the priest as owners of its property. Yet there were limits to the powers of a majority of the membership, for a minority was always free to secede and drift off in its own direction. If the immigrants held together and achieved as much as they did, it was because the longing that moved them sprang from a common stem in their life before emigration.

The transition from establishment to voluntarism was more difficult for peasants than for dissenters. The latter had known, at home, how it was to support a church through their own efforts. In America indeed their situation improved, for the neutrality of the state was better than its hostility. Here all sects were in the same position.

Paradoxically that very equality of situation threatened the survival of the dissenting groups. The sense of election grew weaker in the absence of persecution by a dominating church. Unless constantly reminded of the particularity and uniqueness of their own form of dissent, individuals might be tempted to drift off into other analogous denominations.

Dissenters and peasants both, therefore, saw a danger in the pervasive latitudinarianism of religion in the United States. Too many Americans were ready to believe that salvation could come through any faith or none, that ethical behavior and a good life rather than adherence to a specific creed would earn a share in the heavenly kingdom.

There was a double menace to this delusion. To begin with, it put to nought the sacrifices of establishing the immigrant religions. If all roads led to salvation, why trouble with great difficulty and enormous expense to hack out one's own? Why not follow the well-established easy paths others had already marked? Experience shouted the denial. In the missions, in the chapels, where the strangers came to pray, there the voices were of aliens and the ways were not the same. There were not the satisfactions that a full religion brought. No salvation could be there.

There was also a more subtle threat in latitudinarianism. The American ideas might penetrate the immigrant churches themselves, undermine the old ideas. That would deprive the newcomers, in particular the peasants, of their promised reward. For these people salvation was the compensation for faith and suffering, not for good behavior. They would not have the shift in emphasis.

The problem was, the whole effort, no matter how earnest, was out of context. You can build a church, but you cannot re-create the site, wipe out the surrounding city, restore the village background. You can reassemble the communicants; but can you re-create the communion, wipe out the effects of the crossing, and restore the old piety? A new environment has disorganized the old order. Determined men long for reorganization, struggle to effect it.

Invariably the way seemed to be the complete transfer of the old religious system to the New World. It was not simply the Gospel and priest the immigrants would bring with them, but holidays and processions, ancient costumes and traditional rites, the whole life of religion at home. All these they wished to replant in the unreceptive soil of America. The only way to be sure of survival was to insist on the rigid preservation of the whole.

The process of replanting was arduous, left each of the newer religions a painful history writ not so much in the blood of martyrs as in the sweat of loyal laborers.

Oldest, and ultimately largest, of these churches in the United States was the Roman Catholic Church. By the end of the eighteenth century, American Catholics had outlived the prejudices earlier directed against them. They then constituted a community that was small in size but well-established and secure in social position. Composed primarily of the native-born, the church counted among its communicants some of the wealthiest merchants and planters in the country. The only consequential immigrant group at first were the French, who wielded an influence disproportionate to their numbers because the community was served largely by French clergymen displaced by the revolution in France. Yet these had no significant difficulties with the native Catholics for they shared a common point of view; indeed, American priests were generally trained in French seminaries, and it had earlier seemed possible that a subject of Louis XVI would become the first American bishop.

In the course of the nineteenth century, however, immigration added to the Catholic population a mass of new communicants that quickly overshadowed the original body. Coming from parts of Europe historically distant and separate from each other, from the western coast of Ireland to the eastern slopes of the Carpathians, the newcomers brought with them different and decided notions as to what was the proper form of the Church, wished each to perpetuate the unique qualities of the religious life they had practiced at home. The outcome was a long period of internal dissension.

First to arrive in large numbers were the Irish. In the 1790's there were already disputes in some parishes as to what nationality the priest should be. On scores of petty details the Irish found themselves at odds with the old established Catholics, native and French. And in a few places grievances mounted up until they broke out into open conflicts that called forth the intercession of the civil authorities.

Through the first three decades of the nineteenth century the situation of the Roman Catholic Church remained in balance. The native Catholics had the advantage of respectability and wealth; they added to their strength by occasional conversions from among Protestants and by recruiting the children of immigrants. But they could still hardly hold their own. With few facilities for training priests, there was always a shortage of American clergymen; and some bishops, to their eventual regret, were willing to gamble on the dubious qualifications of stray clerics who wandered up from the West Indies or across from the continent and did much damage before their past records caught up with them.

The Irish on the other hand had behind them the potent resources of an immigration that mounted steadily in volume, and that brought to the New World not only an ever-larger flock of communicants, but also their pastors, made available from the Old Country. Already in the 1830's Irish names were prominent in the priesthood, although not yet among the bishops.

Soon thereafter, the full impact of the great migration transformed American Catholicism. Church membership became overwhelmingly Irish in composition, and Irish-Americans assumed some of the most distinguished places in the

hierarchy in the United States. By the middle of the nineteenth century Catholicism in this county showed a pronounced Hibernian cast.

The scattered parishes still predominantly native American or French fought in vain to retain their autonomy and
distinctiveness. The battle was fought out over the effort of
the laity to retain a determining voice in the management of
church property and thus indirectly of religious affairs. The
practice of some of the earliest Catholics had followed that
of the Protestant denominations and had vested control in
Boards of Trustees. Stubbornly these boards resisted the
demand they relinquish authority, so stubbornly as to precip-
itate a series of schisms from Boston to New Orleans, so
stubbornly that the Church of St. Louis in Buffalo was placed
under an interdict in 1851 and its trustees excommunicated
three years later.

But the bishops won. They were bound to win, for they
had the devoted support of the mass of their Irish communicants to whom the issue was simply that of whose churches
these were to be. With the rights of the laymen the immigrants had little concern; the peasants at home had never
presumed to interfere with the management of the priests'
property, and were only concerned with their rights as wor-
shipers. Those they thought would be less well guarded by
the strange trustees than by bishops and priests of their own
kind. By the time the Third Plenary Council in 1884 ruled
decisively on the question, it was already settled as a practical
matter.

Yet the clerics who gathered for that impressive assembly
in Baltimore already knew that the contest for control of
the Church had not come to an end, had only taken a new
turn. Shortly, the Irish immigrants would face an assault
from two groups of coreligionists eager to purge Catholicism
of its foreign influences, restore its American aspect. Again
the weight of numbers would tell.

Discontent had developed first among native Catholics,
particularly among converts like Isaac Hecker and Orestes
Brownson, who had only a slight understanding of the peasant

faith. Interested above all in proselytizing among Americans, such men regarded the Irish character of the Church as a positive impediment and claimed that Catholicism could only be attractive to native Protestants in the United States if it adapted itself to local conditions. This point of view also gained some adherents among the second generation, among the children of the immigrants who had never lived the life of religion in the Old World, who were impatient of their fathers' ways, and who valued the approval of the American society within which they had grown up.

These were all faithful Catholics, unwilling to deviate in the least from the Church's dogmas. Yet inevitably Americanization involved kinds of compromises. There was a wish to minimize the points of contention with other Americans: perhaps the parochial and the public school could be reconciled; perhaps a formula could be found to make room within Catholic social doctrines for American democracy and liberalism; perhaps the Church could itself participate in or encourage the movements for human amelioration that so absorbed people in the United States. The obstacle was the dull, inert conservatism of the immigrants, their blind adherence to tradition and obedience to the hierarchy. Because of them the Church was *run by a close corporation of discredited foreigners, and what a success they made of it in their own countries!*

Within the hierarchy were some supporters of such views, notably Archbishop Gibbons of Baltimore, Archbishop Ireland of St. Paul, and Bishop Spaulding of Peoria. Their most striking achievement was the creation of Catholic University of America, at Washington, an institution that was to be free of the control of the bishop of any specific diocese, that was not to be bound to any particular teaching order, and that was to provide the scholarly leadership for the new developments in American Catholicism.

Within the hierarchy were also the bitter opponents of the American idea, among them Archbishop Corrigan of New York and Bishop McQuaid of Rochester. Unrelenting in their hostility, they fought every innovation, and saw their resistance crowned with success in 1899 when the Pope, for reasons of his own, condemned what he called the doctrines of Americanism in the Bull *Testem Benevolentia*. Whether the supreme pontiff acted with an eye to American conditions or not the effect of his action was to assure the victory of the conservative wing and with it the continued dominance of the Irish in the Church.

Very likely, that victory would in any case have come; for at that very time the Americans were being driven to close ranks with the Irish against a greater threat to them both. Immigration from Germany, from Italy, and from eastern Europe was bringing to the New World newer groups of Catholics, groups which each insisted on recognition. The desire of so many different people to see re-created the precise forms of their old churches seemed, for a while, a menace to the whole Catholic order in the United States.

The earliest German Catholics had established themselves with relative ease. Arriving at the same time as the Irish, they settled either on farms or in sections of the cities where they could create German parishes. There were in fact a few German bishops. But the Germans who came later in the century found a more complicated situation. Settling in cities where the Irish were already dominant they had trouble setting up churches of their own, often found the bishops unsympathetic or hostile. That was the burden of the complaint thirty-two German priests addressed to the Pope in 1884. That was the tenor of the argument set forth in a tearful pamphlet two years later by Father P. M. Abbelen, Vicar-General of the Diocese of Milwaukee.

The Italians judged their situation more calamitous still. Arriving toward the end of the century, they moved into residential districts that in most cities had formerly been occupied by the Irish. With the intense desire of all peasants, the Italians longed to reconstruct their old village churches. They were Catholics, but the Catholic churches they found in the neighborhoods they occupied were Irish and not Italian —as different from what was familiar to the newcomers as the chapels of the Episcopalians or Methodists. They were not content, and sought to recapture the old authenticity. The result was a struggle, parish by parish, between the old Catholics and the new, a struggle that involved the nationality of the priest, the language to be used, the saints' days to be observed, and even the name of the church.

In this contest, the attitude of the bishops was critical. And there was the greatest grievance of all, for by the 1890's the hierarchy was almost entirely of Irish descent. Do what they could on a local basis, the scattered Germans and Italians were still not strong enough to dispute the control of the diocese. Since power was lodged almost entirely in the hands of the bishops, the fight seemed lost before it was properly begun. Large sectors of the immigrant population were discontented, and there seemed a real possibility that the Church would witness a substantial dropping off in its membership.

Concern with these problems was widespread; but a solution was painfully hard to come at. The most radical proposal was advanced in 1890 in the Lucerne Memorial, a document drawn up under the influence of Peter Paul Cahensly. Cahensly, a German interested in the fate of his coreligionists in America, suggested that the diocese in the United States be based not on geography but on nationality. Instead of following the traditional territorial divisions, the Irish, Germans, and Italians were each to have their own parishes which would then fall into separate Irish, German, and Italian hierarchies. Thus the shock of migration would be eased for Catholics and the dangers of loss of faith minimized. Against this scheme the Irish and American bishops united to secure a condemnation from the Vatican which saw in it an implicit denial of the fundamental catholicity of the Church.

But to reject the proposal was not to solve the problem which rather grew more complicated with the arrival of newer groups of immigrants. The Poles, Lithuanians, Hungarians, and Syrians found themselves minorities within minorities and were therefore more dissatisfied, more open to the temptation of falling away from the Church. Not only were many becoming apathetic and unaffiliated, but such grievances stimulated the proselytizing activities of the Protestant denominations; by 1918 there were some twenty-five thousand Italian converts alone in New York City.

Most distressing of all were the internal dissensions, the breaches of discipline, and the schisms that divided the Church. Always these began with local issues and sometimes were confined within the parish. Thus the Italians of the North End of Boston, dissatisfied with the Franciscans in charge of St. Leonard's, who were partial to the Irish, seceded in 1884 and, on their own, formed the San Marco Society. It took years of controversy before the Archbishop was induced to recognize their church.

But sometimes the divisions became permanent and spread rapidly beyond the localities in which they were initiated. So in the 1890's three independent and spontaneous controversies between Polish parishes and their Irish bishops in Scranton, Buffalo, and Chicago cut loose from the Church a substantial body of communicants who ultimately united under a hierarchy of their own in the Polish National Catholic Church in America. Similar movements created an independent Lithuanian and, for a time, an independent Italian church.

Apart from the heady business of complaining and organizing, there was, though, no satisfaction here. All these efforts at preservation only led to change, and in the change the village church was in any case lost. Generally with time there came a succession of compromises that accepted the Cahenslyite conception of the national parish in practice and enabled each group of immigrants to find a way of worship of its own choosing.

Only sometimes no compromise is possible. Someone must accept the heartache of a radical decision. In 1890, the Right Reverend John Ireland receives the Archpriest Alexei Tovt, pastor within the diocese of a Catholic church in Minneapolis. The Archbishop is shocked because the priest does not kneel, disturbed because the priest is not celibate. There is no violation of doctrine here; the Archbishop knows that Father Tovt is a Uniat, that Uniat Catholics have a dispensation to follow the Greek rites, and that their clergy are free to marry. Yet, knowing all this, the head of the diocese still cannot refrain from upbraiding the seeming breach of decorum. Now Father Tovt is offended; the Archbishop's effrontery seems an invasion of the traditional privileges of his Carpatho-Ruthenian congregation. He and his flock secede and accept the Orthodox faith. In the next half-century, several hundred thousand Uniats follow that lead. In a Pennsylvania mining town, how can an Irishman grow accustomed to meeting the wife and children of a Catholic priest? How long can the Ruthenians accept the slights of misunderstanding, bow to the imputation that their ancient practices are not worthy of preservation?

The centralization, the discipline, and the order of the Catholic Church, its long experience in reconciling national difference, and its international tradition, all were inadequate to contain the peasants' urge to reconstitute their religious life in America exactly as it had been at home in the village.

In the other immigrant churches, where the degree of control was so high, resettlement in America was even more disruptive. Every local variation struggled for expression through the years of bitter confusion.

Immigrants from several regions of Europe brought Lutheranism to the New World. Yet despite an essential uniformity in dogma, they established not one but several Lutheran churches.

The German who came to the United States in the nineteenth century found Lutheran churches already in existence in many parts of the country. These hardly satisfied the newcomer, however. Although they had been founded in the previous century by other Germans, they had lost contact with Europe and been Americanized, tainted with laxity of observance and with latitudinarianism. The growth of the denomination through the addition of immigrants was accomplished by a thoroughgoing reformation. Through the work of the Missouri Synod, organized by C. F. W. Walther, there was a determined effort to return to the purity of practice frittered away by its predecessors.

Nevertheless, succeeding groups insisted upon their own

churches and their own synods. Not, indeed, that the established churches in Europe were much concerned; the Church
of Sweden, for instance, advised its members coming to the
United States simply to join the Episcopal Church. But the
Swedish immigrants could neither accept that advice, nor
move into the German establishments. Everywhere they created churches and bound them into a synod of their own. And
later comers did the same; the Norwegians, the Danes, the
Icelanders, the Finns, and the Volga Germans suffered through
like experiences. They arrived, and were unhappy with the
varieties of Lutheranism they discovered in the United States,
for those seemed to have been diluted by contact with Americanism. Invariably a full religious life seemed to demand the
creation of still newer churches closer to the familiar Old
World models.

So also it was with the various Eastern churches. The period
of immigration was not over before there were five major
Orthodox establishments: the Greek, Hellenic, Russian, Ser-
bian, and Antiochean; and several of these were in turn
divided by schisms. Divisions, the origins of which were lost
in obscure European causes, were here perpetuated through
the devotion of the immigrants and their desire to keep alive
the traditional forms of worship as embodiments of a way of
life.

Dissenters encountered comparable difficulties of adjustment when it came to setting up their churches in the United
States. These people had never been established and were
therefore not disestablished by migration. They were acquainted with the notion of conversion and tended to stress
the ethics of behavior as well as the ceremonial of forms. An
individual who slipped into some American approximation
of his own sect therefore faced not so painful a wrench out
of his earlier religious experience. Nevertheless, the ties to
old ways proved binding for dissenters too. They struggled
stubbornly to maintain their identity as religious groups and
to reconstruct the old faiths in the New World. Little bands
of Welsh Methodists or Scottish Presbyterians or Italian Wal-
densians devoutly held on, and often sought in their settle-

ment in America new justifications for the sense of mission
they bore.

The extreme dissenters, the Jews, followed a pattern of
development much like that of the immigrants who trans-
planted established religions. In the case of this group, the
lack of a hierarchy and of any discipline outside the congregation encouraged very rapid splintering. Any ten Jews were
free to form a synagogue and to worship in what way they
willed. As soon as the numbers were large enough, the multi-
plication of congregations began. Already in the 1850's dif-
ferentiations had appeared among the English, the Germans,
the Poles, and the Bohemians. And when the volume of
immigration increased toward the end of the nineteenth century, the divisions became more minute. The men of a single
province or of a single town assembled to find God in their
old ways.

As for the Catholics and the Lutherans, the New World
for the Jews was a threat to the old ways. In a land where
there was no establishment, they were no longer exceptional
outsiders. Where all people were equally at home, these were
no longer in exile. The Americanism of Judaism was the
Reform Movement, which gathered force at mid-century and
reached its ultimate expression in the two decades after 1880,
at the same time as the analogous trend in Catholicism. The
emphasis on adjustment to conditions in the United States
involved a sacrifice of parts of the traditional ritual, conformity to some of the modes of the Protestant sects, and an
extreme view of religion as primarily a system of ethical
precepts.

Like other newcomers, the Jewish immigrants found such
changes unsatisfactory. Persistently they held to their Ortho-
doxy. The marble temples that arose in the better neighborhoods, the dignified sermons, and the quiet services
attracted them not at all. In ruder buildings, hastily converted
from stores or homes or abandoned churches, they sought the
consoling flavor of familiar worship.

The dissenters too, then, were engaged in the quest for a
religious way of life in the New World that would be the same

as in the Old. This was the common immigrant experience. In the American environment, so new and so dangerous, these people felt more need than ever for the support of their faith. Yet the same environment, in its very strangeness and looseness and freedom, made it difficult to preserve what could be taken for granted at home.

With great hardship and against impressive physical and financial difficulties, the immigrants achieved some degree of success. Out of the scrimped earnings of poor laborers rose monumental edifices capable of serving thousands of communicants.

From time to time, though, they must have reflected, they who came there to seek ease of spirit, that this was still not the Old Country church, that what they had recaptured was more the form, and that out of context, and not so much the way of life. Outside, the crowded street pulsed through the city, disregarding what was within. Here they would never re-establish the old relationship that, back there, had given religion so large a role in their society. Could they then push down the frustrating sense of loss, the fear of emptiness in forms? A possession of infinite value had disappeared in the course of the migration—the inner meaning of their own existence in the universe.

Yet there was no alternative but to continue as before to hold on to what was left, the form; to resist where possible any change in that. Their religious life accordingly grew rigid; they became far more conservative than those of their fellows who had remained in Europe. *I know this much, that I am a Catholic, and I perform the duties of a Catholic as far as I can. I am not devout, for I have no time to pray because every Sunday I must work and—I confess it to you alone—I work even on Easter from 7 until 12. But I will remain a Catholic until I die. . . .* Yield not on the jot or tittle lest the whole writ change—as it must.

This they had learned, however, in the course of their coming and settlement, that adjustment to the circumstances of life in the United States brought them not nearer to but more distant from other Americans. The very process of

getting established revealed to each group the differences
that divided it from every other. The immigrants thus caught
a glimpse of the apartness, the separateness implicit in Americanization. And it would be not long before they saw the
full extent of it.

For Further Reading

An admirable synthesis is Maldwyn Jones' *American Immigration* (1960), while Carl Wittke, *We Who Built America* (rev.
ed., 1964), weaves information on many different ethnic blocs
into his historical narrative. The Report of the United States
Immigration Commission (41 volumes, 1911–1913)—the Dillingham Commission—is an immense storehouse of material
on immigration, but it should be supplemented with Oscar
Handlin's essay on the bias of the commission in his collection
Race and Nationality in American Life (1957). Other useful
collections include Marcus L. Hansen, *The Immigrant in
American History* (1940), David F. Bowers, ed., *Foreign Influences on American Life* (1944), and Henry S. Commager,
ed., *Immigration and American Life* (1961). For the changing
historical opinions on the immigrants, see Edward N. Saveth,
American Historians and European Immigrants (1948). The
classic study on acculturation remains Oscar Handlin's *Boston
Immigrants, 1790–1865* (rev. ed., 1959), which may be supplemented with Robert Ernst's *Immigrant Life in New York
City, 1825–1863* (1949). For the restrictionist movement, John
Higam's *Strangers in the Land* (1955) is thorough, provocative, and persuasive. Roy L. Garis, *Immigration Restriction*
(1927), summarizes the conventional arguments for restriction.

Too many studies of national immigrant groups tend to be
filiopietistic. The more scholarly and objective ones include
Theodore C. Blegen, *Norwegian Migration to America* (2 vols.,
1931–1940); Florence E. Janson, *The Background of Swedish
Immigration, 1840–1930* (1931); Arnold Mulder, *Americans*

from Holland (1947); Albert B. Faust, *The German Element in America* (1927); Rowland Berthoff, *British Immigrants in Industrial America* (1957); William V. Shannon, *The American Irish* (1963); Carl Wittke, *The Irish in America* (1956); Robert F. Foerster, *The Italian Immigration of Our Times* (1919); Peter Wiernik, *History of the Jews in America* (1931); William I. Thomas and Florian Znaniecki, *The Polish Peasant in Europe and America* (1927); Theodore Saloutos, *The Greeks in the United States* (1964); Yamato Ichihashi, *Japanese in the United States* (1932), and Mary Coolidge, *Chinese Immigration* (1909).

The Mysteries
of the Great Plains

Walter Prescott Webb

In the history of nearly every country certain historical eras have become romanticized almost beyond recognition—for example, the Spain of El Cid, the France of Charlemagne and Roland, or the England of Richard the Lion-Hearted. For the American, the Great West in the last half of the nineteenth century, the West of song and story, of cowboys and Indians, of the mountain men and harsh justice is the national adventure.

Who among us has not sat on the edge of his seat, thrilling to the *Garry Owen* while on the flickering screen the cavalry charges down the valley to rescue the wagon train from the screaming Comanches? Or watched the handsome United States marshal slowly and deliberately buckle his gun belt, then step out into the dusty main street of Dodge City or Cheyenne and fill with lead the latest in a seemingly inexhaustible supply of evildoers? Sherwood Anderson in his autobiography wrote of an experience of his youth that surely must have been shared by millions of boys during the past seventy years, the desire for identification with a cowboy hero: "As I sat in

Source: Walter Prescott Webb, *The Great Plains* (New York: Ginn and Company, 1931), pp. 485–515. Copyright 1931 by Ginn and Company. Reprinted by permission of the publisher.

the movie house it was evident that Bill Hart was being loved by all the men and women and children sitting about, and I also wanted to be loved—to be a little dreaded, and feared, too, perhaps. 'Oh, there goes Sherwood Anderson. Treat him with respect. He is a bad man when he is aroused. But treat him kindly and he will be as gentle with you as any cooing dove.' "

What was it about the West that made it so romantic? What effect did the Great Plains have upon American institutions? Was the cowboy a genuine hero? Walter Prescott Webb (1888–1963) suggested answers to these and other questions in his original, imaginative, and fascinating history of the vast central plains of America. He defined the Great Plains as an enormous area running westward from the ninety-eighth meridian to the Rocky Mountains and north to south from Canada to Mexico. Its essential physical characteristics are three: a level land surface, an absence of trees, and a subhumid or arid climate. Early attempts at settlement of the region failed because the first people to cross the line did not realize the imperceptible change that had taken place in their environment. As Webb wrote, "East of the Mississippi civilization stood on three legs—land, water, and timber; west of the Mississippi not one but two of these legs were withdrawn, water and timber, and civilization was left on one by land." So completely different were conditions, so harsh and foreboding did the environment appear that for a long time men concluded the plains were uninhabitable. Up until at least 1860, government cartographers described the region on their maps as the Great American Desert.

Webb tells the story of how this last part of the West was won. It was largely won through ingenuity and inventiveness. The six-shooter, "the most perfect horseman's weapon yet invented," enabled the American to overcome the Plains Indian and to herd cattle. Barbed wire converted the open, free range country into big pasture country and made it possible for the land to be fenced in small areas; the introduction of the windmill helped draw water from beneath the soil. These technological achievements enabled the cattleman to capitalize on the sea of grass, to amass huge herds of longhorns and to drive them over the Chisholm or Western trail to cow towns such as Dodge City or Abilene. Following the cattle kingdom, the farmers overcame their last frontier by adjusting to the lack of water through dry farming and irrigation. In the process of conquering the plains, Webb believed, the character of Anglo-American life changed. He later asserted that conditions on the Great Plains exerted a powerful influence on settlers coming from a humid climate; they came with instruments adapted to a forest environment and "were compelled to modify these instruments, whether tools, weapons, or social and legal institutions, in order to solve the problems they faced on the plains."

Webb's thesis quite obviously owes a great deal to Frederick Jackson Turner's frontier hypothesis. To Turner, among the striking characteristics of the frontier experience was the development of a practical, inventive turn of mind quick to grasp expedients and a dominant individualism. But to a remarkable degree, also, Webb's interpretation of the Great Plains as a hard and hostile country conquered by the ingenuity and inventiveness of its settlers predated the famous hypothesis used by Arnold Toynbee to explain the genesis of civilizations. Calling his theory Challenge and Response, Toynbee argued that the strength of civilization was in direct ratio to the adverse climate or other geographical conditions it had to meet and overcome. Ease, he contended, was inimical to civilization; the greater the difficulty, the greater the stimulus.

Such an idea of history is, of course, largely deterministic and Toynbee has been severely criticized, as has Webb. Fred A. Shannon, in an almost book-length critique of *The Great Plains,* charges him with overlooking important sources, neglecting contrary evidence, and overstating, understating, and misstating facts. He further rejects Webb's thesis that practically every institution that was carried across the ninety-eighth meridian was either broken or remade or greatly altered. Criticizing him for emphasizing differences rather than similarities, he wonders if Webb includes in his category of practically every institution, marriage, the home, forms of government, religion, and capitalism. Shannon disagrees that there was anything singular in the frontier experiences of the Great Plains. Stressing the continuity of culture and similarity of circumstances, he contends that every frontier experience had its share of adaptation and change: "From tidewater to the piedmont and then to the mountain valleys, the Ohio valley and the prairie plains, always there was much that was new in the experiences."

Shannon also accuses Webb of making an apology for Western lawlessness. Part of this apology appears in the following selection. The reader may judge for himself.

"*F*or what do we *know*—and what *do* we know—what do we *really* and *truly* know about what a friend of mine will insist on calling our 'insides'? Meaning not our lights, livers, and other organs, but that part of us where the mysteries are." Thus wrote W. H. Hudson, the field naturalist, who loved to seek the truth, which so often eluded him and so often eludes us all, in the recesses of the unknown. This study of the Great Plains has thus far had little to do with the mysteries, but has been confined to facts which form themselves into what the writer sees as fairly definite patterns of truth. The facts are available to all, but the patterns they form depend upon the point of view of the observer. Surely the patterns are as valid as the facts themselves, because they make rational and comprehensible a way of life which has too often been considered erratic and strange. They are merely a diagram of functional processes, a reconstruction of folk ways. Though the pattern is made up of facts, it differs from them as an assembled machine differs from a dismantled one. The facts are the parts; the pattern is the machine set up with every part in place ready to function. But the patterns made by the historian are never complete. There is always something lacking, a residue, fragments suggestive of other patterns which might be formed if one only knew how to put them together or where to find the missing parts. The quest for the whole truth ends in the "innumerable puzzles, problems, mysteries, one is eternally stumbling against." This chapter is devoted in large part to these mysteries, which may be suggested in the questions What did the Great Plains do to men? How did the experience there affect them? Why did it affect them so? To paraphrase Hudson: What did the Great Plains do to our "insides"?

1. What Immediate Effects Did the Great Plains Have Upon the Anglo-American?

Much evidence of the immediate effects may be found in the reaction of men who came to the Plains. If we again visualize a migrating host suddenly emerging from the forests on an open and boundless plain, we are in position to understand the startled expressions of wonder which involuntarily escaped those who the first time beheld such scenes. The Anglo-American had in his experience no background to prepare him for such a far vision. His momentary surprise and wonder were what we might expect of a person fitted with powerful glasses which opened to him a new and hitherto unseen world.

Herbert Quick has captured the significance of the moment and expressed it in one paragraph of his autobiography. Speaking of his ancestry he says:

> The two lines of descent met and touched in 1857. They met in the forest region, through which they had been for two centuries or more pressing westward. They are examples. They are very significant to America and Americans, and to the world. They were not yet out of the woods, however. In the spring of 1857 they began their last long trek to a *new and different world*. They turned their faces to the west which they had for generations seen at sunset through traceries of the twigs and leafage of the primal forests, and *finally stepped out into the open, where God had cleared the fields,*

and stood at last with the forests behind them, gazing with dazzled eyes sheltered under the cupped hands of toil out over a sea of grassy hillocks, while standing in the full light of the sun. *It was the end of Book One of our history.*

In speaking of the appearance and influence of the plain, Colonel Dodge said:

> Like an ocean in its vast extent, in its monotony, and in its danger, it is like the ocean in its romance, in its opportunities for heroism, and in the fascination it exerts on all those who come fairly within its influence. The first experience of the plains, like the first sail with a "cap" full of wind, is apt to be sickening. This once overcome, the nerves stiffen, the senses expand, and man begins to realize the magnificence of being.

A slightly different view was set forth at a much earlier date by James in his account of Long's expedition:

> These vast plains, in which the eye finds no object to rest upon, are at first seen with surprise and pleasure; but their uniformity at length becomes tiresome. For a few days the weather had been fine, with cool breezes and broken flying clouds. The shadows of these coursing rapidly over the plain, seemed to put the whole in motion; and we appeared to ourselves as if riding on the unquiet billows of the ocean. The surface is uniformly of the description . . . called *rolling,* and will certainly bear a comparison to the waves of an agitated sea. The distant shores and promontories of woodland, with here and there an insular grove of trees, rendered the illusion more complete.

Such quotations could be increased to hundreds. They have these things in common: men expressed surprise, pleasure, and elation, and with one accord they compared the Plains to the sea. This comparison runs throughout the literature from Coronado on. In his *Commerce of the Prairies* Josiah Gregg speaks of the "grand prairie ocean," of the caravans "making port"; he proposed a law based upon maritime law for control of the prairie caravan, and gave the wagons the name of "prairie schooners," which they have borne ever since. Marcy described the Llano Estacado as an "ocean of desert prairie." Van Tramp said of the prairies:

> There is no describing them. They are like the *ocean,* in more than one particular; but in none more than in this: the utter impossibility of producing any just impression of them by description. They inspire feelings so unique, so distinct from anything else, so powerful, yet vague and indefinite, as to defy description, while they invite the attempt.

An example of the similar effect of the plain and the sea is brought out vividly in relation to art in the story of John Noble, the painter. Noble was born in the Panhandle of Texas and was reared in Kansas. His early life was spent on the frontier, where he participated in the melodramatic activities of that region. He began to dabble in colors, and painted pictures for the frontier saloons of the Plains. Later he followed his art East and to Paris. From there he settled down on the coast of Brittany among the fisher-folk, where he found himself a penniless devotee of art. Overcome at last by a longing for home, for the plains of Kansas, he steadfastly refused to go back without having won success.

Noble has given an excellent account of how the Plains affect people not accustomed to them.

> Did you ever hear of "loneliness" as a fatal disease? Once, back in the days when father and I were bringing up long-legged sheep from Mexico, we picked up a man near Las Vegas who had lost his way. He was in a terrible state. It wasn't the result of being lost. He had "loneliness." Born on the plains, you get accustomed to them; but on people not born there the plains sometimes have an appalling effect.
>
> You look on, on, on, out into space, out almost beyond time itself. You see nothing but the rise and swell of land and grass, and then more grass—the monotonous, endless prairie! A stranger traveling on the prairie would get his hopes up, expecting to see something different on making the next rise. To him the disappointment and monotony were terrible. "He's got loneliness," we would say of such a man.

Noble states that his own nostalgia in Brittany was similar to that of the stranger, except that he wanted the Plains. Speaking of his longing, he says:

> I believe it taught me to understand the sea. I began to feel that the vastness, the bulk, the overwhelming power of the prairie is the same in its immensity as the sea—only the sea is changeless, and the plains, as I knew, were passing. . . . It was at this time that some of my fellow artists began to speak of the way I was painting the sea. It was said then, for the first time, I think, I was painting the sea as no one else had painted it.

We cannot solve the mystery of the influence of the plains. It does not help much to say that it is somewhat the same as that of the sea, because that influence is also a mystery. But the evidence indicates that the plain gives man new and novel sensations of elation, of vastness, of romance, of awe, and often of nauseating loneliness.

2. Did Man Originate on the Plains or in the Forest?

It may be permitted to approach the mysterious effect of the Plains upon the human mind through an inquiry into the place of man's origin or differentiation. At present there are two theories as to this. Darwin believed that man's primal home was in a "warm forest-clad land," where he became differentiated from his progenitors. If that be true, then the first man might, upon emerging from his original and accustomed environment into the open plain, experience such strange sensations of fear, wonder, and surprise as those described above. He would be compelled to modify his whole outlook upon life and change his way of living.

Later students are developing a different theory as to the nature of man's original habitat. Joseph Barrell, the geologist, in 1917, and Henry Fairfield Osborn, the paleontologist, in

1923, have advanced the hypothesis that man was differentiated from his progenitors not in Darwin's "warm forest-clad land," but in the central Asiatic plateau. It is this hypothesis that has partly served to guide the Asiatic Expedition, led by Roy Chapman Andrews and supported by the American Museum of Natural History, in its efforts to discover some evidence of man's origin in the arid uplands of Mongolia. Barrell believes that man's physical structure indicates that he originated, or was differentiated, on the plain and not in the forest. His strong padded foot, erect posture, and relatively long legs are departures from adaptation to life in the trees and tend, instead, to fit him for running and tramping long distances; in short, for life on the plain. Osborn thinks that the distant ancestors of man were widespread, extending into the heavy forests which covered central Asia in this early day. Then a wave of elevation and aridity swept over the land, driving the forest southward before the expanding plain and leaving here and there insular groves of trees and isolated groups of man's progenitors to adapt themselves to the new order—the plains—or perish. The horses, cattle, camels, and ancestors of pro-dawn man who perforce or by choice remained in central Asia under the changed and changing conditions adapted themselves to the plain, and in doing so effected the modernization of the mammalian world. According to Osborn man came to the ground because the forest literally melted from under him—he became *man* on the plains and not in the forest.

Osborn first set forth his theory in the *Peking Leader* for October 10, 1923. His statement, to the effect that necessity impels man to invent new weapons and implements on the elevated and semi-arid environment, is illustrated in excellent fashion in the history of the Great Plains.

> An alert race cannot develop in a forest—a forested country can never be the center of radiation for man. Nor can the higher type of man develop in a lowland river-bottom country with plentiful food and luxuriant vegetation. It is on the plateaus and relatively level uplands that life is most exacting and response to stimulus most beneficial.... All recent

ethnologic and physiographic evidence points in the same way; namely, that intelligent, progressive, and self-adaptive types of mankind arise in the elevated upland or semi-arid environments where the struggle for food is intense, where reliance is made on the invention and development of implements as well as weapons.

This theory, or hypothesis as Osborn prefers to call it, is suggestive and stimulates speculation as to the emotions the Great Plains aroused in the American timber dwellers when these first came into the region. If man did become what he is on the plains, and not in the "warm forest-clad land," then perhaps it was natural for him to reënter the old familiar environment with dim stirrings of deeply embedded racial memories; to return with a certain abandon and joy to a closer association with horses and cattle, after an interval of some millions of years in the forests. But, whatever our theory of man's origin, it is certain that he entered the Plains of the United States after a long period of living in the forest.

3. Why Is the West Considered Spectacular and Romantic?

There is no need of argument to show that the West has been looked upon as a land of romance and adventure. The subject has been touched upon in the chapter on literature, but a further brief discussion and analysis may be permissible. Three questions present themselves: *What* period of Plains history had this spectacular and romantic aspect in the highest degree? What were the *elements* in this period that gave it a spectacular and romantic quality? To *whom* did the West appear spectacular and romantic? Why did it appear thus?

The spectacular and romantic period of Western, or Plains, history began with the white man's first knowledge of the country and ended near the close of the nineteenth century, when the cattle kingdom gave way to the agricultural experiment. The spectacular elements and romantic quality were to be found in the physical conditions of the country and in the social situation which obtained there. The physical conditions have been discussed in Chapter II; nothing more will be said of them here. The social situation will now concern us.

The plainsman, as represented by the Indian fighter, the cowboy, the peace officer, and the bad man, led a life that was full of novelty, spiced with danger, and flavored with adventure. At all times he was dependent upon his own resources, which had to be many and varied. His courage and self-reliance are matters of common knowledge. But courage and self-reliance are by no means attributes peculiar to the men who lived and moved on the Great Plains; courageous men have lived in all parts of the country and in all countries. How, then, has it come about that the men of the West have acquired reputations that overshadow those of other men in other sections? It may be the *method* and *equipment* of these men, combined with their courage, that have so distinguished them. In this connection let us consider the influence of the horse and the six-shooter.

The relation between man and horse is one of long standing. It is an association that goes back to Asia, probably to the time when that portion of the world was caught in the wave of elevation and aridity described by Osborn, when the mammalians had to make a choice between forest and plains. According to Osborn the horses and the ancestors of men chose the plain, where men became and remained horsemen until the day of the automobile. But it is unnecessary for us to go so far back in the world's history. Let us stick to the horse in America.

During the period under discussion all men on the Great Plains were mounted, and nearly all travel was on horseback. The horse has always exerted a peculiar emotional effect on both the rider and the observer: he has raised the rider above himself, has increased his power and sense of power, and has aroused a sense of inferiority and envy in the humble pedestrian. The horse glorified the Plains Indian and brought him a golden age of glory, ease, and conquest which he had never known before. Through long ages the horse has been the symbol of superiority, of victory and triumph. The "man on horseback" rides through the military history of the world; and wherever the horseman appears in statuary or painting he is the central or foremost figure. "A good rider on a good horse is as much above himself and others as the world can make him," said Lord Herbert. "When I bestride him, I soar, I am a hawk; he trots the air; the earth sings when he touches it," adds Shakespeare.

What effect did life on horseback have upon the Western men? Did it glorify them as it did the Indian? Did it raise them above themselves and above others? Did it liberate their minds to a freer and more independent thinking? W. H. Hudson has attempted to answer the question.

> The effect of the wind on me, always greatest when it caught me on horseback, when, during the first half of my life, I was constantly riding and sometimes passed weeks at a stretch on a horse every day from morning till night, is now my subject. When in my teens I first began to think, I found that my best time was when on horseback, in a high wind. It was not like the purely agreeable sensation of a soft caressing wind, or of riding in a comparatively quiet air in a genial sunshine; it was a pleasure of a distinctly different kind, if it can be called pleasure. Certainly that word does not give the feeling its characteristic expression, but I have no other. It was a sense of change, bodily and mental, a wonderful exhilaration and mental activity. "Now I can think!" I would exclaim mentally, when starting on a gallop over the great plain —that green floor of the world where I was born—in the face of a strong wind. Nor could it be said that this was only the effect of being mounted and of rapid motion. We know that merely to be on the back of a good horse does give us a sense of power and elation; or, as Lord Herbert of Cherbury says in his autobiography, "It lifts a man above himself."

Hudson thought that this feeling of elation comes only to those who are on horseback occasionally, and that one who is on horseback every day simply has the feeling of being in the right place. He concluded that the effect on him did not come from being on horseback in swift motion, but was "almost exclusively of the wind." It seems probable that his sensations were the result of a combination of effects: a unison between the will of man and the obedience of the horse, the sense of control over great power, the vibrant, swift motion, and the wind. What effect would such influences constantly exerted have on men?

The Western man of this period was not only mounted but was armed with the most effective horseman's weapon yet invented. If the horse elevated man and enlarged his sphere of influence, as it apparently did, the six-shooter increased his power in every situation in which he found himself. The plainsman liked to say (and it was his saying) that God made some men large and some small, but Colonel Colt made them all equal. It would be hard to find a more effective *ensemble* of power than a man on a good horse armed with a six-shooter —the one to conquer space, the other to conquer danger. When someone asked Captain Frank Hamer of the Texas Rangers what was the mental effect of being mounted on a good horse and armed with a six-shooter, he replied, "They just run together like molasses."

Setting aside the question of whether these things of the West—the hard physical conditions, the high altitude, the wind, the use of the horse and of the six-shooter—developed through selection and survival a new and different type of man, a Westerner, let us come to the third part of the inquiry into the spectacular and romantic. This inquiry brings us to a consideration of how the Westerner impressed others.

To *whom* did the West and the Westerner appear spectacular and romantic? To whom did the Westerner appear wild and lawless? Who made the judgments? Who set the standards? These questions lead toward a consideration of the nature of the romantic and the spectacular, but we dare not tackle that problem, involved as it is in abstractions and endless arguments. The matter has already been touched on in the discussion of literature. The West appeared romantic to those who were not of it—to the Easterner, who saw the outward aspects of a strange life without understanding its meaning and deeper significance. The East set the standards, wrote the books, and made the laws. What it did not comprehend was strange, romantic, spectacular. The Easterner did not ride horses as did the Westerner. He did not wear a six-shooter, because the law prohibited it and because law made it unnecessary. He did not herd cattle or wear boots or red handkerchiefs or spurs. He could not quite see that a normal person could do such things. One who did immediately became "interesting," "strange," "romantic," and what not. If things had been reversed as between the Plains and the forest, and American civilization had developed first on the Plains and then had invaded the forests, the ways of life there might have appeared as singular to the Westerner as his did to the Easterner. The cant hook of the lumberjack or the pitchfork of the farm hand might be as romantic to one born and reared on the plains as a lariat or a six-shooter is to a farm hand. Certainly an Eastern "muley" saddle was as strange to a cowboy as the cowboy's Spanish horned saddle was to the Virginia huntsman.

When the Easterner came in contact with this man of the West, whose vision had been enlarged by a distant and monotonous horizon, whose custom it was to live and work on horseback, and who carried at his side the power of life and death over his adversaries, the Easterner was at once impressed with the feeling that he had found something new in human beings. The garb, the taciturnity, the sententious speech redolent of the land and the way of life in it, and the independence, or unconventionality of the Westerner confirmed his first impression. "Ah," said the Easterner, "here is a new species of the genus *homo*. I must observe him carefully and note all his manners and customs and peculiarities. There *is* something romantic about him. He lives on horseback, as do the Bedouins; he fights on horseback, as did the knights of chivalry; he goes armed with a strange new weapon which he uses ambidextrously and precisely; he swears like a trooper, drinks like a fish, wears clothes like an actor, and fights like a devil. He is gracious to ladies, reserved toward strangers, generous to his friends, and brutal to his enemies. He is a cowboy, a typical Westerner."

4. Why Was the West Considered Lawless? Was It Really Lawless or Did It Merely Appear Lawless?

These questions involve us in all sorts of difficulties and elude definite answers. There is, however, some basis for discussion. The most partisan Westerner will admit that the West was considered lawless; the casual visitor from the East was quite certain that it appeared to be lawless; for the sake of this discussion it may be said that the West was lawless and that the Westerner was a persistent lawbreaker. It is to be hoped, however, that the Westerner will withhold his fire until an explanation can be made.

The West was lawless for two reasons: first, because of the social conditions that obtained there during the period under consideration; secondly, because the law that was applied there was not made for the conditions that existed and was unsuitable for those conditions. It did not fit the needs of the country, and could not be obeyed.

The social conditions in the Great Plains have already been discussed. We know, for example, that in the early period the restraints of law could not make themselves felt in the rarefied population. Each man had to make his own law because there was no other to make it. He had to defend himself and protect his rights by his force of personality, courage, and skill at arms. All men went armed and moved over vast areas among other armed men. The six-shooter was the final arbiter, a court of last resort, and an executioner. How could a man live in such a *milieu* and abide by the laws that obtained in the thickly settled portions of the country, where the police gave protection and the courts justice? Could the plainsman go unarmed in a country where danger was ever present? Could a man refuse to use those arms where his own life was at stake? Such men might live in the West, but they could never be of much force. They could not be cowboys or Indian fighters or peace officers or outstanding good citizens.

In the absence of law and in the social conditions that obtained, men worked out an extra-legal code or custom by which they guided their actions. This custom is often called the code of the West. The code demanded what Roosevelt called a square deal; it demanded fair play. According to it one must not shoot his adversary in the back, and he must not shoot an unarmed man. In actual practice he must give notice of his intention, albeit the action followed the notice as a lightning stroke. Failure to abide by the code did not necessarily bring formal punishment for the act already committed; it meant that the violator might be cut off without benefit of notice in the next act. Thus was justice carried out in a crude but effective manner, and warning given that in general the code must prevail.

Under the social conditions the taking of human life did not entail the stigma that in more thickly settled regions is associated with it. Men were all equal. Each was his own defender. His survival imposed upon him certain obligations which, if he were a man, he would accept. If he acted according to the code he not only attested his courage but implied that he was skilled in the art of living. Murder was too harsh a word to apply to his performance, a mere incident, as it were. But how could the Easterner, surrounded and protected by the conventions, understand such distinctions?

Theft was another form of lawlessness common on the Great Plains. But the code of the West had its way of interpreting and punishing theft. Of petty thievery there was practically none on the Plains. Property consisted of horses and cattle. There were horse thieves and cattle thieves.

There was no greater crime than to steal a man's horse, to set him afoot. It was like stealing the sailor's ship or the wings of the bird. There were no extenuating circumstances and little time for explanation or prayer. The penalty was

death. The cow thief was not nearly so bad in public esti-
mation. A cow was mere property, but a horse was life itself
to the plainsman. The code of the West made a strange distinction, one that the East has not understood, between a
cow and a maverick. A cow that bore a brand was the private
property of the man whose brand it bore; a maverick was
public property and belonged to the man that branded it,
just as the buffalo hide belonged to the one that killed the
buffalo. The fact that the maverick was the calf of the
branded cow did not affect the situation very much, especially
in the early days. There were few cattlemen who did not
brand mavericks; but no cattleman considered himself a thief
for having done so.

The lawlessness thus far discussed grew out of the social
situation in the early days. Other forms of lawlessness arose
because the law was wholly inapplicable and unsuited to the
West. Some examples will be noticed here.

The land laws were persistently broken in the West because they were not made for the West and were wholly unsuited to any arid region. The homestead law gave a man
160 acres of land and presumed that he should not acquire
more. Since a man could not live on 160 acres of land in
many parts of the region, he had to acquire more or starve.
Men circumvented this law in every possible way, and managed at last to build up estates sufficient to yield a living.
Major Powell pointed out that the land unit in the arid
region should be 2650 acres, instead of 160 as in the East. But
the lawmakers could never see the force of the argument.

The law of water illustrates with peculiar force the unsuit-
ableness of the old law. The English common law and the
common law as applied in the East prohibited the diversion
of water from a stream or limited it so rigidly that it amounted
to a prohibition. The English common law, strictly enforced,
precluded all possibility of irrigation on an extensive scale.
The Westerner violated the law, and finally evolved a new
one known as the arid-region doctrine of prior appropriation.

Among the cattlemen we find a custom which had the force
of law among them but which was never recognized in law.

This was the recognition of range rights and water rights. A cattleman made his claim to public property, to water and to the land surrounding it, just as the miners in California staked out their mining claims and appropriated water with which to sluice the ore. The law finally recognized, adopted, and protected the miner's claims, including his water rights, but it never recognized the cattleman's claims, although they were almost identical in nature with the miner's claims. Why did the lawmakers recognize the miners and look upon cattlemen as transgressors when their acts were identical? They either had enough knowledge of mining to cause them to recognize its needs, or they had so little knowledge that they were willing to follow the advice of the technical experts and special interests that were ready to advise them. With cattle and the needs of the cattleman the case was different. The lawmakers were familiar with cattle and knew how they were raised in the East. What they were never willing or able to learn was that an entirely different system prevailed in the West.

In the proposed fence legislation, before the invention or extensive use of barbed wire, we see another example of what might be called anti-Plains legislation. In the East men had been in the habit of fencing their crops. When the agricultural frontier emerged on the Plains and it was found to be impossible to build fences, the farmers immediately tried to cure their trouble by legislation. They agitated for a law which would compel men (in this case the cattlemen) to fence their stock so that the farmer could let the fields lie out. The law was actually passed in Texas, though it was made a matter of local option. Eastern Texas counties required that stock be fenced; the western Texas counties, of course, kept the open range. A similar law was passed in regard to carrying a six-shooter. Eastern Texas prohibited it; western Texas was permitted to carry the six-shooter as long as the Indians were there. Any law forbidding it would have been violated.

The law prohibiting slavery in the Plains states is an example of a useless law, as Daniel Webster so eloquently stated. The legislation on Indian affairs was equally inade-

quate and absurd and was wholly unsuited to the nature
of the Plains tribes. At one time the humanitarian policy led
the Department of the Interior to appoint Quakers as Indian
agents! The army regulations and the military system were
unsuited to conditions on the Plains, a fact well recognized
by Jefferson Davis, Sam Houston, and others who took the
trouble to obtain first-hand knowledge of Plains life. One
other example will be sufficient. Congress passed what was
known as the Timber Act, which granted land free—a modified homestead law—on condition that the grantee grow forests
on it. To the credit of Congress be it said that it did not
require the prairie dogs to climb the trees or to live in the
forests. The records do not reveal that Congress passed a
law increasing the rainfall, though it did appropriate considerable sums of money for experiments which were made
for the purpose of producing rain.

Therefore the West was a lawless place. It was turbulent
in the early days because there was no law. It was lawless
in the later period because the laws were unsuited to the
needs and conditions. Men could not abide by them and
survive. Not only were absurd laws imposed upon them, but
their customs, which might well have received the sanction
of law, were too seldom recognized. The blame for a great
deal of Western lawlessness rests more with the lawmaker than
with the lawbreaker.

If the character of the West was spectacular, romantic, and
lawless, its reputation for being so outran the facts. No other
part of the frontier enjoyed the publicity that was given to
the West. There are several reasons for this. First, the West
was late in developing, and its development came at a time
of peace. The nation had become strong enough to handle
its own internal affairs with conscious strength, but it had
not yet begun its vigorous foreign policy of imperial expansion. Its whole attention was centered on itself. The West
was the last stronghold of the frontier to be reduced, and
therefore it loomed high on the egocentric national horizon.
The nation could throw its whole strength into the fray.
Secondly, the West differed from the other sections in its

relation to the path of migration. When the Southern man migrated he moved west but remained in the South; when the Northern man migrated he remained in the North. There was comparatively little movement north and south. There was little common experience until the two invading columns of immigrants struck the Great Plains, where both the Northern men and the Southern men found themselves out of their own section. For the first time they met common problems, whether in western Texas or in North Dakota. There was no North or South in the West. When these men wrote home or returned on a visit, they told a *common* story; for once they agreed. The whole nation came to look on the West in the same way as to Indians, as to cattle, later as to wheat and dry farming, as to its romantic and spectacular aspect, and as to its lawlessness. Thirdly, the Great Plains frontier developed after the means of rapid communication and transportation were highly perfected. The railroads pushed through the land when life was still wild—when the trains were blocked by buffalo herds, and the section hands had to fight Indians as well as dig ditches and lay rails and crossties. The newspapers had developed, the telegraph flashed the news of Indian fights and train robberies all over the nation, and the newspapers carried the accounts to the breakfast table of millions. The Great Plains frontier was a national frontier, nationally advertised. What happened there was magnified in the press and exaggerated in the imagination, and nothing was more magnified than its unconventionality, its romantic aspects, and its lawlessness.

5. Why Is the West Politically Radical?

In this connection John J. Ingalls's statement in reference to Kansas might well be applied to the whole Plains region.

> For a generation Kansas has been the testing-ground for every experiment in morals, politics, and social life. Doubt of all existing institutions has been respectable. Nothing has

been venerable or revered merely because it exists or has endured. Prohibition, female suffrage, fiat money, free silver, every incoherent and fantastic dream of social improvement and reform, every economic delusion that has bewildered the foggy brains of fanatics, every political fallacy nurtured by misfortune, poverty, and failure, rejected elsewhere, has here found tolerance and advocacy.... There has been neither peace, tranquillity, nor repose. The farmer can never foretell his harvest, nor the merchant his gains, nor the politician his supremacy. Something startling has always happened, or has been constantly anticipated.

The radicalism of the Great Plains is but a continuation of that "lawlessness" discussed in section 4, and it arises in part from the same causes. It is the result of an effort at adjustment through political action to new conditions, a searching for the solution of problems where the old formulas fail and the new ones are unknown. The political radicalism has arisen partly from discontent born of suffering.

It may be said, parenthetically, that the political radicalism and innovation of the Great Plains belong primarily if not wholly to the later agricultural period. There is no record of its existence among the men of the cattle kingdom. They accepted the country as God made it, and wanted to keep it in the hands of "God, the government, and us." When the government began a series of legislative acts which dispossessed them or attempted to dispossess them, and turned the country over to the farmers, the cattlemen protested personally, but they never resorted to political action. They were so few in number that they probably could not have made themselves heard.

Political radicalism on the Plains began with the farmers. The prairie region of the Great Plains has been the stronghold of the farmers' movement. Regardless of where the movements began, they always gained their greatest membership in the prairie and Plains region. This was true of the Grange, the Farmers' Alliance, the Farmers' Union, the Nonpartisan League. The Populist party was reënforced from the Great Plains, and the most radical innovator of the Democratic party, William Jennings Bryan, was from Nebraska. His "You shall not press down upon the brow of labor this crown of thorns" may have been inspired by the suffering and poverty which he saw among the homesteaders on the Nebraska plains.

Radicalism is the political expression of economic maladjustment. It has been made clear in the preceding pages that the farmers in the prairies and the Great Plains confronted terrible obstacles. They were far from markets, burned by drought, beaten by hail, withered by hot winds, frozen by blizzards, eaten out by the grasshoppers, exploited by capitalists, and cozened by politicians. Why should they not turn to radicalism? When men suffer, they become politically radical; when they cease to suffer, they favor the existing order. Here is a story that will illustrate:

There was in a certain Western state a community of farmers who were undertaking to farm on alkali land. They became infected by socialistic doctrines, and practically the entire community became socialistic. In the summer the people would hold encampments, bringing speakers from far and near, and neglect their suffering crops to harangue at the government and berate the capitalists. There was nothing vicious about them. They were small landowners who had been caught in a grip of Plains circumstances. Whether or not the mood would have passed by, or whether some new cult would have routed the old one, it is impossible to say. What happened was that oil was discovered in the region, and the whole country found itself in the throes of an oil boom of the most extravagant nature. Money flowed like water, and practically every landowner in the country received for leases and sales of royalty or in fee more money than he ever dreamed of having. If oil were found on his land, his wealth became to him incalculable. From that day until this no word of socialistic doctrine has been heard from any of these people. Wealth or comparative wealth dissolved all those troubles they hoped to cure by radicalism.

Woman's suffrage does not now come under the head of political radicalism, but it was so considered until a few years ago. With the American Revolution the franchise was granted to the common man, provided he was not too common. After the Civil War it was granted to the Negro, and in 1919 it was granted to women. If we examine the history of the woman's movement, we find that it spread practically all over the Great Plains before it was adopted in the East. . . .

Why the men of the West were the first to grant the women the franchise is a problem that remains to be solved. Its final solution will grow out of a better understanding of a peculiar psychology which developed in a region where population was sparse and women were comparatively scarce and re-markably self-reliant. It was not the vaunted chivalry of the South nor the cool justice of the Brahman of the North that gave women the ballot. There is hidden somewhere in the cause the spirit of the Great Plains which made men demo-cratic in deed and in truth.

6. What Has Been the Spiritual Effect of the American Adventure in the Great Plains on Women?

Since practically this whole study has been devoted to the men, they will receive scant attention here. The Great Plains in the early period was strictly a man's country—more of a man's country than any other portion of the frontier. Men loved the Plains, or at least those who stayed there did. There was zest to the life, adventure in the air, freedom from re-straint; men developed a hardihood which made them in-sensible to the hardships and lack of refinements. But what of the women? Most of the evidence, such as it is, reveals that the Plains repelled the women as they attracted the men. There was too much of the unknown, to few of the things they loved. If we could get at the truth we should doubtless find that many a family was stopped on the edge of the timber by women who refused to go farther. A student relates that his family migrated from the East to Missouri with a view of going farther into the West, and that when the women caught sight of the Plains they refused to go farther, and the family turned south and settled in the edge of the timbered country, where the children still reside. That family is significant.

Literature is filled with women's fear and distrust of the Plains. It is all expressed in Beret Hansa's pathetic exclamation, "Why, there isn't even a thing that one can *hide behind!*" No privacy, no friendly tree—nothing but earth, sky, grass, and wind. The loneliness which women endured on the Great Plains must have been such as to crush the soul, provided one did not meet the isolation with an adventurous spirit. The woman who said that she could always tell by sunup whether she should have company during the day is an example. If in the early morning she could detect a cloud of dust, she knew that visitors were coming! Exaggeration, no doubt, but suggestive. The early conditions on the Plains precluded the little luxuries that women love and that are so necessary to them. Imagine a sensitive woman set down on an arid plain to live in a dugout or a pole pen with a dirt floor, without furniture, music, or pictures, with the bare necessities of life! No trees or shrubbery or flowers, little water, plenty of sand and high wind. The wind alone drove some to the verge of insanity and caused others to migrate in time to avert the tragedy. The few women in the cattle kingdom led a lonely life, but one that was not without its compensations. The women were few; and every man was a self-appointed protector of women who participated in the adventures of the men and escaped much of the drabness and misery of farm life. The life of the farm woman was intolerable, unutterably lonely. If one may judge by fiction, one must conclude that the Plains exerted a peculiarly appalling effect on women. Does this fiction reflect a truth or is it merely the imagining of the authors? One who has lived on the Plains, especially in the pioneer period, must realize that there is much truth in the fiction. The wind, the sand, the drought, the unmitigated sun, and the boundless expanse of a horizon on which danced fantastic images conjured up by the mirages, seemed to overwhelm the women with a sense of desolation, insecurity, and futility, which they did not feel when surrounded with hills and green trees. Who can tell us how the Great Plains affected women, and why?

7. In Conclusion, Let Us Inquire What Has Been and What Is to Be the Meaning of the Great Plains in American Life.

This problem may best be approached through a brief résumé. It has been pointed out that the ninety-eighth meridian separates the United States into two equal parts, that the Anglo-Americans who approached the Great Plains from the East came with an experience of more than two centuries of pioneering in the woodland environment, and that when they crossed over into the Plains their technique of pioneering broke down and they were compelled to make a radical readjustment in their way of life. The key to an understanding of the history of the West must be sought, therefore, in a comparative study of what *was* in the East and what *came to be* in the West. The salient truth, the essential truth, is that the West cannot be understood as a mere extension of things Eastern. Though "the roots of the present lie deep in the past," it does not follow that the fruits of the present are the same or that the fruits of the West are identical with those of the East. Such a formula would destroy the variable quality in history and make of it an exact science. In history the differences are more important than the similarities. When one makes a comparative study of the sections, the dominant truth which emerges is expressed in the word *contrast*.

The contrast begins in geology and topography and is continued in climate, reflected in vegetation, apparent in wild animal life, obvious in anthropology, and not undiscernible in history. To the white man, with his forest culture, the Plains presented themselves as an obstacle, one which served to exercise and often defeat his ingenuity, to upset his calculations, to hinder his settlement, and to alter his weapons, tools, institutions, and social attitudes; in short, to throw his whole way of life out of gear. The history of the white man in the Great Plains is the history of adjustments and modifications, of giving up old things that would no longer function for new things that would, of giving up an old way of life for a new way in order that there might be *a* way. Here one must view the white man and his culture as a dynamic thing, moving from the forest-clad land into the treeless plain.

History may take another view of the Great Plains which we may call the static view—a still picture which will show the results of man's efforts at a given time. Such a picture reveals the Great Plains as a land of survival where nature has most stubbornly resisted the efforts of man. Nature's very stubbornness has driven man to the innovations which he has made; but above the level of his efforts and beyond his achievements stand the fragments and survivals of the ancient order. The new and the old, innovation and survival, dwell there side by side, the obverse and the converse of the struggle between man and nature.

The land itself is a survival. The High Plains are, according to Johnson, but fragments of the old plains built up through countless ages by the aggrading rivers swinging down from the desert mountains across the eastward-tilted marine rock sheet. But we are concerned here with a much more recent period—that of the white man's entrance.

The Plains Indians were survivals of savagery, even when compared with the Indians to the east and to the west. They lagged in the nomadic state when practically all other tribes in America had progressed to some form of agriculture and settled village life they were designated as "wild" Indians, to distinguish them from the more docile tribes of the timberland.

It is today, however, that the Plains present the Indians as survivals. Practically all Indians in the United States are found now in the West, most of them within or near the margins of the Plains. They were pushed in there from the east and from the west; and at a time when there was nowhere else to push them they were permitted to settle down on the reservations. The map of the reservations as looked

at by a student a thousand years hence will present the Great
Plains as the region of survival of the native races.

What is true of the Indians is in a measure true of the wild
animals. The Great Plains afforded the last virgin hunting
grounds in America, and it was there that the most characteristic American animal made its last stand against the advance of the white man's civilization.

The West, or the Great Plains, presents also a survival
of the early American stock, the so-called typical American
of English or Scotch and Scotch-Irish descent. The foreign
element is prominent in the prairie region of the Middle
West, as represented by Germans in Illinois and Iowa and by
Scandinavians in Montana and in the eastern Dakotas. But
once we go into the arid region of the Plains, particularly in
the Southwest, we find, or did find until very recent times, the
pure American stock—Smiths, Joneses, McDonalds, Harveys,
Jameses, and so on. The Negroes did not move west of the
ninety-eighth meridian, the Europeans were not attracted by
the arid lands, the Chinese remained on the Pacific coast,
and the Mexican element stayed close to the southern border.

It is in the West that rural life has remained dominant
over urban life. The automobile has tended to obliterate the
difference between rural and urban life, but before its coming
rural ideals, virtues, and prejudices prevailed all over the
Great Plains region. As yet the Great Plains have produced
but few cities, and fewer that do not lie along the timber line.
Minneapolis, Chicago, St. Louis, Kansas City, Fort Worth,
and San Antonio mark the line that separates the East from
the West. These cities owe much of their growth to the fact
that they receive tribute from the Plains. Plains wheat made
Minneapolis and St. Paul; Plains cattle helped to make
Chicago, St. Louis, Kansas City, and Fort Worth. These were
the railheads and distributing centers for the Great Plains.
It is probable that a careful study of the rise of mail-order
houses in Chicago and Kansas City can be shown to have had
a very close relation to the business that came in from the
isolated people of the Great Plains.

The public domain, or public land, has also proved to be

a survival. It is only in the Western states that any considerable portion of public land remains in the hands of the government. A map of national parks and monuments will show that the West is the museum of natural wonders. The Westerner today resents the fact that the government withholds this land from development.

The innovations of the Great Plains are more remarkable than the survivals. The first innovations came in the methods of travel and of fighting. We have seen that until the pioneer reached the Great Plains the favorite and preferred mode of travel was by river boat. The eastward-flowing rivers of the Atlantic slope offered the first highways, and we know that people came by the rivers through the mountain passes into the Mississippi Valley. Once in the valley, the immigrant's way was easy down the Ohio or the Kentucky or the Tennessee, and once on the Mississippi there were hundreds of possibilities before him; but when he went west of the Mississippi as far as the ninety-eighth meridian, he found the way by boat more and more difficult and soon impossible. He left the boat and took to horses or caravans and made the long trails to the Pacific. There was no water travel on the Great Plains. None can deny that the experiment with camels was a novel but futile effort at innovation in travel.

The next innovation came in the methods and implements of war. The six-shooter was invented and adopted as the chief weapon for the mounted man. The Texas Rangers were organized as a mounted force especially designed to fight on horseback.

It was in the edge of the Great Plains region of Texas below San Antonio that the Anglo-American learned to handle cattle on horseback. Cattle-raising is older than history; but so far as the Anglo-American was concerned the method was new. The story of how the method spread with the cattle northward over the long trail and westward to the Pacific slope has been told in considerable detail. Not only was the method of handling cattle on horseback an innovation, but the direction of its development was new. The cattle movement was from south to north, at right angles to the trails

of the Anglo-Americans westward-bound. The cattle kingdom
was a forerunner and an obstacle. It appropriated the Great
Plains when the farmer could not take them, and for a time
it stood in his way to dispute his coming.

In the Great Plains there was an innovation in fencing.
The old materials gave out on the edge of the Plains. Rails
were not to be had, rocks were nonexistent, and hedges were
not wholly satisfactory. Barbed wire was invented opportunely
and provided a cheap and effective fence for the large holdings
of the West.

The introduction of the windmill was an innovation in
providing water. The well-drill and the windmill made the
dry claim tenable and made possible the occupation of the
smaller holdings. Both were at least rare in the East, and both
flourished out of the necessities of the prairie country.

Irrigation was another Western innovation. It was and is
practically unknown in the East, where sufficient rainfall
makes it unnecessary. It was such a novelty that in the more
arid region the English common law had to be abrogated
and the arid-region doctrine of prior appropriations substi-
tuted in its place.

The demand for a large land unit in the Great Plains made
a reorganization of the land system necessary; but since the
land system operated under the inertia of tradition and largely
in accordance with the views of the Eastern agricultural
people, the adjustment was halting and inadequate. The Federal law never conformed to the necessities of the situation
in the West, with the result that the land units had to be built
up by more or less extra-legal means.

Dry farming, which originated in the Great Plains (at least
the name it goes by originated there), presents a vivid contrast
to the farming methods of the East. There has probably been
more experimentation with respect to farming in the Great
Plains region than in all other parts of the country combined.
Along with dry farming has gone the introduction of new
species of crops, chosen for their hardihood and ability to
resist drought. Europe, Asia, and Africa have been combed
for plants that would meet the agricultural needs of the West.

The following quotation brings out in the words of another the agricultural contrast between the East and the West:

THE AGRICULTURAL REGIONS

The United States may be divided into an eastern and a western half, characterized, broadly speaking, one by a sufficient and the other by an insufficient amount of rainfall for the successful production of crops by ordinary farming methods. The North Pacific coast and several districts in California and in the northern Rocky Mountain region constitute exceptions to this statement. The transition zone which separates the East from the West lies, in general, along the one hundredth meridian.... The East is a region of humid-climate farming, based upon tilled crops, small grains, and tame hay and pasture; the West, of wild hay and grazing, dry farming, winter crops in certain localities, and irrigation farming, with only limited areas of ordinary farming under humid conditions such as characterize the East.

The East and the West may each be divided into six agricultural regions. In the East, precipitation being usually sufficient, the classification is based largely on temperature and the crops grown, while in the West rainfall and topography are the important factors. In the East the agricultural regions extend for the most part east and west, following parallels of latitude; while in the West the regions are determined by the mountain ranges and extend north and south. Agriculture in the East varies primarily with latitude and soils, but in the West the principal factors are altitude and rainfall. The average elevation of the eastern half of the United States is less than 1000 feet; that of the western half, over 4000 feet.

In the East corn is the leading crop, constituting over one quarter of the acreage and nearly 3 per cent of the value of all crops....

In the West hay is the leading crop, contributing nearly 37 per cent of the acreage and 26 per cent of the value of all crops in 1919, and the forage obtained by grazing is probably almost of equal value.... The value of all crops in the Western regions, however, constituted in 1919 only 15 per cent of the total for the United States.

The contrast between the East and the West is not as pronounced in live stock as in crops, except that swine are largely

confined to the East, while sheep are much more important in
the West. There is a marked distinction, however, in the manner of management, the live stock in the East being fed in the
barnyards or fields with shelter at night, while in the West
the stock is mostly grazed on the open range. . . .

The farms, or "ranches," in the West are, in general, much
larger in area than in the East. Owing to the low rainfall in
the West, except in the North Pacific Region, the land outside
the irrigated and dry-farming districts is used mostly for grazing, and instead of 80 or 160 acres being sufficient to support
a family, as in the East, 2000 to 4000 acres, or more, are commonly required. In the dry-farming areas half sections of land
(320 acres) and sections (640 acres) are normal-size farms. In
the irrigated districts the farms are no larger than in the East.
The 80- or 120-acre irrigated farms, however, are often worth
as much as the 640-acre dry farms or the 3000-acre stock
ranches.

A larger proportion of the farms in the West are operated
by their owners than in the East, owing, doubtless, to the cattle ranching, the more recent homestead settlement, and the
larger proportion of fruit farms.

The Great Plains region has been a land of political innovation, expressing itself in such vagaries as populism, agrarian crusades, and farm relief.

The literature of the Great Plains, while perhaps hardly
meriting the name, has exhibited a vigor and enjoyed a popularity that command attention if not respect. Aside from the
Wild West literature, which has no counterpart elsewhere,
there is promise of something better. Desert countries have
always been fertile sources of inspiration for literature. They
have contributed a mysticism and a spiritual quality which
have found expression in the lofty and simple teachings of
Jesus and Mohammed, both of whom lived in a region so
like the Great Plains that the similarities have often been
pointed out. The Plains and Prairie literature is sufficiently
developed to enable us to see that it tends toward a portrayal
of high adventure on the one hand and intense suffering on
the other. Out of these elements may come in time a mystical
and spiritual quality contributing much to a civilization that

thus far is notorious for its devotion to material things. Of such innovation Joaquin Miller is the prophet:

> A wild, wide land of mysteries,
> Of sea-salt lakes and dried-up seas,
> And lonely wells and pools; a land
> That seems so like dead Palestine,
> Save that its wastes have no confine
> Till push'd against the levell'd skies.
> A land from out whose depths shall rise
> The new-time prophets. Yea, the land
> From out whose awful depths shall come,
> A lowly man, with dusty feet,
> A man fresh from his Maker's hand,
> A singer singing oversweet,
> A charmer charming very wise;
> And then all men shall not be dumb.

For Further Reading

Fred A. Shannon's "An Appraisal of Walter Prescott Webb's *The Great Plains*" is in *Critiques of Research in the Social Sciences* (1940), which also includes a rebuttal by Webb and the proceedings of a conference which discussed the book and the critique. A recent overall account is James C. Malin, *The Grasslands of North America* (1948), while Frederick L. Paxson's *The Last American Frontier* (1910) is a useful, older work.

Everett Dick's *Vanguards of the Frontier* (1941) and *The Sod House Frontier* (1937) are vivid social histories of life and work on the plains.

The literature on the cowboy is enormous. A scholarly, objective account is Joe B. Frantz and J. E. Choate, *The American Cowboy: The Myth and the Reality* (1955), but see also Philip A. Rollins, *The Cowboy* (1922). Andy Adams' *The Log of a Cowboy* (1903) is probably the best autobiographical account. E. Douglas Branch, *The Cowboy and His Interpreters*

(1926), discusses different perspectives of the hero. For the cattle industry in general consult Ernest S. Osgood, *The Day of the Cattlemen* (1929); Edward E. Dale, *The Cattle Range Industry* (1930); Louis Atherton, *The Cattle Kings* (1961), and Louis Pelzer, *The Cattlemen's Frontier* (1936). The clash between cattlemen and sheep herders is told in Edward N. Wentworth, *America's Sheep Trails* (1948).

For the Indian Wars see the relevant chapters in William T. Hagan, *American Indians* (1961), and two studies by Paul I. Wellman, *Death on the Prairie* (1934) and *Death in the Desert* (1935). Edgar I. Stewart's *Custer's Luck* (1955) is a first-rate account of the famous massacre. Finally, anyone interested in western history is directed to three highly stimulating and imaginative studies: Henry Nash Smith, *Virgin Land: The American West as Symbol and Myth* (1950), Walter P. Webb, *Divided We Stand: The Crises of a Frontierless Democracy* (1937), and Wallace Stegner's distinguished biographical synthesis, *Beyond the Hundredth Meridian: John Wesley Powell and the Second Opening of the West* (1954).

The Farmer's Grievances

John D. Hicks

$\mathcal{D}$uring the presidential campaign of 1896 when a populistic Democrat, William Jennings Bryan, ran against a conservative Republican, William McKinley, a young Kansas editor railed against the Populists and what seemed to him their radical proposals for redistribution of wealth: "That's the stuff! Give the prosperous man the dickens! Legislate the thriftless man into ease. . . . Whoop it up for the ragged trousers; put the lazy greasy fizzle, who can't pay his debts, on the altar, and bow down and worship him." Fifteen years later the same editor, William Allen White, admitted that he had misjudged the farmers' crusade. Then an ardent supporter of the Progressives, he paid the Populists a backhanded compliment: "The Progressives caught the Populists in swimming and stole all their clothing except the frayed underwear of free silver."

Basically the same feeling prevailed among historians thirty years ago. The reform tradition in America was perceived as a straight line running from the prophecies

Source: John D. Hicks, *The Populist Revolt: A History of the Farmer's Alliances and the People's Party* (Minneapolis: University of Minnesota Press, 1931), pp. 54-95. Copyright 1931 by the University of Minnesota Press; renewed 1959 by John D. Hicks. Reprinted by permission of the publisher.

of the Populists through the partial fulfillment of the
Progressive era and culminating in the accomplishments
of the New Deal. The book most responsible for this
interpretation was John D. Hicks' *The Populist Revolt.*
Professor Hicks (b. 1890) brought to his work a deep
sympathy for the farmers; he later wrote that his obser-
vation of "the raw deal that the farmers were getting in
the 1920's" strongly influenced his point of view. Emphasizing the similarity between Populist proposals and
Progressive legislation, Hicks postulated a cause and
effect relationship. Nearly every item in the Populist
platform—government regulation of transportation and
communications, the creation of a subtreasury system,
direct election of U.S. senators, a graduated income tax,
civil service reform, and a substantial increase of the
amount of money in circulation—was enacted into legislation by the Progressives. Despised and rejected for a
season, the Populist doctrines showed an amazing vitality
and won triumphantly in the end. Hicks contended that
Populism, although failing as political rebellion, succeeded in educating the country on the need for reform.

After World War II a historiographical reaction set in
against Populism. Numbers of writers found disquieting
parallels between the agrarian crusade and the European mass political involvements that produced Nazism
and Fascism. They particularly deplored the propensity
of Populist leaders to view history as conspiracy. Populist literature abounds with such titles as S. E. V. Emery's
*Seven Financial Conspiracies Which Have Enslaved the
American People* or Gordon Clark's *Shylock: As Banker,
Bondholder, Corruptionist, Conspirator.* Nor was the
conspiracy theory confined to the fertile imagination of
popular scribblers. It found official expression in the
People's Party platform of 1892: "A vast conspiracy
against mankind has been organized on two continents,
and it is rapidly taking possession of the world. If not
met and overthrown at once, it forebodes terrible social
convulsions, the destruction of civilization, or the establishment of an absolute despotism." Closely related to
this belief in "the devil theory of history," charges
Professor Richard Hofstadter among others, was a kind
of rhetorical anti-Semitism. While admitting that anti-

Semitism did not become a tactic or a program for the
Populists, he nevertheless concludes, "It is not too much
to say that the Greenback-Populist tradition activated
most of what we have of modern popular anti-Semitism
in the United States." By the middle 1950's revisionism
against Populism reached high tide. By then, as C. Vann
Woodward complained, Populists were "charged with
some degree of responsibility for Anglophobia, Negro-
phobia, isolationism, imperialism, jingoism, paranoidal
conspiracy hunting, anti-constitutionalism, anti-intellectualism and the assault upon the right of privacy—these
among others."

Today, the pendulum has swung backward to a more
balanced appraisal of the Populists. Few scholars now
place Populism and Progressivism in the same reform
tradition. Progressivism is now seen as emanating from
the urban areas of America, and while there remains
some dispute over the relative contribution of the urban
gentry of white Anglo-Saxon background as opposed to
the political spokesmen of the immigrant masses, few
identify progressive leadership with agrarian radicals of
the type of "Sockless" Jerry Simpson or Mary Ellis Lease.
Yet much of what is considered essential to our modern
reform tradition is owed to Populism. To a large degree,
the embattled farmers of the 1890's are responsible for
the concept of the interventionist state. Prior to Populism, the belief of the classical or laissez-faire economists
that in social and economic matters the state should act
as a passive policeman had been accepted by both the
Republican and Democratic parties. More than accepted
in fact, for influenced by the popular vogue of Social
Darwinism, the conservative politicians shared the conviction of the business tycoon that Darwin's laws of
natural selection and survival of the fittest operating in
the society make it certain that the poor would be always with us. But the Populists demanded government
intervention to protect the rights of the many against
the interests of the few. From this conviction have developed the modern theories of the welfare state and the
belief in government responsibility to sustain the prosperity of the economy.

On the charges of conspiracy hunting, anti-Semitism,

anti-intellectualism, etc., developed against the Populist,
recent historians have returned a mixed verdict. While
not denying the fanaticism and narrow-mindedness of
many Populist leaders, modern scholars have pointed
out that their conservative opponents also talked wildly
of conspiracies. An Assistant Secretary of Agriculture
warned against "this cunningly devised and painfully
organized cabal of Silverites and demagogues who
would wreck the country's peace, prosperity and honor
all for private gain or political spoils." The Eastern
press reacted hysterically to the relatively moderate
Democratic-Populist platform of 1896. Cried the Philadelphia *Press*, "This riotous platform is the concrete
creed of the mob. It is rank Populism intensified with
hate and venom. It rests upon the four cornerstones of
organized Repudiation, deliberate Confiscation, char-
tered Communism and enthroned Anarchy." Moreover,
the verbal anti-Semitism of the Populists was shared by
many Eastern intellectuals, including Henry and Brooks
Adams and Henry Cabot Lodge, while the anti-Semitism
of certain groups hardly touched by the farmers' crusade—
some eastern immigrant peoples, for example—often went
beyond rhetoric to actual assault upon Jews. Indeed the
Dreyfus case in France appears to indicate that anti-
Semitism was endemic to the age.

Above all, it is essential to judge the Populists in light
of their grievances. True, the farmers protested emotionally, but their frustration was deep. In the following
selection, Professor Hicks vividly describes their plight.
By understanding their grievances, we can better appreciate the intensity of their political reaction.

*I*n the spring of 1887 a North Carolina farm journal stated
with rare accuracy what many farmers in all sections of the
United States had been thinking for some time.

> There is something radically wrong in our industrial system.
> There is a screw loose. The wheels have dropped out of bal-
> ance. The railroads have never been so prosperous, and yet

agriculture languishes. The banks have never done a better or more profitable business, and yet agriculture languishes. Manufacturing enterprises never made more money or were in a more flourishing condition, and yet agriculture languishes. Towns and cities flourish and "boom" and grow and "boom," and yet agriculture languishes. Salaries and fees were never so temptingly high and desirable, and yet agriculture languishes.

Nor was this situation imputed to America alone. Once in an unguarded burst of rhetoric a high priest of the Alliance movement pointed out that similar conditions prevailed in all thickly populated agricultural countries, "high tariff and low tariff; monarchies, empires, and republics; single gold standard, silver standard or double standard." It was true indeed that the blessings of civilization had not fallen upon all mankind with equal bounty. To the upper and middle classes more had been given than to the lower; to the city dweller far more than to his country kinsman. The farmer had good reason to believe, as he did believe, that he worked longer hours, under more adverse conditions, and with smaller compensation for his labor than any other man on earth.

For this condition of affairs the farmer did not blame himself. Individual farmers might be lacking in industry and frugality, but farmers as a class were devoted to these virtues. Those who gave up the struggle to win wealth out of the land and went to the cities so generally succeeded in the new environment that a steady migration from farm to city set in. Why should the same man fail as a farmer and succeed as a city laborer? More and more the conviction settled down upon the farmer that he was the victim of "some extrinsic baleful influence." Someone was "walking off with the surplus" that society as a whole was clearly building up and that in part at least should be his. He was accustomed to regard himself as the "bone and sinew of the nation" and as the producer of "the largest share of its wealth." Why should his burdens be "heavier every year and his gains . . . more meager?" Why should he be face to face with a condition of abject servility? Not himself, certainly, but someone else was to blame.

The farmer never doubted that his lack of prosperity was directly traceable to the low prices he received for the commodities he had to sell. The period from 1870 to 1897 was one of steadily declining prices. As one writer put it, the farmer's task had been at the beginning of this era "to make two spears of grass grow where one grew before. He solved that. Now he is struggling hopelessly with the question how to get as much for two spears of grass as he used to get for one." Accurate statistics showing what the farmer really received for his crops are almost impossible to obtain, but the figures given by the Department of Agriculture for three major crops, given in the table below, will at least reveal the general downward trend of prices.

AVERAGE MARKET PRICES OF THREE CROPS, 1870–1897

Years	Wheat (PER BUSHEL)	Corn (PER BUSHEL)	Cotton (PER POUND)
1870–1873	106.7	43.1	15.1
1874–1877	94.4	40.9	11.1
1878–1881	100.6	43.1	9.5
1882–1885	80.2	39.8	9.1
1886–1889	74.8	35.9	8.3
1890–1893	70.9	41.7	7.8
1894–1897	63.3	29.7	5.8

These prices are subject to certain corrections. They are as of December 1, whereas the average farmer had to sell long before that time, often on a glutted market that beat down the price to a much lower figure. They make no allowance, either, for commissions to dealers, for necessary warehouse charges, nor for deductions made when the produce could not be regarded as strictly first class. They fail to show, also, the difference in prices received along the frontier, where the distance to market was great, and in the eastern states, where the market was near at hand. In 1889, for example, corn was sold in Kansas for as low a price as ten cents a bushel and was commonly burned in lieu of coal. In 1890 a farmer in

Gosper County, Nebraska, it was said, shot his hogs because he could neither sell nor give them away.

So low did the scale of prices drop that in certain sections of the country it was easy enough to prove, statistically at least, that farming was carried on only at an actual loss. It was generally agreed that seven or eight cents of the price received for each pound of cotton went to cover the cost of production; by the later eighties, moreover, many cotton growers were finding it necessary to market their crops for less than they had been getting. The average price per bushel received by northwestern wheat growers dropped as low as from forty-two to forty-eight cents, whereas the cost of raising a bushel of wheat was variously estimated at from forty-five to sixty-seven cents. Statisticians held that it cost about twenty-one cents to produce a bushel of corn, but the western farmer sometimes had to take less than half that sum. Quoth one agitator:

> We were told two years ago to go to work and raise a big crop, that was all we needed. We went to work and plowed and planted; the rains fell, the sun shone, nature smiled, and we raised the big crop that they told us to; and what came of it? Eight cent corn, ten cent oats, two cent beef and no price at all for butter and eggs—that's what came of it. Then the politicians said that we suffered from over-production.

Not politicians only but many others who studied the question held that overproduction was the root of the evil. Too many acres were being tilled, with the result that too many bushels of grain, too many bales of cotton, too many tons of hay, too many pounds of beef were being thrown upon the market each year. As the population increased, the number of consumers had advanced correspondingly, but the increase in production had gone on even more rapidly. It was a fact that the per capita output of most commodities had risen with each successive year. The markets of the world were literally broken down. With the supply so far in excess of the demand, prices could not possibly be maintained at their former levels.

Those who believed in the overproduction theory argued that to some extent this condition of affairs was due to the rapid expansion of the agricultural frontier in the United States and in the world at large. In the United States the opportunity to obtain free lands, or lands at a nominal price, tempted thousands of artisans and laborers to seek their fortunes in the West. This was true not only in the Northwest, where wheat and corn were the chief products, but also in the Southwest, where the main reliance was placed on cotton. The new and fertile lands of the frontier had come into competition with the old and worn-out lands of the East. Minnesota and the Dakotas led the nation in the production of wheat; Kansas and Nebraska, in the production of corn; Texas, whole regions of which had but lately been opened up, in the production of cotton; the western ranges, in the production of beef. The eastern farmer had made an effort to keep pace with the western farmer. He had spent huge sums on fertilizer and machinery, and he had learned to farm more scientifically. But his success merely added to the total output and brought prices tumbling the faster.

Moreover, the revolution in means of transportation that had been accomplished during the latter half of the nineteenth century had opened up world markets for regions that had hitherto had small chance to sell their produce. This was true not only of the American West, which could never have come into being without an elaborate system of railways over which to market its crops, but also of distant regions in Russia, India, Australia, Algeria, Canada, Mexico, and the Argentine, whence, thanks to railways and steamship lines, harvests of surpassing abundance could now find their way to the very centers of trade. Such crops as wheat and cotton, of which the United States had an excess for export, must now often come into competition with these tremendous outpourings from other parts of the world, and the prices must be fixed accordingly. It was the price brought by this exportable surplus that set the price for the entire domestic output.

But the farmers and their defenders refused to place much stock in the overproduction theory. Admitting that the output from the farm had increased perhaps even more rapidly than population, they could still argue that this in itself was not sufficient to account for the low prices and the consequent agricultural depression. They pointed out that, with the general improvement of conditions among the masses, consumption had greatly increased. Possibly the demand attendant upon this fact alone would be nearly, if not quite, sufficient to offset the greater yearly output. There would be, moreover, even heavier consumption were it possible for those who needed and wanted more of the products of the farm to buy to the full extent of their ability to consume. In spite of all the advances of the nineteenth century the world was not yet free from want. "The makers of clothes were underfed; the makers of food were underclad." Farmers used corn for fuel in the West because the prices they were offered for it were so low, while at the same moment thousands of people elsewhere faced hunger and even starvation because the price of flour was so high. Why should the Kansas farmer have to sell his corn for eight or ten cents a bushel when the New York broker could and did demand upwards of a dollar for it? Were there not certain "artificial barriers to consumption"? Were there not "certain influences at work, like thieves in the night," to rob the farmers of the fruits of their toil?

Many of the farmers thought that there were; and they were not always uncertain as to the identity of those who stood in the way of agricultural prosperity. Western farmers blamed many of their troubles upon the railroads, by means of which all western crops must be sent to market. There was no choice but to use these roads, and as the frontier advanced farther and farther into the West, the length of the haul to market increased correspondingly. Sometimes western wheat or corn was carried a thousand, perhaps even two thousand, miles before it could reach a suitable place for export or consumption. For these long hauls the railroads naturally exacted high rates, admittedly charging "all the traffic would bear." The farmers of Kansas and Nebraska and Iowa complained that it cost a bushel of corn to send another bushel of corn to market, and it was commonly believed that the net profit of the carrier was greater than the net profit of the grower. The farmers of Minnesota and Dakota were accustomed to pay half the value of their wheat to get it as far towards its final destination as Chicago. Small wonder that the farmer held the railroads at least partly responsible for his distress! He believed that if he could only get his fair share of the price for which his produce eventually sold he would be prosperous enough. "How long," a Minnesota editor queried, "even with these cheap and wonderfully productive lands, can . . . any agricultural community pay such enormous tribute to corporate organization in times like these, without final exhaustion?"

Local freight rates were particularly high. The railroads figured, not without reason, that large shipments cost them less per bushel to haul than small shipments. The greater the volume of traffic the less the cost of carrying any portion of that traffic. Accordingly, on through routes and long hauls where there was a large and dependable flow of freight, the rates were comparatively low—the lower because for such runs there was usually ample competition. Rates from Chicago to New York, for example, were low in comparison with rates for similar distances from western points to Chicago, while between local points west of Chicago the rates were even more disproportionate. Sometimes the western local rate would be four times as great as that charged for the same distance and the same commodity in the East. The rates on wheat from Fargo to Duluth were nearly double those from Minneapolis to Chicago—a distance twice as great. It cost as much as twenty-five cents a bushel to transport grain from many Minnesota towns to St. Paul or Minneapolis, while for less than as much more it could be transported all the way to the seaboard. Indeed, evidence was at hand to show that wheat could actually be sent from Chicago to Liverpool for less than from certain points in Dakota to the Twin Cities. Iowa farmers complained that it cost them about as much to ship in corn from an adjoining county for feeding purposes as it would have cost to ship the same corn to Chicago; and yet the Iowa rates seemed low to the farmers of Nebraska, who claimed that they paid an average of fifty per cent more for the same service than their neighbors across the Missouri River.

Undoubtedly it cost the railroads more to haul the sparse freight of the West than it cost them to haul the plentiful freight of the East. Railway officials pointed out that western traffic was nearly all in one direction. During one season of the year for every car of wheat hauled out an empty car had to be hauled in, while the rest of the time about ninety per cent of the traffic went from Chicago westward. They asserted that the new roads were often in thinly settled regions and were operated at a loss even with the highest rates. James J. Hill maintained that the roads were reducing rates as fast as they could, and to prove it he even declared himself "willing that the state make any rates it sees fit," provided the state would "guarantee the roads six per cent on their actual cost and a fund for maintenance, renewal and other necessary expenditures." President Dillon of the Union Pacific deplored the ingratitude of the farmers who grumbled about high rates. "What would it cost," he asked, "for a man to carry a ton of wheat one mile? What would it cost for a horse to do the same? The railway does it at a cost of less than a cent." Moreover, he thought that unreasonable rates could never long survive, for if a railroad should attempt anything of the sort competition would come immediately to the farmers' aid, and a parallel and competing line would be built to drive the charges down.

But critics of the railroads saw little that was convincing in these arguments. As for the regulation of rates by competition, it might apply on through routes, providing the roads had no agreement among themselves to prevent it, but competition could scarcely affect the charges for local hauls for the simple reason that the average western community depended exclusively upon a single road. Only rarely did the shipper have a choice of two or more railway companies with which to deal, and even when he had this choice there was not invariably competition. The roads reached agreements among themselves; more than that, they consolidated. "The number of separate railroad companies operating distinct roads in Minnesota was as high as twenty, three years ago," wrote the railway commissioner of that state in 1881. "Now the number is reduced to substantially one-third that number." Nor did Minnesota differ particularly in this respect from any other frontier state. Throughout the eighties as the number of miles of railroad increased, the number of railroad companies tended to decrease. Communities that prided themselves upon a new "parallel and competing line" were apt to discover "some fine morning that enough of its stock had been purchased by the older lines to give them control." Thus fortified by monopoly, the railroads, as the farmer saw it, could collect whatever rates they chose.

How monopoly might operate to increase rates is well shown by a practice common during the early eighties among certain railroads of the Northwest. Selfishly determined to get every dollar of revenue they could from their customers, these roads made use of the device of charging "transit," or through rates, on all the wheat they carried. They demanded that the wheat shipper pay in advance the full rate to Chicago or Milwaukee, or whatever city happened to be the easternmost terminal. They refused entirely to quote local rates to Minneapolis or St. Paul, fearing that if they did so the grain might be transferred at these points to some other road. It was well understood, however, that the shipper who paid transit rates might unload his grain at any milling center or at any mill on the route, have it ground, and then ship it out again as flour on the same rate contract. And if he disposed of his grain finally at such a point, he might sell the balance of his unused freight for what it would bring.

Suppose, for example, that a grain dealer at Milbank, Dakota Territory, wished to sell his wheat in Minneapolis. According to the rules of the Hastings and Dakota road, over which he must ship, he was not allowed to pay local freight to Minneapolis but was compelled to pay full transit rates to Milwaukee, forty cents a hundred pounds instead of the twenty cents a hundred that should normally have been charged. After disposing of his wheat in Minneapolis, the dealer still had on his hands a quantity of unexpended freight from Minneapolis to Milwaukee, for which he had paid approximately twenty cents a hundred. This he offered for sale on the open market, but because "transit," as the unused freight was called, was too plentiful and sold only at a discount of from two and a half to five cents per hundred pounds, the Milbank shipper was fortunate to get fifteen cents —or a little more if the market was good—for transportation that had cost him twenty cents. This loss he learned to look upon as inevitable, and as inevitably he protected himself against it liberally in advance by lowering the price paid the farmer for his grain. "Transit wheat," that is, wheat which had to be shipped over roads quoting transit rates only, always brought from three to five cents a bushel less than "free wheat." Small wonder that farmers living in "transit" regions felt themselves to be defrauded of their rightful profits! There is "probably in no other portion of this country," commented the conservative *Pioneer Press,* "any class of people subjected to such miserable oppression, exercised by a power to which there is no resistance to be offered, and from whose dominion there is no escape. . . . Those who would submit quietly to such outrage must be either more or less than men."

And yet the railroads in much of the frontier area were so greatly overbuilt that, try as they might, they could not always find business enough to enable them to make a reasonable profit on their investment. Some of the new lines had been built by boomers and promoters without thought as to future earning power. Others were projected into sparsely settled regions by established corporations in order to preempt the field for future expansion. In both cases the new roads could in all probability be operated only at a loss, however high they might place their rates. Certainly investments of this sort should never have been made except by corporations fully capable of sustaining a present loss in the hope of future profits. But in any event the farmer was likely to complain. It made little difference to him whether the high rates were charged by the local companies whose lines lay entirely in too thinly settled regions or by the larger companies who demanded from the farmers living in civilization rates high enough to cover the losses attendant upon overbuilding at the fringe of settlement. High rates were the net result in each case.

It was commonly believed also that the practice of stock-watering had much to do with the making of high rates. The exact extent to which the railroads watered their stock, or to which a particular railroad watered its stock, would be a difficult matter to determine, but that the practice did exist in varying degrees seems not to be open to question. A writer in Poor's *Manual* for 1884 stated that the entire four billion dollars at which the railways of the United States were capitalized represented nothing but so much "water." So sweeping a statement seems rather questionable, but the belief was general that railroad companies got their actual funds for investment from bond issues and passed out stocks to the shareholders for nothing. The roads, indeed, did not deny the existence of a certain amount of stock-watering. They argued that their property was quite as likely to increase in value as any other property—farm lands, for example—and that they were justified in increasing their capital stock to the full extent that any increase in value had taken place. Some of their apologists held also that the value of the road was determined by its earning power rather than by the amount actually invested in the enterprise. It followed, therefore, that new capital stock should be issued as fast as the earnings of the road showed that the old valuation had been outgrown.

But to those who suffered from the high rates all these arguments seemed like so many confessions of robbery. The governor of Colorado, considering especially the sins of the Denver and Rio Grande, declared it "incredible that the legitimate course of business can be healthfully promoted by any such inflated capitalization. There must be humbug, if not downright rascality, behind such a pretentious array of figures." The *Kansas Alliance* saw in the prevalent custom of stock-watering an evil "almost beyond comprehension." It placed the total amount of railway overcapitalization at a sum far in excess of the national debt and described these in-

flated securities as "an ever present incubus upon the labor
and land of the nation." Jerry Simpson of Kansas figured that
the 8,000 miles of road in his state cost only about $100,-
000,000, whereas they were actually capitalized at $300,000,000
and bonded for $300,000,000 more. "We who use the roads,"
he argued, "are really paying interest on $600,000,000 instead
of on $100,000,000 as we ought to." Such statements could be
multiplied indefinitely. The unprosperous farmers of the
frontier saw nothing to condone in the practice of stock-
watering. Honest capitalization of railroad property would,
they felt, make possible a material reduction in rates. And, in
spite of the assertion of one who defended the practice of
stock-watering that a citizen who questioned "the right of a
corporation to capitalize its properties at any sum whatever
committed an 'impertinence,' " the farmers had no notion that
the matter was none of their business.

High rates due to overcapitalization and other causes were
not, however, the sole cause of dissatisfaction with the railways. It was commonly asserted that the transportation companies discriminated definitely against the small shipper and
in favor of his larger competitors. The local grain merchant
without elevator facilities or the farmer desirous of shipping
his own grain invariably had greater and graver difficulties
with the roads than did the large elevator companies. These
latter, the farmers contended, were favored by "inside rates,"
by rebates, and by preferential treatment with regard to cars.

Secret rate understandings between the railroads and the
elevator companies were hard to prove, but discrimination
with respect to cars was open and notorious. A regulation in
force in the Hill system was interpreted to mean that "parties desiring to ship grain, whether producers or purchasers,
where there is an elevator, must ship through it, or construct
an elevator of at least 30,000 bushels, or cars will not be furnished." A farmer complained that although a certain railroad had ruined his farm by taking a right of way through it,
there was no means by which he could force the road to "give
him a car to ship his wheat." The small town with its small
shipments was at a disadvantage in competition with the

larger town and its larger shipments. No doubt, as a governor of Minnesota pointed out, the railroads really found it a matter of "economy, profit, and convenience" to receive "large, frequent and easily regulated shipments under contracts with a small number of shippers" rather than to bother with small and irregular shipments from many different sources. But this could not be regarded as a sufficient apology for the failure of supposedly common carriers to give equal treatment to all those who desired to use their lines. "The railways cannot have a choice of customers," declared an impotent state railway commissioner. "Railways, like inn-keepers, must take all that come until the quarters are full. If it is an inconvenience to furnish cars to flat-houses or merchants, the answer is, that is just what the railways are paid for; to serve the public generally is their proper function." "Equality before the law," wrote a prominent publicist, "is a canon of political liberty; equality before the railways should become a canon of industrial liberty."

There were cases in which the railroads were guilty of fairly transparent frauds. The scandal of the *Crédit Mobilier* had not passed so far into history but that critics of the Union Pacific could still find occasion to refer to it. Nor were the thefts that this particular construction company had perpetrated without close parallels in later western road building. There were scandals, too, in connection with the reorganization of roads. Minor stockholders were frozen out in order to benefit a secret clique on the inside; roads were robbed by their operators and forced into a dishonest and avoidable bankruptcy. There were scandals without number in the manipulation of railroad securities. The operations along this line of Jay Gould alone almost baffle description. It is true also that many a western community smarted under heavy taxation levied to pay off subsidies to roads that were unnecessary or in some cases never even built.

The burden of public indebtedness thus incurred to help the railways was indeed staggering. In the days when railroads were not so plentiful the constitutions and laws of the western states were so devised as to permit almost unlimited as-

sistance to the railroads from state and local governmental
units, and skillful railway promoters seldom failed to secure
maximum sums. In Kansas alone during a single period of
sixteen months, from July, 1885, to November, 1886, the total
amount of municipal contributions to the railroads reached
ten million dollars, while by 1890 the grand total of financial
assistance from state and local sources was only a little less
than seventy-five millions. It is estimated that in this state
eighty per cent of the municipal debt was incurred to help
finance the railroads. These colossal debts—for other states
than Kansas were similarly afflicted—the average taxpayer refused to regard as a fair charge upon him. He might have
voted for some of them, but he nevertheless believed that his
vote had been obtained under false pretenses. Resentment in
the West against the high rates that the railroads charged
was thus tinged with something a little more bitter. There
was a firm conviction that the railroads were "crooked," that
they existed not to serve the West but to plunder it.

The indictment against the railroads was the stronger in
view of their political activities. It is not unfair to say that
normally the railroads—sometimes a single road—dominated
the political situation in every western state. In Kansas the
Santa Fe was all-powerful; in Nebraska the Burlington and
the Union Pacific shared the control of the state; everywhere
the political power of one or more of the roads was a recognized fact. Railway influence was exerted in practically every
important nominating convention to insure that no one hostile to the railways should be named for office. Railway lobby-
ists were on hand whenever a legislature met to see that
measures unfavorable to the roads were quietly eliminated.
Railway taxation, a particularly tender question, was always
watched with the greatest solicitude and, from the standpoint
of the prevention of high taxes, usually with the greatest of
success. How much bribery and corruption and intrigue the
railroads used to secure the ends they desired will never be
known. For a long time, however, by fair means or foul, their
wishes in most localities were closely akin to law. Beyond a
doubt whole legislatures were sometimes bought and sold.

In the purchase of men of influence railway passes were ever of the greatest potency. Members of the legislatures pocketed the mileage they were allowed by the state and rode back and forth to the capital on passes furnished by the railroads. Governors, judges, railway commissioners, and all other public officials were given passes and were encouraged to use them freely. Prominent attorneys were similarly privileged and in addition were generally retained by the railroads. The makers of public opinion—editors, ministers, and local politicians— were not neglected; when they were too insignificant to merit the regulation annual pass, they were given occasional free trips or half-fare permits. This "railroad invention for corrupting state officers" was not confined to the frontier but was general throughout the country. "Do they [the railroads] not own the newspapers? Are not all the politicians their dependents? Has not every Judge in the State a free pass in his pocket? Do they not control all the best legal talent of the State?" Thus the *Progressive Farmer* of Raleigh, North Carolina, complained. "To stand in with the railroads in order to get free transportation," wrote a more tolerant observer, "seemed to be the main object in life with about one-half of the population."

It is true enough that there was for a long time a certain blindness on the part of many who accepted the passes to the implications of such gifts. Anti-railroad agitators such as Ignatius Donnelly of Minnesota and "Calamity" Weller of Iowa in their earlier careers not only accepted passes but actually begged for them. Among those who received no passes, however, and paid the bill for those who did, a feeling of hostility to the practice gradually evolved. "A railroad pass," ran one convincing argument, "is not properly a 'courtesy.' It is money. . . . What grocer, plaintiff or defendant in a suit, would venture to give the judge a free pass for his yearly sugar and tea?" "The man who will accept railroad transportation," ran another argument, "which may be worth hundreds of dollars every year, and feel under no sort of obligation for it is a very contemptible sort of a man, and as rare as he is contemptible." By 1886 Donnelly was returning his passes and,

along with others of similar views, was denouncing the pass
evil as a system of covert bribery.

But from the standpoint of the western pioneer the crowning infamy of the railroads was their theft, as it appeared to
him, of his lands. Free lands, or at least cheap lands, had
been his ever since America was. Now this "priceless heritage"
was gone, disposed of in no small part to the railroads. To
them the national government had donated an area "larger
than the territory occupied by the great German empire,"
land which, it was easy enough to see, should have been pre-
served for the future needs of the people. For this land the
railroads charged the hapless emigrant from "three to ten
prices" and by a pernicious credit system forced him into a
condition of well-nigh perpetual "bondage." "Only a little
while ago," ran one complaint, "the people owned this
princely domain. Now they are *starving for land*—starving for
an opportunity to labor—starving for the right to create from
the soil a subsistence for their wives and little children." To
the western farmers of this generation the importance of the
disappearance of free lands was not a hidden secret to be un-
locked only by the researches of some future historian. It was
an acutely oppressive reality. The significance of the mad
rush to Oklahoma in 1889 was by no means lost upon those
who observed the phenomenon. "These men want *free land*,"
wrote one discerning editor. "They want *free land*—the land
that Congress squandered . . . the land that should have formed
the sacred patrimony of unborn generations." Senator Peffer
of Kansas understood the situation perfectly. "Formerly the
man who lost his farm could go west," he said, "now there is
no longer any west to go to. Now they have to fight for their
homes instead of making new." And in no small measure, he
might have added, the fight was to be directed against the
railroads.

Complaints against the railways, while most violent in the
West, were by no means confined to that section. Practically
every charge made by the western farmers had its counterpart elsewhere. In the South particularly the sins that the
roads were held to have committed differed in degree, per-

haps, but not much in kind, from the sins of the western roads. Southern railroads, like western railroads, were accused of levying "freight and fares at their pleasure to the oppression of the citizens" and of making their rates according to the principle, "take as much out of the pockets of the farmers as we can without actually taking it all." Southerners believed, in fact, that the general decline in freight rates that had accompanied the development of the railroads throughout the country was less in the South than anywhere else and that their section was for this reason worse plagued by high rates than any other.

Local rates were certainly as unreasonably high, when compared with through rates, as anywhere in the country. North Carolina farmers claimed that such articles as turnips, potatoes, cabbages, and apples could be brought to the city of Raleigh from northern markets and sold for less than the similar products of near-by farms. Competition was stifled as relentlessly in the South as in the West. A group of southeastern railroads, for example, "abdicated" their rate-making functions in favor of one supreme rate umpire, whose decisions were not to be questioned. There were discriminations as to persons and as to places. The individual or the company that had capital and could do business on a large scale received favors denied to individuals or companies of less importance. Cities of consequence were given rates that unimportant towns and villages similarly situated could not obtain. There was the usual abundance of stock-watering. There were frauds—frauds of construction companies like the *Crédit Mobilier,* frauds of stock manipulations, frauds of enforced bankruptcies. Nor were the operators of southern railroads novices at the political game. They gave away passes freely and with satisfactory results. Politicians pointed with pride to the railroads and urged that "no embarrassing restraint upon their development or prosperity should be imposed by a legislative body." State railway commissions were nonexistent or relatively innocuous, and the taxation of railways was light.

These common grievances of South and West against the railroads promised to supply a binding tie of no small consequence between the sections. Whether they were westerners or southerners, the orators of revolt who touched upon the railway question spoke a common language. Moreover, the common vocabulary was not used merely when the malpractices of the railroads were being enumerated. Any eastern agitator might indeed have listed many of the same oppressions as typical of his part of the country. But the aggrieved easterner at least suffered from the persecutions of other easterners, whereas the southerner or the westerner was convinced that he suffered from a grievance caused by outsiders. In both sections the description of railway oppression was incomplete without a vivid characterization of the wicked eastern capitalist who cared nothing for the region through which he ran his roads and whose chief aim was plunder. This deep-seated antagonism for a common absentee enemy was a matter of the utmost importance when the time came for bringing on joint political action by West and South.

In the northwestern grain-growing states the problem of the railroads was closely related to the problem of the elevators. Some grain houses were owned by individuals or local companies who ran one or more elevators in neighboring towns. A few were owned by the railway companies themselves. Still others were the property of large corporations that operated a whole string of elevators up and down the entire length of a railway line. These larger companies naturally built better and more commodious houses than the smaller ones; they were more efficient in their manner of doing business; and they were easily the favorites of the railroads. All the companies, large or small, must obtain on whatever terms the railway companies saw fit to impose such special privileges as the right to build upon railroad land and the right to proper sidetrack facilities. By refusing these favors the roads could prevent, and did prevent, the erection of new elevators where they deemed the old ones adequate, but once an elevator was authorized it could usually count on railway support.

Thanks mainly to their satisfactory relations with the railroads, the first elevator companies to cover a territory enjoyed in their respective localities almost a complete monopoly of the grain business, both buying and selling. Wherever elevators existed the roads virtually required that shipments of grain be made through them, for in practice if not in theory cars were seldom furnished to those who wished to avoid the elevator and to load their grain from wagons or from flat warehouses. On the face of it this rule seemed harmless enough, for the elevator companies were supposedly under obligations to serve the general public and to ship grain for all comers on equal terms. This they might have done with fair impartiality had they not been engaged themselves in the buying and selling of grain. But since it was the chief concern of the elevator operator to purchase and ship all the grain he could get, he could hardly be expected to take much interest in providing facilities for the farmer who wished to ship directly or for the competitive grain merchant who lacked an elevator of his own. The result was that the independent buyer was speedily "frozen out," and the farmer found that if he was to get rid of his grain at all he must sell to the local elevator for whatever price he was offered. He claimed rightly that under such a system he was denied a free market for his grain. To all except the privileged elevator companies the market was closed.

This absence of a free market was the chief reason assigned by many farmers for the low prices they were paid for their grain. Since the elevator men had a monopoly of the grain-buying business, what was to prevent them from paying only such a figure as their pleasure and interests might dictate? If there was only one elevator at a station it was clear that the operator was a law unto himself and might pay what he chose. Even if there were several elevators there was only rarely competition as to price. Pooling was sometimes resorted to, but usually agreements with regard to prices could be reached without this device, each elevator taking its share of grain without attempting to capture the business of its neighbor.

When the elevator companies paid lower prices than were justifiable, they naturally made an effort to conceal the fact. They knew that the price of wheat in Minneapolis or Chi-

cago at any given time was public information. The railway
rates to such a terminal were also known to all. If, therefore,
they openly exacted more than a reasonable profit for handling grain their practice would be subjected to an unpleasant and "pitiless" publicity. So they generally quoted as good
prices as could be reasonably expected, considering the high
freight they had to pay and the current market values of
wheat at the terminals to which they shipped. For their long
profits they relied upon more skillful means. Wheat, as presented for sale, was of course of uneven quality and must be
graded before a price could be assigned. Custom had established certain standards of grading; for example, wheat
ranked as number one hard must weigh fifty-eight pounds or
more to the bushel, must be clean, of a good color, and at
least ninety per cent pure hard wheat. Grain that was too
light in weight, contained foul seed, or was dirty, off color,
or frosted was graded accordingly. It was in determining these
grades that the elevator men had the best opportunity to reduce the price paid to the farmer, for the buyer fixed the
grades at will, after making such an examination of the wheat
as he saw fit. The farmer had nothing to say about it. If he
objected to the grade and price he was offered, he had no recourse but to take his grain to another elevator, probably
only to find that there the same condition prevailed. Moreover, another elevator was not always available.

Undoubtedly there was great irregularity and unfairness in
the grading of grain. Farmers at one station claimed that they
had never received a grade of number one hard and very little, if any, of number one regular. They therefore appointed
a committee of three to follow a shipment of thirty cars from
their town to Duluth, where they found that four of the cars
had been graded number one hard, ten number one regular,
and nearly all above the grades the farmers received. The
local elevator had profited accordingly. It was alleged in another community that of a shipment of wheat from the same
field, grown from the same seed, and harvested at the same
time, some had been graded number one, some number two,
and some rejected. At best the elevator operators were anx-

ious to grade low enough to protect themselves against losses. Charles A. Pillsbury, one of the most prominent elevator men in the Northwest, himself admitted that at the beginning of the crop season grades at Minneapolis and Duluth were much more liberal than later, when the supply was greater and the demand had diminished. Often enough elevator operators graded according to their honest judgment in the early part of the season, but later on, when inspection at the terminal points had tightened up, they became frightened and refused "for days at a time to grade anything above number two hard, no matter what the quality offered." The state railway commissioner of Minnesota estimated, conservatively he believed, that the farmer lost on an average about five cents a bushel through unfair grading. Many said it was twice that amount.

If the farmer had little part in fixing the price at which his produce sold, he had no part at all in fixing the price of the commodities for which his earnings were spent. Neither did competition among manufacturers and dealers do much in the way of price-fixing, for the age of "big business," of trusts, combines, pools, and monopolies, had come. These trusts, as the farmers saw it, joined with the railroads, and if necessary with the politicians, "to hold the people's hands and pick their pockets." They "bought raw material at their own price, sold the finished product at any figure they wished to ask, and rewarded labor as they saw fit." Through their machinations "the farmer and the workingman generally" were "overtaxed right and left."

One western editor professed to understand how all this had come about. The price-fixing plutocracy, he argued, was but the "logical result of the individual freedom which we have always considered the pride of our system." The American ideal of the "very greatest degree of liberty" and the "very least legal restraint" had been of inestimable benefit to the makers of the trusts. Acting on the theory that individual enterprise should be permitted unlimited scope, they had gone their way without let or hindrance, putting weaker competitors out of business and acquiring monopolistic privileges for themselves. At length the corporation "had absorbed the liberties of the community and usurped the power of the agency that created it." Through its operation "individualism" had congealed into "privilege."

The number of "these unnatural and unnecessary financial monsters" was assumed to be legion. An agitated Iowan denounced the beef trust as "the most menacing" as well as the most gigantic of "about 400 trusts in existence." A Missouri editor took for his example the "plow trust. As soon as it was perfected the price of plows went up 100 per cent . . . who suffers? . . . Who, indeed, but the farmer?" Senator Plumb of Kansas held that the people of his state were being robbed annually of $40,000,000 by the produce trust. Southern farmers complained of a fertilizer trust, a jute-bagging trust, a cottonseed oil trust. Trusts indeed there were: trusts that furnished the farmer with the clothing he had to wear; trusts that furnished him with the machines he had to use; trusts that furnished him with the fuel he had to burn; trusts that furnished him with the materials of which he built his house, his barns, his fences. To all these he paid a substantial tribute. Some of them, like the manufacturers of farm machinery, had learned the trick of installment selling, and to such the average farmer owed a perpetual debt.

The protective tariff, while not universally deplored in farm circles, met with frequent criticism as a means of "protecting one class at the expense of another—the manufacturer against the farmer, the rich against the poor." Because of the tariff the American market was reserved for the exclusive exploitation of the American manufacturer, whose prices were fixed not in accordance with the cost of production but in accordance with the amount of protection he was able to secure. The genial system of logrolling, which on occasion made Democrats as good protectionists as Republicans, insured a high degree of protection all around. And so the tariff became a veritable "hot-bed for the breeding of trusts and combines among all classes of men thus sheltered by the law." This situation was the more intolerable from the farmer's point of view for the reason that he must sell at prices fixed by foreign competition. The protective tariff gave the eastern manufacturer "the home market at protective prices," but the prices of western and southern farm produce were "fixed by the surplus sold in foreign free-trade markets." Thus the farmers were as a class "*a priori* 'unprotected,' the victims of a system of free-trade selling and 'protected' purchasing—in their economic relation as consumers paying heavy prices for high tariff goods, and as producers most of them selling against the competition of the world's markets." Southern farmers were probably more keenly aware of the oppressive nature of the tariff than the westerners, and they denounced it roundly as an important contribution to their distress. They could see plainly enough that because of the tariff they were effectively debarred from exchanging their cheap farm products for the cheap manufactured goods of European nations. Westerners, while by no means silent on the subject, were inclined to regard the tariff as "subordinate to ... finance, land, and transportation."

It was the grinding burden of debt, however, that aroused the farmers, both southern and western, to action. The widespread dependence upon crop liens in the South and farm mortgages in the West has already been described. In the South as long as the price of cotton continued high and in the West as long as the flow of eastern capital remained uninterrupted, the grievances against the railroads, the middlemen, and the tariff-protected trusts merely smouldered. But when the bottom dropped out of the cotton market and the western boom collapsed, then the weight of debt was keenly felt and frenzied agitation began. The eastern capitalists were somehow to blame. They had conspired together to defraud the farmers—"to levy tribute upon the productive energies of West and South." They had made of the one-time American freeman "but a tenant at will, or a dependent upon the tender mercies of soulless corporations and of absentee landlords."

There are ninety and nine who live and die
  In want, and hunger, and cold,
That one may live in luxury,
  And be wrapped in a silken fold.

The ninety and nine in hovels bare,
The one in a palace with riches rare.
And the one owns cities, and houses and lands,
And the ninety and nine have empty hands.

As one hard season succeeded another the empty-handed farmer found his back debts and unpaid interest becoming an intolerable burden. In the West after the crisis of 1887 interest rates, already high, rose still higher. Farmers who needed money to renew their loans, to meet partial payments on their land, or to tide them over to another season were told, truly enough, that money was very scarce. The flow of eastern capital to the West had virtually ceased. The various mortgage companies that had been doing such a thriving business a few months before had now either gone bankrupt or had made drastic retrenchments. Rates of seven or eight per cent on real estate were now regarded as extremely low and on chattels ten or twelve per cent was considered very liberal, from eighteen to twenty-four per cent was not uncommon, and forty per cent or above was not unknown. Naturally the number of real estate mortgages placed dropped off precipitately. Instead of the six thousand, worth nearly $5,500,000, that had been placed in Nebraska during the years 1884 to 1887, there were in the three years following 1887 only five hundred such mortgages, worth only about $650,000, while only one out of four of the farm mortgages held on South Dakota land in 1892 had been contracted prior to 1887. When the farmer could no longer obtain money on his real estate, he usually mortgaged his chattels, with the result that in many localities nearly everything that could carry a mortgage was required to do so. In Nebraska during the early nineties the number of these badges of "dependence and slavery" recorded by the state auditor averaged over half a million annually. In Dakota many families were kept from leaving for the East only by the fact that their horses and wagons were mortgaged and could therefore not be taken beyond the state boundaries.

Whether at the old rates, which were bad, or at the new, which were worse, altogether too often the western farmer was mortgaged literally for all he was worth, and too often the entire fruits of his labor, meager enough after hard times set in, were required to meet impending obligations. Profits that the farmer felt should have been his passed at once to someone else. The conviction grew on him that there was something essentially wicked and vicious about the system that made this possible. Too late he observed that the money he had borrowed was not worth to him what he had contracted to pay for it. As one embittered farmer-editor wrote,

> There are three great crops raised in Nebraska. One is a crop of corn, one a crop of freight rates, and one a crop of interest. One is produced by farmers who by sweat and toil farm the land. The other two are produced by men who sit in their offices and behind their bank counters and farm the farmers. The corn is less than half a crop. The freight rates will produce a full average. The interest crop, however, is the one that fully illustrates the boundless resources and prosperity of Nebraska. When corn fails the interest yield is largely increased.

What was the fair thing under such circumstances? Should the farmer bear the entire load of adversity, or should the mortgage-holder help? Opinions varied, but certain extremists claimed that at the very least the interest should be scaled down. If railroads were permitted to reorganize, reduce their interest rates, and save their property when they got into financial straits, why should the farmer be denied a similar right?

The only reorganization to which the farmer had recourse, as a rule, was through foreclosure proceedings, by which ordinarily he could expect nothing less than the loss of all his property. Usually the mortgagor was highly protected by the terms of the mortgage and could foreclose whenever an interest payment was defaulted, whether the principal was due or not. In the late eighties and the early nineties foreclosures came thick and fast. Kansas doubtless suffered most on this account, for from 1889 to 1893 over eleven thousand farm mortgages were foreclosed in this state, and in some counties as much as ninety per cent of the farm lands passed into the ownership of the loan companies. It was estimated by one alarmist that "land equal to a tract thirty miles wide and ninety miles long had been foreclosed and bought in by the loan companies of Kansas in a year." Available statistics would seem to bear out this assertion, but the unreliability of such figures is notorious. Many farmers and speculators, some of them perfectly solvent, deliberately invited foreclosure because they found after the slump that their land was mortgaged for more than it was worth. On the other hand, many cases of genuine bankruptcy were settled out of court and without record. But whatever the unreliability of statistics the fact remains that in Kansas and neighboring states the number of farmers who lost their lands because of the hard times and crop failures was very large.

In the South the crop-lien system constituted the chief mortgage evil and the chief grievance, but a considerable amount of real and personal property was also pledged for debt. Census statistics, here also somewhat unreliable because of the numerous informal and unrecorded agreements, show that in Georgia about one-fifth of the taxable acres were under mortgage, and a special investigation for the same state seemed to prove that a high proportion of the mortgage debt was incurred to meet current expenditures rather than to acquire more land or to make permanent improvements. Similar conditions existed throughout the cotton South. Chattel mortgages were also freely given, especially by tenants, but frequently also by small proprietors. Interest rates were as impossibly high as in the West, and foreclosures almost as inevitable. Evidence of foreclosures on chattels could be found in the "pitiful heaps of . . . rubbish" that "commonly disfigured the court house squares." Foreclosures on land, or their equivalent, were numerous, serving alike to accelerate the process of breaking down the old plantations and of building up the new "merchant-owned 'bonanzas.'" Many small farmers lapsed into tenantry; indeed, during the eighties the trend

was unmistakably in the direction of "concentration of agricultural land in the hands of merchants, loan agents, and a
few of the financially strongest farmers."

Taxation added a heavy burden to the load of the farmer.
Others might conceal their property. The merchant might
underestimate the value of his stock, the householder might
neglect to list a substantial part of his personal property, the
holder of taxable securities might keep his ownership a secret, but the farmer could not hide his land. If it was perhaps
an exaggeration to declare that the farmers "represent but
one-fourth of the nation's wealth and they pay three-fourths
of the taxes," it was probably true enough that land bore the
chief brunt of taxation, both in the South and in the West.
Tax-dodging, especially on the part of the railroads and other
large corporations, was notorious. Some North Carolina railroads had been granted special exemptions from taxation as
far back as the 1830's, and they still found them useful. In
Georgia the railroads paid a state tax but not a county tax.
Nearly everywhere they received special treatment at the
hands of assessors, state boards of equalization, or even by
the law itself. Western land-grant railroads avoided paying
taxes on their huge holdings by delaying to patent them until
they could be sold. Then the farmer-purchaser paid the taxes.
Meantime the cost of state and local government had risen
everywhere, although most disproportionately in the West,
where the boom was on. In the boom territory public building
and improvement projects out of all proportion to the capacity of the people to pay had been undertaken, and railways,
street-car companies, and other such enterprises had been
subsidized by the issuing of state or local bonds, the interest
and principal of which had to be met by taxation. For all
this unwise spending the farmers had to pay the greater part.
The declaration of one Kansas farmer that his taxes were
doubled in order "to pay the interest on boodler bonds and
jobs voted by non-taxpayers to railroad schemes and frauds
and follies which are of no benefit to the farmer" was not
without a large element of truth. The farmer was convinced
that he was the helpless victim of unfair, unreasonable, and

discriminatory taxation. Here was another reason why he was "gradually but steadily becoming poorer and poorer every year."

Beset on every hand by demands for funds—funds with which to meet his obligations to the bankers, the loan companies, or the tax collectors and funds with which to maintain his credit with the merchants so that he might not lack the all-essential seed to plant another crop or the few necessities of life that he and his family could not contrive either to produce for themselves or to go without—the farmer naturally enough raised the battle cry of "more money." He came to believe that, after all, his chief grievance was against the system of money and banking, which now virtually denied him credit and which in the past had only plunged him deeper and deeper into debt. There must be something more fundamentally wrong than the misdeeds of railroads and trusts and tax assessors. Why should dollars grow dearer and dearer and scarcer and scarcer? Why, indeed, unless because of the manipulations of those to whom such a condition would bring profit?

Much agitation by Greenbackers and by free-silverites and much experience in the marketing of crops had made clear even to the most obtuse, at least of the debtors, that the value of a dollar was greater than it once had been. It would buy two bushels of grain where formerly it would buy only one. It would buy twelve pounds of cotton where formerly it would buy but six. The orthodox retort of the creditor to such a statement was that too much grain and cotton were being produced—the overproduction theory. But, replied the debtor, was this the whole truth? Did not the amount of money in circulation have something to do with the situation? Currency reformers were wont to point out that at the close of the Civil War the United States had nearly two billions of dollars in circulation. Now the population had doubled and the volume of business had probably trebled, but the number of dollars in circulation had actually declined! Was not each dollar overworked? Had it not attained on this account a fictitious value?

Whatever the explanation, it was clear enough that the dollar, expressed in any other terms than itself, had appreciated steadily in value ever since the Civil War. The depreciated greenback currency, in which all ordinary business was transacted until 1879, reached by that year a full parity with gold. But the purchasing power of the dollar still continued its upward course. For this phenomenon the quantity theory may be—probably is—an insufficient explanation, but . . . the fact of continuous appreciation can hardly be denied.

For those farmers who were free from debt and were neither investors nor borrowers such a condition might have had little meaning. The greater purchasing power of the dollar meant fewer dollars for their crops, but it meant also fewer dollars spent for labor and supplies. Conceivably, the same degree of prosperity could be maintained on the smaller income. But in the West and in the South the number of debt-free farmers was small indeed, and for the debtor the rising value of the dollar was a serious matter. The man who gave a long-term mortgage on his real estate was in the best position to appreciate how serious it was. Did he borrow a thousand dollars on his land for a five-year term, then he must pay back at the end of the allotted time a thousand dollars. But it might well be that, whereas at the time he had contracted the loan a thousand dollars meant a thousand bushels of wheat or ten thousand pounds of cotton, at the time he must pay it the thousand dollars meant fifteen hundred bushels of wheat or fifteen thousand pounds of cotton. Interest, expressed likewise in terms of produce, had mounted similarly year by year so that the loss to the borrower was even greater than the increase in the value of the principal. What it cost the debtor to borrow under such circumstances has been well expressed by Arnett in the table on the following page, which is based on statistics taken from the census of 1890.

Add to this the unreasonably high interest rates usually exacted and the commissions and deductions that were rarely omitted, and the plight of the debtor farmer becomes painfully clear. He was paying what would have amounted to about a twenty or twenty-five per cent rate of interest on a non-appreciating dollar.

It was, moreover, far from comforting to reflect that in such a transaction what was one man's loss was another's gain. Nor was it surprising that the harassed debtor imputed to the creditor, to whose advantage the system worked, a deliberate

DEBT APPRECIATION, 1865–1890

Average Five-year Debt Contracted in	Appreciation (in terms of dollar's purchasing power)
1865–1869	35.2
1870–1874	19.7
1875–1879	4.5
1880–1884	11.7
1885–1890	11.6

attempt to cause the dollar to soar to ever greater and greater heights. Had not the creditor class ranged itself solidly behind the Resumption Act of 1875, by which the greenback dollar had been brought to a parity with gold? Was not the same class responsible for the "crime of 1873," which had demonetized silver and by just so much had detracted from the quantity of the circulating medium? Was there not, indeed, a nefarious conspiracy of creditors—eastern creditors, perhaps with English allies—to increase their profits at the expense of the debtors—western and southern—by a studied manipulation of the value of the dollar? "We feel," said Senator Allen of Nebraska, "that, through the operation of a shrinking volume of money, which has been caused by Eastern votes and influences for purely selfish purposes, the East has placed its hands on the throat of the West and refused to afford us that measure of justice which we, as citizens of a common country, are entitled to receive." And the grievance of the West against the East was also the grievance of the South.

Nor was this grievance confined to resentment against the steadily mounting value of the dollar. There was in addition an undeniable and apparently unreasonable fluctuation in its purchasing power during any given year. At the time of crop movements, when the farmers wished to sell—indeed, had to sell, in most cases—the dollar was dear and prices were correspondingly depressed. When, on the other hand, the crop had been marketed and the farmers' produce had passed to other hands, the dollar fell in value and prices mounted rapidly. Wall Street speculators and others bought heavily when prices were low and sold later when prices were high at handsome profits—profits which, the farmers firmly believed, should have gone to the original producer. Why should these things be?

Southerners and westerners who studied the question found an answer in the inelasticity of the currency. In agricultural sections, they reasoned, money was needed most when crops were harvested, for at such times the fruit of an entire year's productive effort was thrown upon the market. The farmer could not hold his crop, for he must have money with which to meet pressing obligations—store debts, interest charges, mortgages. Sell he must, and sell he did. But this tremendous demand upon the currency increased the value of the dollar, since there were no more dollars in circulation at crop-moving time than at any other time! When at last the crop was moved and the abnormal demand for money had subsided, then the value of the dollar declined and prices rose correspondingly. These fluctuations within a given year were often large enough to make the difference between prosperity and adversity for the farmer. Could he have sold at the maximum price, or even at the average price, instead of at the minimum, he would have had far less of which to complain. As it was, he could see no good reason why the supply of money should remain constant when the need for it was variable. Unless, perchance, this were the deliberate intent of those who stood to profit from the situation. Was this not another device by which it was ordained that those who had might profit from those who had not?

This inelasticity of the currency, as well as its inadequacy, was blamed in large part upon the national banking system, against which every critic of the monetary situation railed.

According to these critics, the laws establishing national banks were "of the same character of vicious legislation that demonetized silver." They were "conceived in infamy and ... for no other purpose but to rob the many for the benefit of the few." It was at least susceptible of demonstration that the national bank-note circulation had steadily dwindled. The law of 1864 provided that national bankers must buy bonds of the United States to the extent of not less than one-third of their capital stock. These bonds were then deposited with the government and upon them as security the banks might issue notes up to ninety per cent of the par value of the bonds. This right to issue paper money, however, was exercised more freely in the years directly following the Civil War than later on, and in 1873 the total bank-note circulation had mounted to $339,000,000. From that time on it tended to decline. In 1876 it was $291,000,000; in 1891 it was only $168,-000,000. By just so much was the volume of the currency diminished, and, if the quantity theory held, the appreciation of the dollar was correspondingly accelerated.

The explanation of this cut in the note issues of national banks is not hard to find. The national debt was being paid off and some of the bonds upon which note issues had been based were retired on this account. Indeed, with its yearly revenues far in excess of its necessary expenditures, the government relaxed the rule with regard to the minimum bond deposit required of the banks and even entered the market to buy back national bonds before they were due. Naturally the bonds rose to a heavy premium, and national bankers found that they could make a greater profit by selling their bonds and retiring their notes than by keeping their notes in circulation. But in the whole proceeding the western and southern debtors saw something sinister. Was not the government in league with the money sharks to increase the value of the dollar? Why should the government bonds be paid off in gold, or its equivalent, rather than in new issues of greenbacks, the kind of money that had been used ordinarily in the purchase of these bonds? Why should there be any national banks at all? Why should "the business of issuing money and controlling its volume" be turned over "to a few persons who used their power to their own interest?" Why should not the government itself issue money direct to the people and at reasonable rates?

The argument for government issues of greenbacks had at least one dependable leg to stand upon. Such a policy would promote flexibility in the currency. The volume of note issues might then be regulated in accordance with the demand, whereas under the national banking system the volume was regulated chiefly by the possible profit to the bankers concerned. If it paid the banks to buy bonds and turn them into currency, then the banks could be expected to follow that course. If it paid better, however, to keep their bond holdings static or even to dispose of bonds and retire notes, then they followed that course. Not the needs of the country but the probable profits of the bankers determined the amount of the currency. The charge was made that at certain critical times, especially during crop-moving seasons, scarcity of money was deliberately connived at, since higher rates of interest could then be charged, presumably with greater profits. Probably this charge was baseless in the main, but that the currency was virtually inflexible under the national banking system is a matter of common knowledge.

Hostility to the national banks was increased by the argument, plausible enough but fallacious, that these institutions were able to exact double interest, once on the bonds they purchased from the government and once on the notes secured by these bonds and lent to their customers. As a western editor put it:

> If a man is worth a million and wants to start a national bank, he buys one million in bonds which he deposits with the government who pays him interest for every dollar in gold twice a year. These bonds are not taxed one cent to help defray the expenses of the government. Now then, the government carrying out its policy to make the rich richer issues him $900,000 in greenbacks to bank on and get all the interest he can and charge [*sic*] him 1 per cent on the greenbacks to cover expense of engraving, etc. The man was worth $1,000-

ooo, the government makes him worth $1,900,000, and untaxed. Is this right farmer? You bear the burden and your land cannot escape taxation.

Moreover, the attitude of the farmer towards the bankers was not improved by the reflection that the men who bought Civil War bonds in the first instance had bought at a low price and with depreciated paper currency.

Such were the grievances of which the farmers complained. They suffered, or at least they thought they suffered, from the railroads, from the trusts and the middlemen, from the money-lenders and the bankers, and from the muddled currency. These problems were not particularly new. Always the farmer had had to struggle with the problem of transportation. He had never known a time when the price of the things he had to buy was not as much too high as the price of the things he had to sell was too low. He had had his troubles with banks and bankers. But those earlier days were the days of cheap lands, and when things went wrong the disgruntled could seek solace in a move to the West. There was a chance to make a new start. Broader acres, more fertile fields, would surely bring the desired results. And with the restless ever moving to the West, the more stable elements of society left behind made pleasing progress. Now with the lands all taken and the frontier gone, this safety valve was closed. The frontier was turned back upon itself. The restless and discontented voiced their sentiments more and fled from them less. Hence arose the veritable chorus of denunciation directed against those individuals and those corporations who considered only their own advantage without regard to the effect their actions might have upon the farmer and his interests.

For Further Reading

After nearly forty years, Hicks' monograph retains its position as the basic work on Populism. Other full-length studies include Solon J. Buck, *The Agrarian Crusade* (1920), and Carl

C. Taylor, *The Farmer's Movement 1620–1920* (1953). Ches-
ter M. Destler traces Populist efforts to unite with labor in
American Radicalism, 1865–1901 (1946) as do Murray S. and
Susan W. Stedman in *Discontent at the Polls: A Study of
Farmer and Labor Parties 1827–1948* (1950). Theodore Salou-
tas and John D. Hicks, *Agricultural Discontent in the Middle
West, 1900–1939* (1951), deal with important effects of Popu-
lism in the twentieth century. Significant state studies include
Alex M. Arnett, *The Populist Movement in Georgia* (1922);
William D. Sheldon, *Populism in the Old Dominion* (1935);
John B. Clark, *Populism in Alabama* (1927), and Francis B.
Simkins, *The Tillman Movement in South Carolina* (1926).
An excellent general survey of agriculture after 1860 is Fred
A. Shannon, *The Farmer's Last Frontier* (1945).

Most of the discussion in recent years about the nature of
Populism has been provoked by Richard Hofstadter's *The
Age of Reform* (1955). Among the scholars rejecting Hof-
stadter's criticisms of the farmers are Norman Pollack, *The
Populist Response to Industrial America* (1962), and Walter
T. K. Nugent, *The Tolerant Populists: Kansas Populism and
Nativism* (1963). C. Vann Woodward's "The Populist Heri-
tage and the Intellectual" in *The Burden of Southern History*
(1963) is a convenient summary of the recent arguments pro
and con Populism.

Two excellent biographies of populist leaders are C. Vann
Woodward, *Tom Watson: Agrarian Rebel* (1938), and Mar-
tin Ridge, *Ignatius Donnelly: Portrait of a Politician* (1962).
Another informative biography is Elmer Ellis' *Henry Moore
Teller: Defender of the West* (1941). Paolo E. Coletta, *William
Jennings Bryan* (3 vols.; 1964–1969) is the major full-length
study of Bryan. Paul W. Glad's *The Trumpet Soundeth,
William Jennings Bryan 1896–1912* (1960) provides some addi-
tional insights into the man. Social-history buffs will enjoy
Lewis Atherton's cultural and economic history of the Midwestern country towns, *Main Street on the Middle Border*
(1954).

The Triumph of Bryanism

Allan Nevins

Few substantial issues differentiated the Democratic and Republican parties in the two decades following the end of Reconstruction. Most presidential campaigns centered on personalities or emotional appeals. Republican politicos, for example, continually "waved the bloody shirt" to remind the electorate of its successful defense of the Union and its emancipation of the slaves. To underline the identification of the Democracy with rebellion and Negro repression, the G.O.P. consistently chose as its presidential candidate veterans of the war; every Republican aspirant from 1868 until 1904, with the exception of James G. Blaine, had served in the war. The Democrats responded to the Republican challenge with "me-tooism," none of their standard-bearers being markedly different in political outlook from their opponents. Indeed, in 1880 the Democrats went so far as to nominate a war hero of their own, General Winfield Scott Hancock.

Of the chief executives of these years, Rutherford B. Hayes, James A. Garfield, Chester A. Arthur, and Benjamin Harrison are chiefly remembered as conservative

Source: Allan Nevins, *Grover Cleveland: A Study in Courage* (New York: Dodd, Mead & Company, Inc., 1932), pp. 678–712. Copyright 1932; © 1960 by Allan Nevins. Reprinted by permission of the publisher.

defenders of the status quo who, although not personally involved in the pervasive corruption of the Gilded
Age, individually and collectively left an indistinct impression on their contemporaries and a preciously small
legacy to posterity. Just two pieces of significant legislation date from their administrations: the Pendelton
Civil Service Act (1883), enacted in response to public
indignation following the assassination of Garfield by a
disappointed office seeker, and the Sherman Anti-Trust
Act, widely regarded at the time of its passage in 1890
as a meaningless gesture to appease the antitrust agitation.

All the Presidents of the age rate no higher than
"average" in the polls that historians are so fond of taking among themselves. Only Grover Cleveland, who
served two terms (1885–1889, 1893–1897), the lone Democrat in the half century between James Buchanan and
Woodrow Wilson, seems to stand a head higher than his
contemporaries. This distinction derives solely from his
personal qualities of political courage and independence, for his enunciated political philosophy of applying "business principles to public affairs" coincided perfectly with the conservatism of the Republicans. Allan
Nevins (b. 1890), perhaps our most masterful and pro-
lific biographer, in his Pulitzer Prize-winning study concluded that Cleveland was indeed too conservative to
become a great constructive statesman. Aside from awak-
ening the nation to the dangers of the protective tariff
system, his first administration is remembered chiefly for
its negative actions—for example, Cleveland's veto of
the dependent pension bill and his strong stand against
the railroads, the lumber companies, and other preda-
tory interests attempting to feast on the public lands.
Nevins finds Cleveland bequeathing "to subsequent generations an example of courage that never yields an
inch in the cause of truth, and that never surrenders an
iota of principle to expediency." But where Nevins sees
courage, others have seen a foolish obstinacy; where he
discerns a devotion to principle, others have charged a
complete absence of perception of or concern with the

economic and social questions convulsing the nation, particularly during his second administration.

The ferocious battle over free silver provides a good example of the divergence of opinion on Cleveland. To briefly sketch the history of the silver question, Congress in 1832 had established the ratio of silver to gold at 16 to 1; in other words, there was sixteen times as much silver in a silver dollar as there was gold in a gold dollar. Until the California gold discoveries of 1848, this ratio more or less satisfactorily measured the value of the two metals, but after 1850, 16 to 1 severely undervalued silver and since most producers obtained a better price from silversmiths, jewelers, and other commercial users, they stopped offering silver to the Treasury. Hence, with little opposition, Congress ended the coinage of silver in 1873. But within a few years, discoveries of tremendous new deposits of silver in the Western United States led to a clamor from these areas for a return to the unlimited coinage of silver at the old ratio. Many farm organizations endorsed the demand for free silver believing an influx of the cheaper metal into the money market would cause a currency inflation that would in turn drive up commodity prices. In times of inflation anyone dealing in real property—corn, cotton, hogs— stands to profit, but those who deal in personal property, that is, currency bonds, etc., tend to suffer losses. Free silver therefore encountered the vehement opposition of Eastern bankers and creditors. The silverites gained partial victories with the passage of the Bland-Allison Act in 1878 and the Sherman Silver Purchase Act of 1890. The latter success proved short-lived, however, for one of Cleveland's first acts in his second administration was to secure repeal of the Sherman legislation. This immediately produced a rebellion against the President by the silver Democrats led by Representative Richard "Silver Dick" Bland of Missouri and the eloquent young congressman from Nebraska, William Jennings Bryan. In the following selection, Nevins praises Cleveland for refusing to accept a compromise on the silver purchase act and holding the breach against fi-

nancial error. But while the silverites unquestionably
went too far in demanding a return to 16 to 1 coinage
(the market ratio in 1896 was close to 32 to 1), Cleveland ignored the basic shortage in the money supply. By
resting the country's financial system entirely upon a
metal in such short supply, he severely restricted a growing economy. Notwithstanding the urging of wiser Democrats than himself, he stubbornly refused to consider
any of several alternatives. One such option, international bimetallism, would have—if it could have been
achieved—simultaneously increased the nation's currency, converted many advocates of free silver, and
strengthened the Democratic Party. Cleveland's negative, defeatist approach to international bimetallism, observed another biographer, Horace Merrill, "reflected
more than anything else his stubborn pride that prevented him from voluntary change or conspicuous concessions." More than anyone else, Grover Cleveland
contributed to the triumph of Bryanism.

*C*leveland was often charged with being no political manager,
and always accepted the charge lightly, for he had little desire
to figure in that light. Yet in the spring of 1895 he took
shrewd steps in an effort to hold the party in line. While it
was obvious that most of the West was irretrievably lost, there
was still hope for the sound money cause in the South. That
section had maintained a loyal front against the Populist
invasion in 1892. If it could be induced, even in part, to
stand by the Administration in 1896, the silverite frenzy of
the trans-Mississippi regions might yet be dammed back.
Cleveland knew how desperately poor the South was, and
what tinder for the flame of agitators the small farmers of
that region presented. The political barometer there was the
price of cotton. Beginning in 1891 prices had declined, the
average New York rate that year being two and a half cents
lower than in 1890. In 1892 occurred a further decline. There
was a short crop in 1893, and despite the panic a reaction to

higher levels. But in 1894 an enormous crop again surfeited the
market, the world demand fell on account of the depression,
and prices dropped sickeningly; while the next year the decline continued. In 1894 the New York market touched a low
level of 6⅞ cents a pound, and in 1895 it actually fell to 4⅞
cents. One of Cleveland's friends sent him a little dialogue
as reported by a student at the University of North Carolina:

STRANGER TO FARMER: "What do you-all live on down here?"

FARMER: "Mostly by barter."

STRANGER: "Don't you ever see any money?"

FARMER: "Well, I have had as much as half a dollar."

FARMER'S SON: "You lie, dad, I never see you have more'n a
quarter."

And Tom Watson, the perfect type of the demagogue, was
arousing Georgians in meeting after meeting with colloquies
of the following kind:

"Well, boys, I'm going to turn this gathering today into a
school. . . . I'll start with the head pupil, who ought to know.
Mr. Barnes [Watson's sound-money opponent], when a national bond is deposited, how much of its value does the government issue in money?"

No answer.

"Tell him, boys."

"Ninety per cent," roars a sea of voices.

"All right. Now, how much interest does the national
banker pay on the money he gets on his bonds?"

"One per cent," the crowd yells in unison.

"All right. Now, how much interest do the farmers have to
pay the banker every time they borrow a little money?"

"Eight per cent," the audience shouts.

"You bet they do. Then how much has the national banking system in Washington robbed the farmers of?"

"Seven per cent," roars the crowd.

"Yes, and then when the government goes and pays the
banker four per cent on his bonds, his profit on his money
becomes how much?"

"Eleven per cent," they shout.
"And what do you ever get?" Watson hurls at the crowd.
"Nothing!" they yell back.

Yet to Cleveland the South seemed worth fighting for. His letter to Governor Stone was part of a systematic campaign for that region. It embodied a direct argument to the cotton growers. They grew products which were exported for gold; yet they were willing to submit to all the loss which would arise from a fluctuating and depreciated silver currency, for buyers of cotton would have to insure themselves in every transaction against a sudden drop in silver, and the farmers would have to pay for this insurance. Cleveland declared that he simply could not understand their attitude. At the same time he began corresponding with such sound-money Southerners as Senator Caffery of Louisiana and Gov. C. O'Ferrall of Virginia. When Representative Patterson of Tennessee made a sound-money speech in the House, Cleveland asked Fairchild if he could not distribute it broadcast in the Southern States. "I am entirely certain," he wrote, "that section can be dislodged from their association with the West on the currency question. They have heard but one side and there is plenty of proof at hand that they will respond properly if the other side is made plain. A campaign of education such as was waged for tariff reform would produce quick and abundant results—in the South especially." He saw to it that sound-money Southerners were brought into close coöperation with the sound-money Democrats of Northern centres. For example, he introduced to Fairchild, by letter, the able Representative from the Mobile district, just reëlected on a gold platform:

> Mr. R. H. Clarke I understand will go to New York this evening to confer with certain parties there, in relation to an attempt to start an aggressive movement in the South on the subject of sound money.... I have no information concerning the details of his plan, but can do no less than to say to you that few if any men in Congress from the South (I think I may say no Representative from the South) has a better ap-

preciation of public duty or sounder ideas on public questions. Without any prompting, and, so far as I have been
able to see, without any reference to selfish interests, he has
been faithful and sound among many faithless and unsound.
There is no man in Congress whom I hold in higher esteem,
and if anything is to be done to win his section back from
error and misconception it must be done through just such
men.

Most important of all, Cleveland arranged that Secretary
Carlisle should make a tour of the border States in May,
delivering sound-money speeches at Bowling Green, Coving-
ton, Louisville, and Memphis. The Memphis speech was made
at a much-advertised sound-money convention on May 23,
before nearly seven hundred delegates representing every
Southern State except Virginia and North Carolina. Never
had Carlisle's lucidity of mind and expository charm appeared to better advantage than in these four discourses.
Avoiding repetition, he linked the speeches into a matchless
presentation, historical and economic, of the case for sound
money. That the national financial system was unsound and
needed reorganization he frankly admitted, and he gave his
ideas upon this reorganization. But he exposed in masterly
fashion the weakness of the chief free silver arguments. The
market ratio of silver to gold was now 32 to 1; free coinage
at 16 to 1 would halve the value of the dollar, and heavily
reduce all wages; gold would be driven from circulation, and
silver monometallism would mean a contracted as well as
depreciated and fluctuating currency. Mine-owners and those
debtors who had not agreed to pay in gold might profit, but
the great mass of workmen, merchants, and farmers would
lose. The 21,000,000 Americans who had put money into
savings banks, insurance companies, and building and loan
associations would be repaid in fifty-cent dollars. The Eastern
press warmly praised Carlisle's speeches. So did the Memphis
delegates, who were almost entirely business men, with few
politicians, and who adopted resolutions praising "the un-
flagging courage and sturdy patriotism of President Cleveland."

Cleveland himself made a trip to the South in the autumn. On October 24, with Vice-President Stevenson, Secretary Carlisle, and five other members of his Cabinet, he received a cordial reception at the Cotton States Exposition in Atlanta. After reviewing a military parade he made a speech to 50,000 people in which, while avoiding the currency question, he decried all sectional and selfish interests in politics. Free-coinage and gold men alike could endorse his general attack on those who strove to gain some private advantage at the expense of their fellow-citizens; but what he specifically had in mind were the demands of mine-owners in the silver States.

Yet it proved impossible to raise money in New York or other cities for a systematic Southern campaign; and a succession of events in 1895 rendered it clear that Cleveland's struggle to hold that section was hopeless. The sound-money convention in Memphis was quickly followed, in June, by a silver convention in the same city; and a long list of political leaders were prominent among the thousand delegates. Senator Turpie of Indiana was made permanent chairman. Among those prominent on the floor were Senators Bate and Harris of Tennessee, Jones and Berry of Arkansas, George and Walthall of Mississippi, and Marion Butler of North Carolina. Tillman, the veteran Warner, and the youthful Bryan were all conspicuous. A number of Southern governors attended, the enthusiasm was marked, and many speakers favored placing the silver question above party allegiance. During the summer one State convention after another went on record for free coinage. In a single week the Texas, Mississippi, and Missouri conventions declared for silver at 16 to 1, and adopted resolutions hostile to the financial policy of the government. Senator Morgan published in the *Arena* a long article on "Why Does the South Want Free Silver?"—reaching a new level of absurdity in such assertions as that "gold is the money of the speculator and miser, while silver fructifies industry as the rains do the earth." Large silver conventions at Salt Lake City, Des Moines, and Springfield, Ill., encouraged the South.

The only important Southern election this year was in Mississippi, and in the struggle of the silver and gold forces the advantage lay wholly with the former. The Cleveland Democrats at first urged that the currency question, being a national and not a State issue, should be excluded from consideration; but a Senator was to be chosen, and the argument was rejected. Though the officeholding Democrats, with many local newspapers, fought gallantly, they were outnumbered. Governor Stone wrote Cleveland charging that Federal officials were being improperly used. The county conventions proved overwhelmingly for silver, and the State convention declared for free coinage and against bond issues. The final election was simply a contest between the silver Democrats and Populists, the former of course winning, with no ticket for which gold Democrats could honestly vote. Autumn saw Speaker Crisp opening a senatorial campaign in Georgia on a 16-to-1 platform; Senator Harris announcing that the Democrats the next year must take up silver or accept defeat; and strong movements under way for electing silver delegations to the national convention. On August 14–15 a conference of free coinage Democrats met in Washington to effect an organization within the party strong enough to control the convention. Among the leaders were Senator Jones, Harris, Jarvis of North Carolina, Call of Florida, and Daniel of Virginia; a group who denounced Cleveland and his "panic-breeding, corporation-credit currency," and appointed an executive committee to keep up the fight. The "Senatorial clique" of the Chicago convention was thus born.

In great parts of the Middle West the conflagration was now getting beyond control. The silverites were well organized, and thanks to the mine-owning interests of the mountain States, well financed. W. A. Clark and Marcus A. Daly of Montana had helped pay for the delivery of the Omaha *World-Herald* to Bryan. Reprints of free-coinage speeches in Congress flooded the country, many pamphlets were sold or given away, and even books were distributed by the hundreds of thousands. The *National Bimetallist* and the *Arena* were gaining large circulations. *Coin's Financial School* was followed by a plausible imitation—Ignatius Donnelly's *American*

People's Money, which reported an imaginary conversation between a stupid banker and a brilliant farmer on a railroad journey. The chairman of the Wisconsin Democratic Committee wrote Cleveland's secretary as early as April, 1895, that he was astonished to find so much growth in the silver movement. "The difficulty in the nation is that the free silver advocates are active. They have been circulating literature rather freely and seem to have a fairly good organization throughout the country, while on the other hand those who believe in sound money and endorse Mr. Cleveland's views on the subject have apparently done very little systematic work." Teller, Weaver, Bland, Boies, Ebenezer Wakely, Sibley of Pennsylvania, and others were constantly active. Throughout 1895 Bryan was lecturing in the West and South, welcomed in many places, as the British journalist Sidney Brooks said, as almost a second Messiah; and as he travelled he wrote rough outlines for editorials on the backs of envelopes or torn bits of paper, and mailed them to the *World-Herald* office. David F. Houston, who heard him at Fort Worth, discovered that a prairie schooner could be driven through any part of his argument, but he was unrivalled in winning adherents.

Here and there the Cleveland forces, like a besieged garrison, threw back the attackers. In Ohio, for example, Senator Brice took the field against Allen W. Thurman and the other free silver men, used his large fortune in the battle, and mustered 538 sound money delegates in the State convention of 808 men. The result was a conservative nominee for governor, and a platform which congratulated Cleveland on his policies. But there was truth in the Chicago *Inter-Ocean's* remark that the victory was brought about by patronage and money; "Cleveland furnished one, Brice the other, and the hoops were knocked right off both barrels." And in general all the Western omens indicated that the national convention would be speedily captured by the silverites. In Missouri a convention was called by special action, and with Bland as chairman proved overwhelmingly for free coinage. In Nebraska the Bryanites won an equally despotic control over the State convention. When some reckless delegate offered a resolution endorsing Cleveland and the national platform of 1892, the roof was lifted by a roar of protest, and order was not restored for ten minutes.

Congress met in December—now an overwhelmingly Republican Congress, but no more hostile than before—amid gossip that Cleveland, in a last effort to stem the tide, would enter the lists for a third term. This talk was taken seriously by men who ought to have known better. Cleveland really wanted Carlisle, or failing him, William E. Russell. Senator Gray of Delaware declared that the President would be the logical nominee the following year, and kindly explained that it would not really be a third term—only his second consecutive term. Chauncey Depew thought the nomination a certainty, and a good thing too, for like other railroad men, he remembered the defeat of the Chicago strike gratefully. Even Roosevelt, writing his *fidus Achates*, Lodge, believed that Cleveland might be named. "I think we should beat him if he was; but I am by no means sure that he would not give us a good deal of a fight. People are crazy over him; though I think it is more our kind of people than the 'masses.'" When the subject was first mentioned, Cleveland indulged only in indignant grunts. But as it grew irksome, he let the trusted correspondent of the *Evening Post* know that as soon as the third term business got beyond mere talk, he would put a stop to it.

The thousand indications that the silver movement had completely escaped from control, that it was almost certain to capture the Democratic party, and that it would probably split the next Republican convention, greatly alarmed business and finance. Late in the summer the vigor which the Morgan-Belmont syndicate had imparted to the Treasury began to ebb. During August legal-tenders again began to be offered in large quantities at the Treasury for gold. Secretary Carlisle hurried back from a lighthouse-inspection trip he was making on the Great Lakes. In the uneasy state of the public mind the slightest indication of another run on the Treasury gold was bound to cause anxiety and arouse discussion of a fourth bond issue. By September 14, 1895, the gold reserve had been reduced to $96,300,000, and was falling more than a million dollars a day. J. P. Morgan then announced that the syndicate would continue to aid the government and was constantly accumulating gold for the purpose, and this eased the tension. In October withdrawals almost ceased. But they recommenced in November, when $16,000,000 was taken out, and in December the situation became dangerous. The head of the New York sub-treasury wrote Carlisle in alarm on December 20. " 'The Philistines are upon us'—in other words, private hoarding has begun—and we must stand both foreign and interior drains." He had lost more than $4,000,000 on that single day.

Once more, and again vainly, Cleveland asked Congress for helpful legislation. He mentioned the subject in his annual message, and on December 20 sent a special appeal. But it was generally agreed that no new legislation for a bond issue that would be acceptable to the House, or the Senate, or the President, would be approved by either of the other branches. The silverites were as obstructive as ever, and the Republican majority in the House joyously took the position that the real trouble lay in the tariff—that if there were a higher tariff there would be more revenue, and more revenue was what the Treasury really needed. It was necessary to plan once more for a bond-sale under the old legislation. For a time in late December the conditions seemed highly unfavorable. Cleveland's message on Venezuela caused a disastrous flurry, sending rates for call money to 80 per cent, forcing several brokerage houses to suspend, and giving Carlisle sleepless nights.

The great question was how the bonds should be sold. For a few days, as 1895 closed and 1896 opened, it was generally believed that the fourth issue, like the third, would have to be disposed of by secret negotiation to a banking syndicate. No one believed this more strongly than J. P. Morgan. He took steps to form a great international syndicate, including other New York bankers, the Deutsche Bank of Berlin, and Morgan, Harjes Company of Paris, which was to purchase the bonds, retail them in America, Germany, France, and other countries, and deliver gold coin to the Treasury in exchange.

Late in December he went to Washington and talked with Carlisle. On January 4, with the approval of the bankers associated with him, Morgan sent Cleveland a frank offer. He would buy from $100,000,000 to $200,000,000 of bonds on substantially the same terms as his purchase a year earlier, would furnish the Treasury an equivalent sum in gold coin, and would take steps to prevent gold exports. James Stillman of the City Bank vigorously supported the scheme, writing Cleveland that he could supply $22,000,000 in gold from the vaults of his own and one other bank, and could guarantee that the Deutsche Bank would furnish $25,000,000 more. He and Morgan insisted that a sale to their syndicate would serve in every way the best interests of the people.

Still another plan was suggested by Jacob H. Schiff, who opposed selling any bonds abroad. He wrote the President that he should lose no time in asking the national banks to buy $100,000,000 worth of four per cent bonds, pledging their gold stocks in return but actually paying the gold only in instalments. This, he said, would give Americans the profit that foreigners would otherwise take, and would "prove our own strength in the face of the unparalleled crisis."

But Cleveland and Carlisle never intended to sell this fourth issue except by public offer; they were determined from the outset on a popular loan. They had disposed of the first two issues in this way; they had deeply regretted the exigency which made a public sale of the third issue impossible; and now they went back to their old method. Morgan was dimly aware of this purpose, and in making his offer of January 4, he wrote Cleveland that if he decided to sell the bonds to the public instead of the syndicate, then the House of Morgan would give the issue its fullest support and strive to make it a success. Yet, ignorant of the Administration's consistent intention of asking for public bids, Pulitzer and the *World* on December 26 launched a noisy campaign to force it to that course! The paper blazed forth with excited denunciation of "bond rings," of "greedy financiers" who "cornered" the government, of "credulous" public officials; it appealed to Cleveland in double-leaded editorials to avoid this "colossal scandal"; it inveighed against a government by syndicates for syndicates. This clamor was echoed in the halls of Congress.

On January 6 Cleveland and Carlisle quietly announced that the fourth bond issue of $100,000,000 would be sold by public subscription. The previous day Cleveland had written a letter to Senator Caffery in which he put the *World* and its Congressional allies right. "The Secretary of the Treasury," he stated, "from the first moment that the necessity of another sale of bonds seemed to be approaching desired to offer them, if issued, to the people by public advertisement, if they could thus be successfully disposed of . . ." The mere fact that Morgan had formed a syndicate, he remarked, proved nothing. If Morgan was convinced that the government would be forced to sell its bonds again by private negotiation, he had a perfect right to put himself in a position to make a bid; indeed, he might regard it as a patriotic act. And there was a shot for the *World* in Cleveland's locker. "I am amazed," Cleveland wrote, "at the intolerance that leads even excited partisanship to adopt as a basis of attack the unfounded accusations and assertions of a maliciously mendacious and sensational newspaper." Yet Cleveland had made a mistake in not letting the public know in better time of his intentions. Because of this mistake, the absurd legend that the *World* had defeated another syndicate sale persisted for years.

Cleveland spent much thought on means of making this popular bond sale a success. By no means content to entrust all the details to Carlisle, he corresponded with Fairchild on the subject, and his letters—one of them beginning "It is horribly late and I am dreadfully tired"—indicate that he was shaping various features of the loan himself. "I have already written one or two of our friends that the period between the instalments of gold (for payment) might be extended," he concluded, "and I have invited suggestions as to what extension should be made and intimated to Mr. Stewart that your knowledge of Treasury loans would make you a good man to advise with." After the period for subscriptions opened, he sat far into the night at his desk, writing friends and urging them to work for the loan. When the bids were unsealed at the Treasury on February 5, it was found there were 4,640 offers aggregating $568,269,000, most of them being at 110 to 112. The *World's* bid for a million dollars at 114 was the highest for any considerable amount. In the end, about $66,-800,000 of the bonds went to 780 persons who had made subscriptions at various rates above 110.6877, and $33,179,250 went to Morgan at that figure. Cleveland was vastly pleased. As Robert L. O'Brien, who had now become Washington correspondent of the Boston *Transcript,* wrote that paper:

"Seldom if ever have I taken so much interest in anything as I have in the success of this bond issue," said President Cleveland this morning. "Both Secretary Carlisle and myself have had it very much at heart." In response to a reference by your correspondent to the syndicate contract of last year, the President remarked that he had never had reason to question the wisdom of that arrangement under the conditions then existing. "That contract," he added, "helped us out at a time when 48 hours' delay might have produced serious results. I sympathize, nevertheless, with some of the objections made to that form of placing a loan. The difference between the price obtained by the syndicate and the price currently quoted can be twisted into an argument which will appeal to people who do not stop to calculate the actual cost to the syndicate of floating the loan at that time.

"My preference would have been to have the present loan much more popular than it appears on its face, but we have done the best we could. . . . If we could have sold them a three per cent gold bond at par I think it would have brought out a good deal of this gold, but the only bonds the law allows us have to be sold considerably above par in order to keep the net rate of interest within reasonable limits. But from such information as comes to me from various private sources I am convinced that more small holdings of gold will come into the Treasury by the present arrangement than appear on the surface. The small country banks, for instance, which are buying bonds for their customers, have made their bids through their New York and Boston correspondents, and this gives the loan the appearance of having been taken up by the big financial institutions at the money centres."

The issue quickly lifted the Treasury's gold reserve, which had fallen as low as $44,500,000, to a high point of $128,713,-000. It was now permanently safe, and Cleveland might consider one of his greatest labors finally accomplished. Just what was the value of that labor no one can say, for no man knows what would have been the result if the country had suspended gold payments. But even if we appraise the service lightly—as few will—it is obvious that the struggle was heroic in character, and that Cleveland's courage and determination in the face of multiform obstacles and harsh abuse were never more worthy of honor from posterity.

The country could now quickly forget about the Treasury in the excitement of the opening presidential campaign; for the last act in that fateful drama, the rising of the West and South, was about to be enacted. The silver forces, frustrated in Washington, appealed to the court of last resort—the voters of the land. On January 16, while the bond issue was pending, the Democratic national committee met to select a convention city. The free coinage men demanded St. Louis, the gold men New York; and by a compromise which gave every advantage to the silverites, Chicago was chosen. A few days later another great conference of silver delegates was held at the capital. The Senate at the moment was whipping into shape a free coinage bill, which it passed on February 1 by a vote (counting pairs) of 48 to 41, the Democrats furnishing 24 yeas and only 15 nays. Cleveland watched with something like despair when a fortnight later the House defeated this bill by a vote to non-concur; for the defeat was accomplished by the Republicans, and the Democrats voted almost two to one—58 to 31—in favor of silver. It was all too plain that these Democratic Congressmen represented the sentiment of the party.

The Democratic movement toward silver in the last six months before the Chicago convention was like an avalanche: a mere whisper at first, then a half-imperceptible shift in the landscape, and suddenly a roar, a crash, an irresistible cataclysm. During February and March there were no State conventions. The Administration forces, still cherishing a hope of saving some of the Middle Western States, made Chicago the centre of earnest activities. "Carlisle," wrote William L. Wilson in his diary for April 10, "read to us at Cabinet meeting today parts of the speech he is to make next Wednesday in Chicago on free silver as it affects the workingman. This, it seems to me, is one of the strongest arguments we have, but it has been very incompletely presented heretofore, and as in the beginning of the tariff fight, the workingmen, especially those in the protected industries, were against us, so now I believe the labor organizations of the country are largely for free silver, not understanding how disastrous its effect would be on the wage-earner." Champ Clark called this address, given April 15, the best single gold-standard speech ever delivered. But it had little effect on the silver men, and the Chicago *Record* described Carlisle as coming "fresh from the banquet table of Wall Street goldbugs to tell the idle and starving workingmen" that robbery was no crime. In April, moreover, disquieting news began to come in. The Missouri convention, after riotous proceedings, overwhelmed the handful of gold delegates from St. Louis and declared for free coinage. Mississippi went for silver, and in Nebraska, where the two factions held separate conventions, the silver men were far stronger. In the East, Pennsylvania, which endorsed Pattison for the nomination, and the Massachusetts and Rhode Island conventions, which came out for William E. Russell, adopted gold planks. But this had been discounted in advance.

Late in April Cleveland was particularly concerned over Michigan. He had written several times to encourage Dickinson in the struggle. The convention was held in Detroit on the 29th, and that night news came that the gold men had carried their platform, and that 17 of the 28 delegates to Chicago would be for gold. "Light out of darkness!" rejoiced Wilson, adding next day: "The silver men seem dazed by the victory of the Administration forces." Cleveland sent Dickinson a heartfelt letter of thanks for the achievement. But their joy was short-lived, for on May 7 the Tennessee convention voted for silver and there came bad news from Illinois.

Altgeld had seized control of the party machinery and expected to carry the delegates for silver. "What ups and downs we are having in this fight!" wrote Wilson. "Before the Michigan convention we were very blue. After that the fight seemed won. With Illinois under Altgeld's control we may yet lose the convention."

Thereafter there were two defeats for every victory. In the last ten days of May the Democrats of Iowa declared 675 to 270 for silver and endorsed Boies for the nomination; the South Carolina Democrats, with Tillman in control and only four dissenting votes, denounced the Administration as tyrannical and un-Democratic; and Wyoming and Oklahoma went overwhelmingly for silver. At the beginning of June the Virginia convention, after instructing the 24 national delegates to vote as a unit for free coinage, greeted Cleveland's name with hisses, while the gathering in Kentucky hooted every mention of both Cleveland and Carlisle. "The sun of Austerlitz rises this morning," exclaimed Senator Blackburn to the Kentuckians. "Having captured the convention of Kentucky, we will go on and capture the convention of Chicago." Cleveland in Cabinet meeting sadly congratulated Carlisle that he had escaped humiliation by not attending. Kansas on June 2, and North Dakota, Utah, and California soon afterward, all fell into line for silver.

Yet many conventions sat late, and hope was not completely given up to the very end. One of the worst blows to the gold forces occurred in Indiana. Here the fatal prostration of Voorhees, with the activity of the capable Tom Taggart, had seemed to open a roseate chance for success. But the county conventions went steadily against gold, and the State convention in Indianapolis on June 24 adopted a silver plank. The previous day 1065 delegates in Illinois had voted unanimously for free coinage. Kenesaw M. Landis wrote that "the God's truth is, the Democratic party in Indiana and Illinois is wildly insane on this subject of silver." A little group of Northwestern States—Wisconsin, Minnesota, and North Dakota—gave partial aid to sound money. But the Democratic organization in New York, dominated by the jealous and indifferent Hill, once more struck Cleveland from the rear. The leaders should have imitated the Massachusetts Democrats by calling an early State convention, adopting a rigid sound-money plank, and commending the Administration. Instead, they did nothing to stem the silver tide and sat inactive until a few days before the Chicago convention was to assemble. On June 24 the convention met at Saratoga, with Hill, Whitney, and John Boyd Thacher in charge, and voted a platform which struck most gold men as weak and colorless. It called for international bimetallism along with the gold standard, and endorsed "gold and silver as the standard money of the country." In short, New York had faltered in the fight. Meanwhile, on June 23–25 Ohio (where Brice too was sulking), Texas, Georgia, and North Carolina all went into the silver column.

The silver men now possessed far more than a majority of the delegates, but they were not yet sure of two-thirds; they could write the platform, but it was not certain they could name the candidate.

As the excitement mounted the rancors and passions of recent years all came frothily to the surface. The hotheaded Tillman had set an evil example in January by a speech to the Senate in which he arraigned Cleveland with the harshest epithets, calling him "bull-headed," "self-idolatrous," a "besotted tyrant," and an "arrogant and obstinate ruler," and going so far as to term Carlisle "this Judas from Kentucky." Worse still, he declared that "millions are on the march," and that unless speedy relief arrived they would "come to Washington with rifles in their hands to regain the liberties stolen from them." The Eastern press gave back adjective for adjective, the New York *Times* calling Tillman a filthy baboon, and the *Mail and Express* describing him as a political ruffian. But the agrarian Democrats rose behind him with loud cheers, and General Weaver wrote him to strike again: "Keep your whip in your hand; it is the same one twice used in the temple scene at Jerusalem, and you struck the same set of scalawags." It happened that in March Cleveland went to New York to attend a rally in Carnegie Hall in behalf of the home missions of the Presbyterian Church. In the course of his speech he referred to the lawlessness, the dramshops and gambling-dens, to be found on the frontier, and excited the wrath of a host of Westerners by adding:

> These conditions, if unchecked and uncorrected, fix upon the new community, by their growth and expansion, a character and disposition which, while dangerous to peace and order in the early stages of settlement, develop into badly regulated municipalities, corrupt and unsafe Territories, and undesirable States. . . . These churches and this religious teaching were never more needed than now on our distant frontiers, where the process of forming new States is going on so rapidly, and where newcomers who are to be the citizens of new States are so rapidly gathering together.

These words, which doubtless in part reflected Cleveland's irritation with the selfish silver-mining States, aroused an absurdly exaggerated storm. Senator Teller gathered bundles of statistics on the comparative number of jail inmates, paupers, prostitutes, and murderers in the East and West, and flung them at Cleveland's head. Senator Dubois accused him of ignorance, narrow-mindedness, and sectional pharisaism. According to Senator Vest, he had stood with the ghastly light of the hell-holes and rum-cellars of New York shining on his face and had cantingly said that home missions must be used to civilize the heroic pioneers. Western nerves, it was clear, were badly on edge.

In both West and South, indeed, more than one observer has described the temper of the hour as a veritable frenzy. Representative Henry St. George Tucker of Virginia, for standing loyally by Cleveland, was cut by old friends, and even feared physical violence as he went about his district. Former supporters shook their fists in his face. In Georgia the general feeling among small farmers, small shopkeepers, and laborers was of sullen rage. Survivors of that era laugh at the idea that by any possible measures Cleveland could have checked the silver forces. "All hell," states Senator Cohen, "couldn't stop them." When Hoke Smith in the spring of

1896 engaged in a series of joint debates with Crisp, his reception varied between icy coldness and almost mob-like hostility. William L. Wilson, hopelessly battling against the craze in his old West Virginia district, wrote that "I have never seen the masses of the people so wild over a question they know little or nothing about. To reason with them is as impossible as to talk down an angry cyclone, and they turn away from all those whom they have been wont to follow in public matters with contempt." On the western plains men talked with confidence of what they would do to the bloated money-holders when they came into power. Multitudes were convinced that they were the victims of a gigantic conspiracy by the money interests of Wall Street and Lombard Street, and that only a sharp change in the standard of values could stop their exploitation.

During June Cleveland was besought on every hand to say something. The Chamber of Commerce of the State of New York, through its committee on financial legislation, urged him to address a letter to some prominent Westerner or Southerner, pointing out again the folly of debasing the currency. "We feel," they wrote, "that there is a great lack of leadership, political and national, for the sound money forces." After much hesitation, Cleveland yielded to the pressure and on June 16 gave the country a statement through the New York *Herald*. Declaring that he did not wish to pose as a party dictator, he confessed that he could not forbear making a last appeal in behalf of the grand old organization, so rich in honorable traditions, so justly proud of its achievements, and so undaunted in its battles for the people's welfare:

> I have made no figures as to the probable action of delegates already chosen or to be chosen to the Democratic National Convention, but I refuse to believe that when the time arrives for deliberate action there will be engrafted upon our Democratic creed a demand for a free, unlimited, and independent coinage of silver. I cannot believe this, because I know the Democratic party is neither unpatriotic nor foolish, and because it seems so clear to me that such a course will inflict a very great injury upon every interest of our coun-

try, which it has been the mission of Democracy to advance, and will result in lasting disaster to our party organization. There is little hope that as a means of success this free silver proposition, after its thorough discussion during a political campaign, will attract a majority of the voters of the country. It must be that many of the illusions influencing those who are now relying upon this alleged panacea for their ills will be dispelled before the time comes for them to cast their ballots, which will express their sober second thoughts. The adoption by the Democracy of this proposition would, I believe, give to our opponents an advantage, both in the present and future, which they do not deserve. . . .

In my opinion no effort should be spared to secure such action of the delegates as will avert party demoralization. It is a place for consultation and comparison of views, and those Democrats who believe in the cause of sound money should there be heard and should be constantly in evidence. A cause worth fighting for is worth fighting for to the end.

A chorus of commendation came from the conservative press. Most of the sound-money newspapers said yes, fight to the end, there was still hope. But others asserted that the cause of free coinage had gained such headway that little short of a miracle could stop it. Any chance that the statement would affect the Western Democrats had been destroyed by the systematic abuse of Cleveland there. "No President," as the Indianapolis *Sentinel* said, "was ever so persistently and malignantly lied about as Grover Cleveland has been. The judgment of thousands of men has been warped by whispered stories that are too silly to discuss."

William C. Whitney had arranged to sail for Europe on June 17, but after consultation with Senators Hill and Gorman and other Democratic leaders, he cancelled his passage and announced that he would go to Chicago and join others in a tremendous effort to insert a gold plank instead of a free coinage plank in the platform. He would not be a delegate, but would simply use his personal influence. Various silver men instantly accused him of plotting to buy up Democratic delegates as Mark Hanna had been accused of buying up Republican delegates. But Whitney, who had recently spent several months in Europe studying the currency question, and who was a staunch believer in bimetallism by international agreement, issued a conciliatory statement. "I am not foolish enough," he said, "to suppose that any Eastern man could be nominated by this convention, much less that I could be. I sympathize thoroughly with the feeling in the South that has caused the uprising and that will find expression in Chicago; but as to the principles which the uprising has brought forth and the issues being framed, I entirely disagree." His appearance in the lists revived flagging hopes. William E. Russell, everywhere regarded in the East as the logical successor of Cleveland, wrote a friend on the 18th that "it is of the utmost importance that the Democratic Party should take an absolutely sound position on the money question, and I am hopeful of that result in Chicago, although I admit at present the chances seem against it." Winslow Warren, in a sudden access of enthusiasm, thought that Whitney himself might be the Ney of this Friedland. "Only one man can have a chance of turning the tide back and that is Whitney. The saving of the party, and the nation perhaps, seems to me to demand from him the sacrifice. If he would avow himself a candidate upon a good platform pledged to use his utmost efforts, if elected, for international bimetallism (whatever that may be), his wonderful popularity South and West might turn things yet."

These momentary and delusive hopes gained a certain color from the result of the Republican convention which opened in St. Louis on the 16th. The rout there of the silver men, who fell far below the numbers with which they had been credited, was complete. Hanna, who had long before determined on a gold plank, sat in his rooms at the Southern Hotel inwardly chuckling as one Eastern leader after another—Platt, Lodge, Lauterbach—demanded that he accept such a plank. The gold standard sentence was actually in the platform by Friday night before the convention opened; these men, making their speeches to the omnipotent Hanna on Saturday and Sunday, went away afterwards bragging that they had forced his hand. The actual writer of Hanna's plank was Melville E. Stone, head of the Associated Press, chosen because he was

the only man present at the time who could spell "inviolable."
When the platform was formally adopted the silver delegates,
in one of the dramatic moments of Republican party history,
formed behind Teller and Dubois and marched from the hall.
"Go to Chicago!" shrieked the convention, and Hanna yelled
"Go! Go!" with the rest. The whole event, thought the New
York *Times,* "increases immensely the probability of a like
triumph for the gold standard at the Chicago convention."
And, said the *World,* "McKinley's triumph is Democracy's
opportunity. . . . Shall it be a campaign—or suicide?"

The gossip that Cleveland might yet be presented for a
third term continued, and embarrassed him and his friends.
William L. Wilson tells us in his unpublished diary that he
and the President repeatedly talked the matter over. Cleveland said in April that he was getting scores of letters every
day appealing to him to run, and that some public disclaimer
seemed necessary from him, but he had never found the fitting
time and person to make it. He did not like to speak when
the prospects of the sound money wing were increasingly
gloomy, and he thought it better to remain quiet for a time
if his doing so inspired anyone to work who might otherwise
become inactive. Once he was about to make a flat announce-
ment that he would under no circumstances be a candidate,
but Justice Peckham dissuaded him. Just after the gold forces
carried the Michigan convention William L. Wilson urged
him to issue the statement, and again he almost made up his
mind to do so; but this time Dickinson successfully inter-
vened. He was the more easily persuaded because he felt that
the idea of his running again was preposterous, and he was
reluctant to dignify the rumors by noticing them.

Nevertheless, his failure to speak out was a great tactical
blunder. It would have strengthened the gold forces if in
April or early May he had said that he would refuse a nomination; for the third-term talk injured the sound money
cause more in the South and West than it helped it in the
East. It irritated Hill; it irritated Brice of Ohio. There was a
dinner-table conference at Hill's home, Wolfert's Roost, in
April, at which Hill, Brice, Gorman, Alton B. Parker, Adlai

E. Stevenson, and John R. McLean all considered the possibility of stopping the silver movement. When McLean urged Brice to go to Chicago to help in the fight, Brice burst out explosively: "I don't propose to pull any more chestnuts out of the fire for Grover Cleveland. If you will get a statement from him that he will not be a candidate, I will do it." Late in June McLean came to Carlisle, and said: "There is yet a way for the President to smash free silver." "How is that?" asked Carlisle. "Well, I care nothing about silver, but I hate Cleveland. Let him say he is not a candidate, and the Ohio convention can be controlled." Carlisle told Cleveland of the conversation, the President pooh-poohed McLean's demand, and the Ohio convention declared for silver. It was Carlisle's own opinion that a timely utterance would have been of great benefit to the gold forces, and Wilson agreed.

Cleveland simply did not realize how intense was now the hatred which many men had for him. An illustration of its violence was presented by an altercation this spring between Dickinson and Senator Pugh of Alabama. The scene was John Chamberlain's restaurant in Washington, where Dickinson was dining. Pugh was sitting at a table near by, and observing his presence, began a malignant and vile tirade against Cleveland for the purpose of offending him. As Dickinson rose at the close of his meal, Pugh's companion, Benton McMillin, who was half tipsy, dragged him over to be introduced to "my friend, Senator Pugh." Dickinson said, "I don't want to know the d——d old blatherskite!" Pugh retorted, "You are a scoundrel!" Dickinson came back with "You are a d——d old wart!" and as Pugh pretended to be drawing a weapon the former Postmaster-General shouted at him, with another epithet, "Sit down!" Pugh sat down.

Yet Cleveland all through these stormy and disastrous weeks somehow maintained his spirits. Wilson wrote in his diary that he was much pleased by Whitney's decision to stay and fight it out. "He does not comprehend the madness of the free silverites nor the hopelessness of trying to accomplish anything by reason, appeal, or entreaty. Yet he is not specially hopeful of staying the lunacy of the convention." Particularly significant was a statement which he made at the beginning of June. The President and Wilson were talking of the work the Administration had done. Their conversation was not cheerful, though they felt they had performed their duty. "I told the President," writes Wilson "that history would put in its true light his great but unpopular fight for public credit. He answered jocularly and half seriously, 'I am not concerning myself about what history will think, but contenting myself with the approval of a fellow named Cleveland whom I have found to be a pretty good sort of fellow.' "

Cleveland left for Gray Gables on the evening of June 29. At that hour delegates were already beginning to gather in Chicago for the convention, which was to open on July 7. Before the doors of the White House closed behind him he had written a final appeal to the party—a letter read at the Tammany celebration of the Fourth. Remarking that the situation was one which invested the national celebration with more than usual impressiveness, he added: "The high and firm financial ground which we have thus far been able to hold should not be abandoned in the pursuit of a policy never attempted without national injury, and whose bright promise of individual benefit has never been fulfilled." Having penned this letter, he commended the fight at Chicago into the hands of Whitney.

Whitney's special train of three handsome parlor cars left New York on Thursday afternoon, July 1, reaching Chicago at 4:40 P.M. the following day. He had made plans for the trip with his usual care. "Now is the time," he had written Russell a fortnight earlier. "Come with me to Chicago and we will do one of two things—either beat down this craze or save the *esprit de corps* of the Eastern Democracy by most emphatic action. This last is probably all we can do, but there is more duty in that at the present time than in anything else." Russell had responded with equal enthusiasm—he would be heart and soul in the battle at Chicago. But he had laid down one condition. "I must go to Chicago to aid in the fight for sound money with no idea in the public mind that I am to have a personal interest in the success of the cause; and therefore before going I shall disclaim any candidacy and announce that my name will not be presented to the convention as a candidate, otherwise it certainly would seem as if I were fighting for a cause in the hope of some personal benefit out of its success. This I will not do under any circumstances." To this Whitney, quite properly, objected. He did not wish Russell to disclaim his candidacy, for the sound money forces might find it necessary to centre their fight about him. And he insisted that Russell prepare a speech with the utmost care. He had arranged a mass meeting in the Auditorium on the Saturday night before the convention opened, and "It will be the opportunity of your life. . . . You have beyond any man in this country the ability to utilize this great occasion."

Plainly, Whitney hoped against hope not only for a sound money platform, but for the nomination of Russell on it. The special train, well stocked with comestibles and drinkables, carried a strange array of men. David B. Hill was there, for once reconciled with Cleveland's best friends. So was "Blue-eyed Billy" Sheehan, chatting amiably with Senator Gray of Delaware. Ex-Mayor Hughie Grant, leader of Tammany, and Charles R. Miller, editor of the *Times,* contrived to endure each other. George Harvey and Senator Smith of New Jersey, two men who were to help make Woodrow Wilson's career, fraternized with Thomas Fortune Ryan and Smith M. Weed. At Detroit Don M. Dickinson, mutton-chop whiskers and all, climbed aboard. These men cheered each other up wonderfully. "It was evident," wrote a reporter for the Chicago *Tribune* who joined them at Jackson, Mich., "that they hitherto had underestimated the strength of the silver element in the West, and the fact that almost for the first time in the history of Democratic conventions New York and the East generally were to be systematically ignored."

But this ignorance was quickly dissipated. The train rolled into the station under the stares of a hostile crowd, and the little group emerged upon streets alive with silver badges and gay with silver banners. Within half an hour, they knew that their fight was utterly hopeless. Whitney had taken a suite in the Auditorium Hotel, and acting as chief of staff, ordered his associates to scatter and size up the situation. They came back profoundly impressed by the mad enthusiasm, the crusading energy, that swirled around them. One silver delegation after another was arriving with its supporters. Men bitter with a sense of injustice and burning with a desire for redress—not all politicians, but in part plain farmers, storekeepers, and labor representatives—were filling every lobby. "These men are mad," declared John R. Fellows. "We should get out a writ of *de lunatico inquirendo*." And Warren remarked to Whitney: "For the first time I can understand the scenes of the French Revolution!"

Whitney, imitating his tactics of 1892, had quietly summoned a group of trustworthy leaders—Harrity of Pennsylvania, Everett of Massachusetts, Francis of Missouri, Faulkner of Georgia, and others—to Chicago. They held a secret meeting in the "hoodoo" room of the Auditorium, where four years earlier the Tammany delegates had drawn up a round-robin of protest and denunciation against Cleveland's nomination; but they were as dispirited as the silver leaders at their headquarters in the Sherman House were elated. On Saturday evening, July 3, the sound-money forces held their rally in the Auditorium theatre. Franklin MacVeagh of Chicago presided. Russell spoke with fluent persuasiveness, and with all the irresistible personal charm which, as he moved about the lobbies and streets, led hostile Southerners and Westerners to say, "We'd like to vote for you, Governor, but not this year!" As a means of making converts to the gold standard, however, the meeting was a total failure. Meanwhile, few men mentioned Cleveland's name anywhere except to assail him. His portrait mysteriously disappeared from the New York headquarters, where it was replaced by pictures of Flower, Murphy, and Hill.

On Sunday the 4th, amid exploding firecrackers, the trains poured fresh crowds into the city. Every few minutes a distant band would announce the approach of some new delegation or club. Among the first was the Bland Silver Club of St. Louis, five hundred men in linen suits. Then came the Blackburn Club of Lexington, the Matthews Club of Indiana, the Jacksonian Club of Omaha, and noisiest of all, the Bryan Club of Lincoln. At the Sherman House, under the portraits of the four Western heroes, Bland, Boies, Blackburn, and Pennoyer, the silverites surged about the pale and taciturn Governor Altgeld, who might well have been nominated had not his foreign birth made him ineligible. He supported the "Senatorial clique" which, led by Vest, Harris, and Tillman, had decided upon Bland as the nominee.

On Tuesday, a cool and cloudless day, the convention was called to order by National Chairman Harrity in a great hall of 20,000 seats. Senator Hill had been proposed by the national committee for temporary chairman, but he was now regarded as a gold man, and his name was the signal for an outbreak. "Will you turn down David B. Hill?" indignantly shouted Waller of Connecticut. "We will," shrieked the delegates—and by a vote of 556 to 349, they placed Senator Daniel, who with his air of courtesy and dignity looked like a second Edwin Booth, in the chair. It was evident that the silver wing still lacked the two-thirds vote necessary to control the nomination. On Wednesday, therefore, the silverite committee on credentials made sure of it by increasing the delegations from all the Territories, and ejecting a number of the gold delegates from Michigan and Nebraska. Hats, flags, and newspapers flew in the air as the newly-seated Nebraskans, headed by Bryan, marched in and took their places.

Thursday, again cool and clear, brought the crisis of the convention. As Senator Jones read the platform reported by the committee on resolutions, the planks which were aimed directly at Cleveland's policies—those condemning the bond issues, the "trafficking with banking syndicates," the use of injunctions, and Federal interference in local affairs—seemed to stun even many of the silver delegates. The party was not merely repudiating its President, but insulting him. Tillman took the floor in defence of the new doctrines. He declared that the Southern people were tired of being mere hewers of wood and drawers of water, while New York and the other great Eastern States were eating up their substance. "You ask us to endorse Cleveland's fidelity," he said. "In reply, I say he has been faithful unto death, the death of the Democratic party." As he closed, he read a set of resolutions which condemned the Cleveland Administration as "undemocratic and tyrannical," as abhorrent to liberty-loving Americans, and as one which had sought to plant a plutocratic despotism "on the ruins of the republic." Hill followed with an admirable defence of the Administration, tactful but emphatic. Vilas spoke. Then Russell, pale and worn, his fine voice choked with emotion, rose to make the last speech of his life—a speech pleading rather in sorrow than in anger against the destruction of the party to which he had devoted his brief and crowded career. And as he sat down there climbed the steps to the platform a tall, robust figure, with the elastic step of youth, and with a strikingly handsome head—William Jennings Bryan.

Tillman and Jones had treated Cleveland with contumely, but not a single hostile reference to the President marred the beauty of Bryan's discourse. Indeed, every reference to his opponents was courteous. "It is not a question of persons," he said: "it is a question of principle; and it is not with gladness that we find ourselves brought into conflict with those who are now arrayed upon the other side." We know now how assiduously Bryan had for years practised almost every passage of this speech; we know how carefully he had laid his plans to stake everything upon it and sweep the convention before him. But to nearly everyone in the huge hall it had the charm of novelty. He spoke with deliberation, with dignity, and with a sonorous eloquence that drove every word home. From the outset he held the attention of his hearers. The passage that first fired them to exultant enthusiasm was his rhetorical reference to McKinley: "Why, that man who used to boast that he looked like Napoleon, that man shudders today when he thinks that he was nominated on the anniversary of the battle of Waterloo!" Thereafter almost every sentence was followed by a burst of wild applause from twenty thousand throats. He spoke of the farms as the basis of American prosperity; of the way in which the petitions of the people had been scorned and their entreaties mocked; of the issue of 1776 and the new contest for national independence. Amid a painful silence, he came to his climax, delivered in tones of labored and solemn protest: "Having behind us the producing masses of the nation and the world, the laboring interests and the toilers everywhere, we will answer their demand for a gold standard by saying to them: 'You shall not press down upon the brow of labor this crown of thorns—you shall not crucify mankind upon a cross of gold!' "

The roar that followed these words was the signal that Cleveland was no longer the head of the party he had twice led to victory; that he was thrust aside and its future leadership lay with the young orator from Nebraska.

Cleveland's friend Otto Gresham, who was in the audience, has told us what ensued: "State after State planted its banner alongside of the Nebraska standard until there were two-thirds of the convention represented. John E. Lamb with a drawn face stood holding to the Indiana banner while the other Indiana delegates sat mute in their places. Senator Voorhees was home sick and he died a few months later. 'He is nominated without a roll-call,' was the cry. To my mother and Mrs. Potter Palmer, who sat beside me, I said, 'Uncle Grover will pull the sound-money men out before there is a roll-call. They will bolt as soon as they vote on the platform.' Whether Mr. Cleveland attempted to pull them out I never learned. But that night after the convention adjourned, I learned that Tammany was willing to go out but that the other New Yorkers and the New England men—men like William C. Whitney and Governor Russell of Massachusetts—were unwilling to go that far." This was correct. The gold men sat in sullen silence as pandemonium raged for thirty-five minutes after Bryan sat down. They sullenly answered to the roll-call as the platform was carried, 628 to 301, and the old Democratic party, the party of Tilden and Cleveland, passed out of existence.

That evening the nominating speeches began. Bryan's name was on every tongue; the animosity toward the Eastern delegates was such that the slightest incident might have produced an explosion. But no incident occurred, for again the gold delegates sat silent as the roll of the States was called, or stated in brief and bitter words why they had no candidates to offer. William F. Harrity alone presented Pattison of Pennsylvania. The next day the balloting began. Most of the gold leaders left early, and when on the fifth ballot Bryan was named for the presidency, they were at their hotels sadly packing up and making ready to catch the first train. But Otto Gresham remained, and as Bryan's nomination was announced he heard Senator Vest ejaculate triumphantly, "Now we are even with old Cleveland!"

And Cleveland? Nearly a thousand miles distant he was gazing out on the waters of Buzzards Bay, his heart filled with we know not what bitterness. We know only that he denied himself to most callers, and answered few letters; that when C. S. Hamlin, returning from the convention, spoke of running up to Gray Gables, he was told he had better not go; and that he burst out in a letter to Dickinson, "If ever there was a penitentiary devoted to the incarceration of those who commit crimes against the Democratic party, how easily it could be filled just at this time!"

The first question which Cleveland and his Cabinet had to face was whether they should bolt the Chicago nominations. Their decision was difficult to make. Almost every Democratic newspaper in the East sharply disavowed a candidate who was described by the *World* as the product of hysteria, and a platform that the *Evening Post* declared was baser than any adopted since slavery days. But considerations of party honor and loyalty made it difficult for the President to issue an open repudiation of the Democratic organization or to give even tacit support to McKinley and the Republicans. A third ticket was obviously required. Some of the sound money men before leaving Chicago agreed upon a statement rejecting Bryan and his doctrines and calling for a new convention, and this was published on July 14 over the signatures of Senator Palmer, Comptroller Eckels, two former Representatives from Illinois, Forman and Cable, and others. The Re-

form Club of New York gave Eastern leadership to the
movement. On July 15 it was announced that Secretary Herbert had bolted and that Olney would not support Bryan.
Postmaster-General Wilson and other Cabinet members were
besieged by reporters demanding a statement of intentions.
The newspapers were full of names of prominent Democrats
in private life who turned their backs on Bryan, and full also
of endorsements of the ticket by men who might have been
thought hostile. Such leaders as Gorman and Hill proved
more interested in keeping control of their State machines
than in maintaining the former principles of the party. For
a time some thought of Hill as a possible sound-money nominee. He retired to Wolfert's Roost and to silence, refusing to
be interviewed. Then, having announced that "I am a Democrat still—very still," in August he gave a dinner for Bryan
and his wife.

Cleveland thought of Bryan as a Populist pure and simple,
without the remotest idea of true Democratic principles; but
he exhibited his usual caution. "I have an idea, quite fixed
and definite," he wrote Lamont, "that for the present at least
we should none of us say anything. I have heard from Herbert
today. He says he has declared he will not support the ticket.
I am sorry he has done so. We have a right to be quiet—
indeed I feel that I have been invited to that course. I am
not fretting except about the future of the country and
party . . ." The President, who felt hurt that Whitney had
not consulted him just before leaving for Chicago, was not
in communication with him or with many others. William L.
Wilson agreed that Cleveland and the Cabinet would be wise
to keep silent and act together, and wait and see if a sound-
money ticket was not later nominated which they could
support. Already a movement toward that end was on foot,
for in accordance with the Palmer-Eckels call all national
committeemen belonging to the gold wing of the party were
being urged to meet in Indianapolis on August 7.

Meanwhile, Cleveland was called from Gray Gables to attend the funeral of William E. Russell in Boston. The Massa-

chusetts leader, after days and nights of exhausting labor in
Chicago, the first of Whitney's party to rise and the last to
go to bed, had departed for a short vacation in the woods
near Little Pabos, Quebec. For years he had overtaxed his
frail body. On the morning of July 16 his friends at the
fishing camp found him cold in bed, where he had died peacefully in his sleep. It was a loss that conservative Democracy
could ill afford. As Charles Eliot Norton said, he was the most
persuasive and effective of all the younger men in the party
because his great abilities were matched by a complete sin-
cerity. He had written his wife from the convention on July 8
that "I had no idea how hard and distasteful this task would
be. I have but one comfort in it: I have done my duty with
fidelity"—and as the *Nation* remarked, this last phrase might
be taken as the summary of his laborious life. To the newspaper men at the funeral Cleveland, carefully dressed in a
long frock coat and silk hat, and tanned a brick red by the
Cape Cod sun, looked worn and discouraged. "His face apparently was as full as ever, but there was a look of added
age; the lines seemed harder and the gray mustache, for all its
bristling, had less color than even a few months ago."

The conference of Gold-Democratic committeemen in Indianapolis early in August resulted in the call for a national
convention to be held in the same city on September 2.
Palmer, Vilas, and Dickinson were the men most active in
the movement, while the Louisville *Courier-Journal* office
became a headquarters for the labor of bringing delegates
together. It was an uphill task; but a fortnight before the
convention met the principal owner of that newspaper, Walter
N. Haldeman, wrote Watterson that, after much hard but
effective work, the promise at last was for a large convention
of first class men, the delegates representing every State and
Territory in the American Union except possibly "three of
the rotten boroughs of the West." For a time the leaders were
in great perplexity as to whom they should nominate. Vilas
and Bragg of Wisconsin were suggested; a small group favored Watterson, who was in Europe at the time, and another

small group J. Sterling Morton; while there was an insistent demand from various quarters for William L. Wilson. When Oscar S. Straus told Wilson that Carl Schurz and others were vigorously recommending his nomination, Wilson demurred. He did not want the honor, others were willing and eager to grasp it, and he feared that he would be accused of using the patronage of the Post Office Department to help his candidacy. "I shall do all I can to direct attention to Senator Palmer," he confided to his diary, "and in any event away from myself."

Palmer, in the end, was the man. He was nominated on the first ballot by a huge majority over Bragg, and Gen. Simon B. Buckner of Kentucky, a Confederate veteran, was named for the vice presidency. Delegates from forty-one States and three Territories were present, and the name of the National Democratic Party was adopted. Cleveland was pleased by the candidates and still more by the declaration of principles, for the convention praised his patriotism and courage in the heartiest terms, and denounced protection and free silver in the same plank as schemes to enrich a few at the expense of the masses. "I feel grateful," he wrote Vilas, "to those who have relieved the political atmosphere with such a delicious infusion of fresh air. Every Democrat after reading the platform ought to thank God that the glorious principles of the party have found defenders who will not permit them to be polluted by impious hands." He could have had the nomination for himself by acclamation, but he had peremptorily refused it.

Everyone, including Cleveland, understood that the Palmer-Buckner ticket would not obtain a single electoral vote. The two old soldiers, invested with the pathetic nobility of the past, made a vigorous campaign and were a stirring sight as they appeared together on the platform; but they were sacrificial figures, whose real mission was to divert enough votes from the Bryan column to make certain of the election of McKinley. Cleveland was quite willing that, in States like Kentucky, the Gold-Democratic ticket should throw the electors to McKinley. He never believed for an instant that the

Chicago ticket was Democratic at all, and as between Bryan and McKinley he unquestionably preferred the latter. It was with some difficulty that he refrained from making a public attack on the silver candidates, and he wrote Lamont:

> I am perplexed concerning the course I should pursue. My inclination, of course, is to join the chorus of denunciation, but I am doubtful as to the wisdom of such action, in the light of a chance that [it] might do more harm than good. My position cannot be misunderstood by any man, woman, or child in the country. I am President of all the people, good, bad, or indifferent, and as long as my opinions are known, ought perhaps to keep myself out of their squabbles. I must attempt to cooperate with Congress during another session in the interest of needed legislation, and perhaps ought not to unnecessarily further alienate that body and increase its hatred of me, and if I take an active and affirmatively aggressive position it may aid the cause we have *not* at heart, in increasing the effectiveness of the cry of presidential interference. In addition to all this, no one of weight or judgment in political matters has advised me to speak out— though I shall be surprised if Palmer does not urge it soon.
>
> If you say anything, I do not care how plainly you present the inference that I am in accord with your views.

Yet very wisely, for in good taste he could pursue no other course, he avoided all active participation in the campaign. When the Gold-Democrats held their notification meeting at Louisville, he declined to attend. He merely permitted the publication of a letter to the national chairman, saying that as a Democrat devoted to the integrity of his party he should greatly have liked to be present and to mingle with those who insisted that its glorious standard should still be borne aloft as of old in faithful hands. Late in October he went to Princeton, where the college (just becoming a university) was holding its sesquicentennial celebration. Here, in the presence of a large body of scholars and public men, he delivered one of the most carefully prepared addresses of his career. He spoke on the themes usual for such an occasion—the duty of educated men, the responsibility of institutions of learning to the state, and the dangers of public ignorance concerning the fundamental principles of economics and politics. Some of the passages of the address had a direct application to the campaign then approaching its close. It was as important, he said, for a nation to show honesty and fidelity to its obligations as for an individual to do so. "Neither the glitter of its power, nor the tinsel of its commercial prosperity, nor the gaudy show of its people's wealth, can conceal the cankering rust of national dishonesty, and cover the meanness of national bad faith." A constant stream of thoughtful, informed men, he believed, should come from our colleges to preach national honor and integrity. And later in the address he touched on the perils which lurked in social or political intolerance. "When popular discontent and passion are stimulated by the art of designing partisans to a pitch perilously near to class hatred or sectional anger, I would have our universities and colleges sound the alarm in the name of American brotherhood and fraternal dependence." This speech, which received much commendation from the conservative Eastern press, both Democratic and Republican, brought Cleveland as near the verge of an actual political utterance as he came.

While he thus kept out of the campaign, he had to deal with what he regarded as the treachery of important Federal officeholders who got into it on the Bryan side. Of these there were many. He was disappointed, for example, by the course of Holmes Conrad, the Solicitor-General, who immediately espoused the silver ticket. Early in September Cleveland wrote Vilas that he was exceedingly angry and humiliated by the actions of these false Democrats, and was anxiously considering his duty in the matter. He realized that many of the renegades—for so he thought of them—had powerful political sponsors, and that to make many dismissals would accentuate the schism in the party. "I am hesitating," he concluded, "but it must not surprise some of these people if they run against unpleasantly sharp corners." In the end tolerance won the day, and he rejected a proscriptive policy.

A particularly difficult question, however, was presented by the defection of Secretary Hoke Smith. The able Georgian had, in the face of immense pressure, steadily supported the gold standard, arguing for it in many speeches in his native State and upholding it through his Atlanta *Journal*. But like other Southerners, he felt that to lead a revolt against his party would be to run the risk of a Republican victory and the restoration of negro rule—an intolerable prospect. Reluctantly, he fell into line behind Bryan; though he never accepted free silver, and during the late summer and fall repeatedly said so in public speeches.

Smith wrote frankly to Cleveland on July 20, explaining that he had promised the people of Georgia before the convention that he would support the nominee, and that the "local situation" made it necessary for him to do so. At the same time he began to show constraint in his relations with the other Cabinet members. He had been wont to ride around nearly every evening on his bicycle to Carlisle's house for a chat, but now ceased doing so. Cleveland sent him a rather tart reply, combining both rebuke and expostulation. He did not understand, he wrote, how Smith could accept the Chicago nominees and reject the platform—it was straining at a gnat and swallowing a camel; he did not see how he could take off his coat to help elect men whose nomination largely depended upon the virulence of their hatred of the Administration; and he was not impressed by Smith's argument on the local situation—"I suppose much was said about the 'local situation' in 1860." Though it was a natural position to take, it was not very considerate. Smith accepted the reference to 1860 in good part, writing Cleveland that while he was devoted to the nation, in the year named he would have gone with his State, and now he must stand by it. Other Cabinet members, and especially Carlisle and Wilson, hoped that he would not be forced out of the official family. As Carlisle well said, Smith had been an able Secretary; the Administration had but a few months to continue, and for the present was without organized support; his retirement would make an unpleasant stir

in the country, and give him the position of a man perse-
cuted for party's sake—and then he was such a bluff, likable
fellow!

But Cleveland was adamant, and Smith's resignation, offered on August 6, was accepted ten days later to take effect
on September 1. In his place Cleveland named David R.
Francis of Missouri. "I hope I need not say," he wrote Smith,
"how deeply I regret your retirement, and how much I appreciate the devotion, industry, and ability which have characterized your discharge of duty as a member of my official
family." Wilson always thought that if Smith had gone to
Gray Gables just after the convention, and explained how
delicate was his position as a good Georgian and the editor
of a daily newspaper, the difficulty might have been smoothed
over without a rupture. However, there was no ill feeling.
Cleveland the next winter kindly invited Smith to attend the
annual Cabinet dinner at the White House, and Smith accepted.

The result of the election was hardly in doubt after the
middle of September. Lamont, who was in close touch with
Hill and the situation in New York, told the Cabinet a fortnight later that the Bryan movement was on the wane, and
that while the regulars and Tammany men made a great
show of enthusiasm for the ticket, this was utterly hollow.
Many who shouted the loudest in public for Bryan were
saying in private that they would not vote for him. Cleveland
returned to the White House on October 9, "looking thoroughly well and in excellent spirits, being fully convinced
that there is no danger of Bryan's election." In the last week
of the canvass a certain undercurrent of uneasiness was visible
among sound-money people because of numerous reports that
much of the labor vote was drifting to Bryan. There was a
sharp squeeze for money on October 29, call rates in New
York going to one hundred per cent; and withdrawals of gold
took place in the metropolis and in San Francisco. But this
flurry passed. On the evening of election day all the Cabinet
officers who were in the capital met at eight o'clock at the

White House to hear the returns. They soon came pouring in on a special wire, announcing immense Republican gains from the Northeast and Central West, and it was easy to discern that a great tidal wave was carrying McKinley to victory. Cleveland and his associates then fixed their attention particularly upon the returns from the border States—Kentucky, in which Carlisle was interested, West Virginia, Wilson's State, and Maryland. While the evening was still young Maryland was pronounced safe. At one in the morning, when the gathering broke up, West Virginia as well was in the McKinley column, and it was all but certain that Kentucky was to be placed there.

Cleveland could not but be pleased by the decisive nature of the result. In a total vote of almost fourteen million, McKinley had a plurality of 602,000 over Bryan. Though the Gold-Democratic ticket had polled only 135,000 votes, it had been the means of transferring many more to the McKinley column. In State after State in the South—Alabama, Georgia, Louisiana—Bryan's vote ran behind that of Cleveland in 1892. Cleveland was pleased even more by the fact that the verdict at the polls was quietly and peacefully accepted. The Bryan movement had represented an attempt on an unprecedented scale to array the poor, the neglected, the unemployed, and the discontented against the "plutocratic" elements in America; it had aroused a depth of sectional feeling unknown since Reconstruction days; and yet the decision was accepted without a ripple of protest. And what gratified the President most of all were the voices, not a few in number, which declared that the victory for sound money was rather his than Hanna's or McKinley's. Dr. Fabian Franklin wrote in the Baltimore *News:*

> When the history of the present time comes to be seriously written, the name of the hero of this campaign will be that of a man who was not a candidate, not a manager, not an orator; the fight which has just been won was made possible by the noble service of one steadfast and heroic citizen, and the victory which was achieved yesterday must be set down as

the crowning achievement of his great record. . . . It is impossible to overestimate the value of the service Grover Cleveland has done through his twelve years of unswerving fidelity to the cause of honest money.

For Further Reading

In addition to the Nevins biography, students interested in Cleveland should consult Horace S. Merrill, *Bourbon Leader: Grover Cleveland and the Democratic Party* (1957), which emphasizes Cleveland's defense of the status quo; and Rexford G. Tugwell, *Grover Cleveland* (1968), which makes a strong case for his failure as President. Robert McElroy's *Grover Cleveland, The Man and the Statesman* (2 vols., 1923) is the authorized life. A useful compilation is George F. Parker, *The Writings of Grover Cleveland* (1892), which may be supplemented with Allan Nevins, ed., *Letters of Grover Cleveland* (1933). Good biographies of other political leaders of the era are Harry Barnard, *Rutherford B. Hayes and His America* (1954); Alexander C. Flick, *Samuel Jones Tilden* (1939); Theodore Clark Smith, *Life and Letters of James Abram Garfield* (1925); George F. Howe, *Chester A. Arthur: A Quarter Century of Machine Politics* (1934); Harry J. Sievers, *Benjamin Harrison: Hoosier Statesman* (1959); David S. Muzzey, *James G. Blaine* (1934); Margaret Leech, *In the Days of McKinley* (1959); W. A. Robinson, *Thomas B. Reed: Parliamentarian* (1930), and Mark C. Hirsch, *William C. Whitney: Modern Warwick* (1948).

For studies of party organization, internal party politics, and pressure groups, see Wilfred Binkley, *American Political Parties* (1943); Herman S. Merrill, *Bourbon Democracy of the Middle West 1865–1896* (1953); Matthew Josephson, *The Politicos 1865–1896* (1938); Mary R. Dearing, *Veterans in Politics: The Story of the G. A. R.* (1952); C. Vann Woodward, *Origins of the New South 1877–1913* (1951), and J. R.

Hollingsworth, *The Whirligig of Politics* (1963). A good general study is Ray Ginger, *Age of Excess* (1965), while Leonard D. White's *The Republican Era 1869–1901* (1958) is solid administrative history. Also recommended are the relevant chapters in Eric Goldman, *Rendezvous with Destiny* (1952), and Richard Hofstadter, *The American Political Tradition* (1948).